KIDS LOVE OHIO

A PARENT'S GUIDE TO EXPLORING
FUN PLACES IN OHIO WITH
CHILDREN...YEAR ROUND!

GEORGE & MICHELE ZAVATSKY
U.S. VOICE COMMUNICATION
7438 SAWMILL ROAD, SUITE 500
COLUMBUS, OHIO 43235

Dedicated To The Families Of Ohio

Second Printing 5/98

© Copyright 1998, U.S. Voice Communication

Sequel to KIDS ♥ COLUMBUS ™ Marchele Publishing

© Copyright 1991, 1992, 1994, 1997

All rights reserved. No part of this book may be reproduced or transmitted in any form or by any means, electronic or mechanical, including photocopying, recording or by any information storage and retrieval system without the written permission from the authors, except for the inclusion of brief quotations in a review. Any library use must be marked "Reference Only" not to be circulated.

Although the authors have exhaustively researched all sources to ensure accuracy and completeness of the information contained in this book, we assume no responsibility for errors, inaccuracies, omissions or any other inconsistency herein. Any slights against any entries or organizations are unintentional.

ISBN: 0-9663457-0-3

KIDS ♥OHIO (KIDS LOVE OHIO) ™   U.S. Voice Communication

Acknowledgements

We are most thankful to be blessed with our parents, Barbara Darrall and George and Catherine Zavatsky who helped us every way they could – researching, proofing and babysitting. More importantly, they were great sounding boards and offered loving, unconditional support.

We are thankful for the Crawford and Starr Families who have helped and encouraged us along the way. Bryce Crawford, Adam Hoyt, Allison Hoyt, Toby Starr, Tony Starr and our own Jenny Zavatsky have decorated our chapter cover pages with their illustrations. We are both thankful to them for their precious artwork. Our own young kids, Jenny and Daniel, were delightful and fun children during all of our trips across the state.

We especially thank and very respectfully acknowledge, Marcia Grant Berlin, the original co-author of our first book, KIDS ♥ COLUMBUS. Her strong commitments to friendship and effort in our first project were tremendously beneficial to the completion of this project.

We both sincerely thank each other – our partnership has created a great "marriage of minds" with lots of exciting moments and laughs woven throughout.

Above all, we praise the Lord for His many answered prayers and special blessings throughout the completion of this project.

We think Ohio is a wonderful, friendly area of the country with more activities than you could imagine! Our sincere wish is that this book will help everyone "fall in love" with Ohio!

- George & Michele

INTRODUCTION

HOW TO USE THIS BOOK

If you are excited about discovering Ohio, this is the book for you and your family! Become a Buckeye state expert! Know your home state well and proudly discuss fun trips with friends and relatives. We spent over a thousand hours doing all the scouting, collecting and compiling so that you could spend less time searching and more time having fun.

Here are a few hints to make your adventures run smoothly:

- Consider the **child's age** before deciding to take a visit.
- Know **directions** and parking. Call ahead if you have questions and bring this book. Also, don't forget your camera! *(please honor rules regarding use)*
- **Estimate the duration** of the trip. Bring small surprises (favorite juice boxes) and travel books and toys.
- Call ahead for **reservations** or details, if necessary.
- Most listings are **closed major holidays** unless noted.
- Keep a **journal** of your visits in a notebook (*or in the blank pages in the back of this book*).
- Make a **family treasure chest**. Decorate a big box or use an old chest. Store memorabilia from a fun outing, pictures, brochures and souvenirs. Once a year, look through the box and reminisce.
- Plan **picnics** along the way. Many Ohio Historical Society sites and state parks are scattered throughout Ohio. Pull off an exit or take a rural/scenic route to take advantage of these free picnic facilities.
- Some activities, especially tours, require **groups** of 10 or more. To participate, you may either ask to be part of

another tour group or get a group together yourself (neighbors, friends, school organizations). If you arrange a group outing (usually 10 or more people), most places offer discounts.

❏ Each chapter is listed by area (*see map below*), then by city. This makes it easier for you **to plan** your days **strategically** by location.

AREA CHART

C = Central	NC North/Central	SC= South Central
CE = Central/East	NE = North/East	SE = South/East
CW =Central/West	NW = North/West	SW = South/West

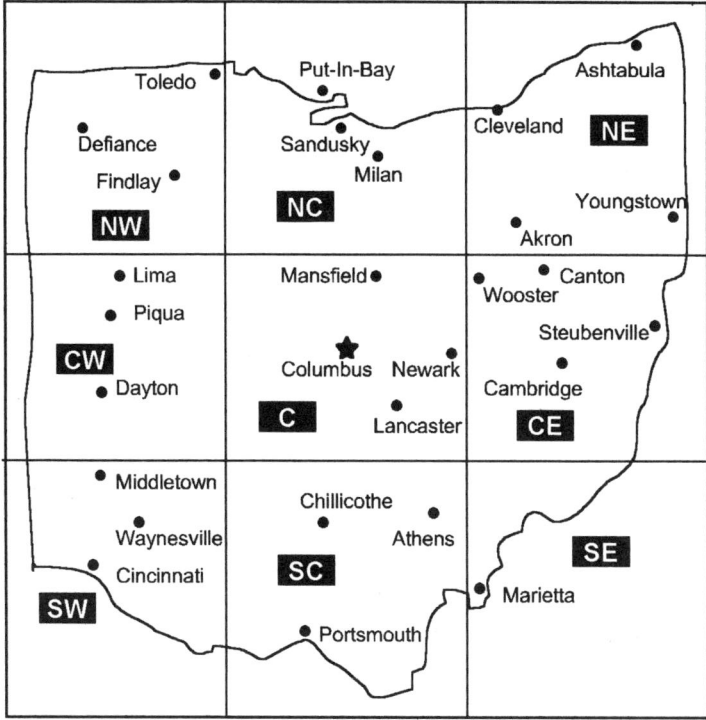

Cities You Will Find Listed In This Book

Area C
Amlin
Ashville
Baltimore
Brownsville
Buckeye Lake
Bucyrus
Butler
Canal
Circleville
Columbus
Delaware
Dresden
Dublin
Granville
Grove City
Hebron
Killbuck
Lancaster
Lexington
Lodi
London
Loudonville
Mansfield
Marion
Medina
Millersport
Mt. Gilead
Mt. Sterling
New Albany
Newark
Obetz
Pataskala
Perrysville
Pickerington
Reynoldsburg
Roseville
Spencer
Upper Sandusky
Utica
Westerville
Worthington
Zanesville

Area CE
Barnesville
Belle Valley
Belmont
Berlin
Byesville
Cadiz
Cambridge
Canton
Carrolton
Coshocton
Cumberland
Delphos
Dennison
Dover
East Liverpool
Freeport
Gnadenhutten
Martin's Ferry
Massillon
Middlefield
Millersburg
Mount Pleasant
New Concord
New Cumberland
New Philadelphia
North Canton
Norwich
Orrville
Port Washington
Powhattan Point
Senecaville
St. Clairsville
Steubenville
Strasburg
Sugarcreek
Walnut Crk
Wilmont
Wooster
Zoar

Area CW
Arcanm
Beaver Crk
Bellefntaine
Celina
Centerville
Clifton
Dayton
Delphos
Eaton
Fairborn
Germantown
Greenville
Huber Hts
Kenton
Lakeview
Lima
Lockington
Miamisburg
Minster
Moraine
New Bremen
Piqua
Springfield
St. Mary's
Troy
Urbana
Versailles
Wapakoneta
West Liberty
Wilberforce
Xenia
Yellow Spgs
Zanesfield

Area NC
Ashland
Bay Village
Bellevue
Brunswick
Catawba Island
Elyria

Area NC
Fremont
Kelley's Island
Lakeside
Locust Point
Lorain
Marblehead
Milan
N. Ridgeville
Norwalk
Oak Harbor
Oberlin
Olmsted Falls
Port Clinton
Put-In-Bay
Sandusky
Tiffin
Vermilion
Wellington
Willard

Area NE
Akron
Alliance
Andover
Ashtabula
Aurora
Barberton
Bath
Berea
Burton
Canal Fulton
Canfield
Chardon
Chesterland
Cleveland
Columbia Stn
Conneaut
Cuyahoga Falls
Eastlake
Fairport Hbr.
Geneva
Geneva On Lk
Hartville
Hinckley
Independence
Jefferson

NE *(cont)*
Kent
Kirtland
Lake Milton
Lakewood
Mentor
Newbury
Niles
N. Kingsville
Painesville
Parma Hts
Peninsula
Portage
Ravenna
Shaker Hts.
Stow
Twinsburg
Unionville
Warren
Willoughby
Youngstown

Area NW
Archbold
Bluffton
Bowling Green
Defiance
Findlay
Grand Rapids
Maumee
Perrysburg
Sylvania
Toledo
Van Buren
Van Wert
Wauseon

Area SC
Adelphi
Athens
Bainbridge
Chillicothe
Gallipolis
Hillsboro
Ironton
Jackson
Logan

SC *(cont)*
Mcarthur
Millville
Nelsonville
Portsmouth
Rio Grande
Rockbridge
Wshngtn CH
Waverly
Wellston
West Union

Area SE
Marietta
MConnlsvile
Reedsville
Stockport

Area SW
Cincinnati
Hamilton
Harrison
Harveysburg
Hillsboro
Kettering
Kings Mills
Lebanon
Loveland
Mason
Middletown
Moscow
Oregonia
Oxford
Pt. Pleasant
Ripley
Sharonville
Springboro
Waynesville
West Union
Wilmington
Winchester

George Zavatsky and Michele (Darrall) Zavatsky were raised in Ohio and have lived in many different cities throughout the state. They currently reside in a suburb of Columbus, Ohio. They are both graduates of The Ohio State University (where they met) and have been happily married since 1987. Along with writing and self-publishing several books, each of them also own and operate a catalog marketing company and a courier business. Besides the wonderful adventure of marriage, they place great importance on being loving parents to Jenny and Daniel.

Table of Contents

Chapter 1 – AMUSEMENTS...1

Chapter 2 – ANIMALS & FARMS....................................13

Chapter 3 – FUN INTERACTIVE LEARNING....................33

Chapter 4 – MUSEUMS..47

Chapter 5 – OHIO HISTORY & GOVERNMENT................73

Chapter 6 – OUTDOOR EXPLORING.............................117

Chapter 7 – SEASONAL & SPECIAL EVENTS..................143

Chapter 8 – SPORTS..179

Chapter 9 – THE ARTS...187

Chapter 10 – THEME RESTAURANTS............................213

Chapter 11 – TOURS..221

Chapter 12 – TRANSPORTATION ADVENTURES............267

Index...281

Chapter 1
AMUSEMENTS

Toby & Tony

AREA "C"

HOMESTEAD PARK

4675 Cosgray Road, (I-270 to State Route 33 to Plain City exit), **Amlin**

- Area: **C**
- Telephone Number (614) 846-9554
- Hours: Dawn to Dusk
- Admission: FREE

Homestead Park is a fabulous adventure for everyone. The country setting, pond, trails, shelter houses, picnic area and grill provide a great place for an all day picnic. The special feature for the children is the elaborate playground with everything from a sandpit to concrete tunnels, swings and bridges, towers and cranes. Separate from this play area is "Fort Washington", a fully equipped fort featuring seasonal wet activities. The attached squirt guns have a continuous supply of water!

WYANDOT LAKE AMUSEMENT AND WATERPARK

10101 Riverside Drive (I-270 to Sawmill Road Exit), **Columbus**

- Area: **C**
- Telephone Number: (614) 889-9283 or (800) 328-9283
  Mid-May – Labor Day
  Admission: $14.00 and up
  Under Age 3 FREE
  Season Pass – Individual - $39.99, Family - $139.99
- Miscellaneous: Concessions, Kiddie rides, and Gift Shops

AMUSEMENTS

This is great fun for a summer day. Wyandot offers a huge wave pool, numerous thrilling water slides and a water fun area for the little ones. Then, put on your shoes and get on the roller coaster or one of the amusement rides available. All this for one admission charge. Life vests and rafts are available.

<u>Christopher Island</u> – Tree house, lagoons, abandoned ships, heated water guns and sprayers, jet steams, and dark speed tunnels.

<u>RICHLAND CAROUSEL PARK AND CAROUSEL MAGIC FACTORY</u>

I-71 Exit State Route 13 North to downtown, **Mansfield**

- Area: **C**
- Telephone Number (419) 522-4223
- Hours: Factory Weekdays, 10:00 a.m. – 4:00 p.m.
  Carousel Daily, Rain or Shine
- Admission: Factory Tour $2.50 Adult
  $1.00 Children (5-12)
  Carousel $1.00 – (2) ride tokens

Watch the wood carousel horses being made starting from a "coffin box" with a hollow center, then the carving with special tools, and finally the painting. The artisans are friendly and enjoy showing off their skill and love of the art (Factory at 44 West 4th Street). Now that you know how they're made, walk over to the wonderful carousel in the center of town. For lunch, stop at the Coney Island Diner with its genuine old-time tables, stools and "Blue Plate" specials.

AREA "NC"

PREHISTORIC FOREST

8232 East Harbor Road - Route 163. (8 miles East of Port Clinton off State Route 2), **Marblehead**

- Area: **NC**
- Telephone Number: (419) 798-5230
- Hours: Daily, 10:00 a.m. – Dark (Summer) June – August Weekends Only, 10:00 a.m.–Dark (May and September)
- Admission: Yes

Learn the eating habits and lifestyles of dinosaurs in a forest full of them. Take a walk through a volcano, dig for dinosaur footprints and bones or get your picture taken with Reggie, the 14' Python snake! Also included is the Reptile House (pythons, lizards, and alligators) and Mystery Hill (the "Illusion of Nature" House where water runs uphill and chairs stick to the walls).

CEDAR POINT

State Route 4 (I-80 to Exit 7 or Exit 6A. Follow Signs), **Sandusky**

- Area: **NC**
- Telephone Number: (419) 627-2223 or (419) 626-0830
- Hours: Vary by season. May – October
- Admission: $7.00 - $30.00, Small children – General (4-59). Separate admission for Soak City and Challenge Park. Starlight rates too!
- Miscellaneous: Stroller rental. Picnic area. Food Service Soak City – wave pool, water slides, Adventure Cove, Eerie Falls (get wet in the dark), swim-up refreshment center.

AMUSEMENTS

Challenge Park – Rip cord Sky coaster (fall 150 feet and then swing in a 300-foot arc. Grand Prix Raceway. Miniature Golf.

Amusement extravaganza on the shores of Lake Erie including:
12 Roller Coasters
Chaos – turn sideways & upside down at the same time
Live Shows – 50's, Motown, Country
Bear County – Berenstain Bears motif with piped-in kids music and child sized play buildings

AREA "NE"

GEAUGA LAKE
State Route 43 (9 miles north of Turnpike Exit 13), **Aurora**

- Area: NE
- Telephone Number: (800) THE-WAVE
- Hours: Open 10:00 a.m. Weekends, 11:00 a.m. Weekdays, (Summer)
  Weekends Only (May, September, October)
- Admission: $8.00 - $22.00.
  Kids age 2 and under FREE. $4.00 for Parking
- Miscellaneous: Lockers and changing rooms. Paddleboat and Aquacycle rentals. Stroller and wagon rental. Picnic area. Food service. Towel rental. Proper swimwear required. Swimwear available in gift shops.

Take a ride on a backward loop or 13-story plunge roller coaster. Water play at The Wave (2-½ acre pool with surfs) or any of the other water chutes, wet slides, toboggan run, or Grizzly Run (white water rapids). Little ones can splash at Turtle Beach with its' mini waterfalls and slides (even a feeding area for babies). Hooks Lagoon is a 5-story tree house with 150+ water gadgets to shoot.

PIONEER WATERLAND
10661 Kile Road, (Route 6 to Route 608), **Chardon**

- Area: **NE**
- Telephone Number: (440) 951-7507
- Hours: Daily, 10:00 a.m. – 8:00 p.m.
  Memorial Day – Labor Day
- Admission: $9.00 and up
  Less than 40" tall FREE
- Miscellaneous: Picnic Area, Food Service, and Video Arcade

Little ones frequent the toddler play area and waterland. Others can explore the water slides, paddleboats, inner tube rides, volleyball nets, Indy raceway, batting cages, miniature golf or driving range. All adjoining a chlorinated crystal clear lake with beaches.

CONNEAUT LAKE PARK
I-90 to Albion Exit, Conneaut – **Cleveland**

- Area: **NE**
- Telephone Number (800) 828-9619
- Hours: Daily, Noon – 9:00 p.m. or 10:00 p.m. (Weekends) (Summer)
- Admission: $2.00 - $15.00
- Miscellaneous: Stroller rental. Food Service. Picnic Areas

A small amusement park with an old time charm. Some classic featured rides include the Merry-Go-Round, Dodge-Em-Cars, and Tilt-A-Whirl. Also included are a swimming beach, sightseeing cruises, boat rentals, and fishing tournaments.

AMUSEMENTS

I-X CENTER INDOOR AMUSEMENT PARK
6200 Riverside Drive (Brookpark), **Cleveland**

- Area: **NE**
- Telephone Number: (216) 676-6000
- Hours: Only open in April, Hours vary daily (Call for details)
- Admission: $12.00 General, $7.00 Senior
- Miscellaneous: Food service

After riding the World's Tallest Indoor Ferris Wheel (10 stories high) you can SCREAM through 150 rides! Also features a video arcade, miniature golf, laser kareoke, kiddie area and live entertainment.

MEMPHIS KIDDIE PARK
10340 Memphis Avenue (I-71 to West 117th/Memphis Avenue Exit), **Cleveland**

- Area: **NE**
- Telephone Number: (216) 941-5995
- Hours and Admission: Call for details, seasonal

Little tots rides like a ferris wheel, roller coaster (our little girl's first!), carousel and miniature golf.

WILDWOOD WATERPARK
11200 East River Road (Route 252), **Columbia Station**

- Area: **NE**
- Telephone Number: (440) 236-3944
- Hours: Daily, Daytime. (Mid June – Labor Day)
- Admission: $9.95 (ages 5+)

A waterpark in the woods with sandy beaches and waterslides, paddle boats, miniature golf, and canoe rides.

ERIEVIEW PARK
5483 Lake Road (I-90 to Geneva Exit 218 to State Route 531), Geneva-on-the-Lake

- Area: **NE**
- Telephone Number: (440) 466-8650
- Hours: Daily to 10:00 p.m. (Memorial Day – Labor Day)
- Admission: "Day Pass", Group Rates
- Miscellaneous: Food Service, Picnic Area

Located on the "strip" with old-fashioned classic rides, kiddie rides, bumper cars and water slides.

AREA "SW"

CONEY ISLAND
6201 Kellogg Avenue. (Off I-275), Cincinnati

- Area: **SW**
- Telephone Number (513) 232-8230
- Hours: Daily (Memorial Weekend – Labor Day)
  Pool, 10:00 a.m. – 8:00 p.m.
  Rides, Noon – 7:00 p.m.
- Admission: $9.00- $11.00, Ages 4+
  Free Parking

Sunlite, the world's largest re-circulating pool with a huge slide and 7 diving boards, is one of the many fun attractions. Also, Zoom Flume water toboggan, Pipeline Plunge tube water slide, kiddie rides, miniature golf, bumper boats, pedal boats and picnic areas.

AMUSEMENTS

LINDER FAMILY OMNIMAX THEATER
I-71/I-75 to Ezzard Charles Drive, **Cincinnati**

- Area: **SW**
- Telephone Number: (513) 287-7000
- Hours: Monday – Friday, 11:00 a.m. – 4:00 p.m., 7:00 p.m. – 8:00 p.m. (Friday 8:00 p.m. – 9:00 p.m.) (Summer)
  *Saturday, Sunday and Holidays, 11:00 a.m. – 5:00 p.m. (Saturday 7:00 p.m. – 9:00 p.m.) (Summer)
  *Monday – Friday, 1:00 p.m. – 3:00 p.m., (Tuesday/Thursday 7:00 p.m. – 8:00 p.m.) (Rest of the Year)
  *Saturday, Sunday and Holidays, 11:00 a.m. – 4:00 p.m. (Saturday, 7:00 – 9:00 p.m.) (Rest of the Year)
- Admission: $6.50 Adult, $4.50 Children (3-12)

Shows on the hour viewed on a 5 story, 72-foot wide domed screen.

SURF CINCINNATI
11460 Sebring Drive, (Off I-275, 5 miles West of I-75), **Cincinnati**

- Area: **SW**
- Telephone Number: (513) 742-0620
- Hours: Daily, 10:30 a.m. – 8:30 p.m.
  Memorial Day - Labor Day
  Admission: $11.00 and up (ages 3+)
  Reduced rates after 3:30 p.m.

Waterpark with a ½ acre wave pool, kid's pool, waterslides, inner tube rides, sundeck, beach, miniature golf, go carts, and concessions.

PARAMOUNT'S KINGS ISLAND
I-71 to Exit 25A, (24 miles North of Cincinnati), **Kings Mills**

- Area: **SW**
- Telephone Number: (800) 288-0808
- Hours: Daily, 9:00 a.m. – Dark (Memorial Day – Late August)
  Weekends Only (April, May, September, October)
- Admission: $16.00 - $29.00
  Child (3-6) –Reduced rates
  Parking Fee
- Miscellaneous: A theme park with professional service attitude! Plan a day or two at this world class amusement adventure. Features:

WaterWorks – heated wave pool, children's play area, lazy river plus 16 water slides and rides.

9 Top Roller Coasters – The Beast (longest wooden coaster), The Outer Limits (1st indoor coaster to catapult in the dark at high velocity), Days of Thunder (racing car simulator of high speed stock car racing).

Hanna Barbera Land – Scooby Doo's Magic-To-Do, Cartoon characters.

Nickelodeon Splat City – Green Slime Zone (water spray, pipe work maze, Mess-A-Mania). Most popular with school age kids.

THE BEACH
2590 Waterpark Drive. (I-71 Exit 25B - 20 miles North of Cincinnati), **Mason**

- Area: **SW**
- Telephone Number: (800) 886-SWIM
- Hours: Daily opens 10:00 a.m. Closing varies.
  Memorial Weekend – Labor Day

AMUSEMENTS

- Admission: $11.00 – 18.00 Children – Senior – Adult
- Miscellaneous: Food Service

Over 40,000 square feet of beach and two million gallons of water and waves await you! Favorites include the Pearl leisure pool, Aztec Adventure watercoaster, Thunder Beach Wave Pool and the Lazy Miami River inner tube ride. The young children's water area has Splash Mountain with warm water!

AMERICANA AMUSEMENT PARK
5757 Middletown-Hamilton Road (State Route 63 to State Route 4 South) (I-75 to Exit 29), **Middletown**

- Area: **SW**
- Telephone Number (800) 486-3070
- Hours: Daily (except Monday) opens at 11:00 a.m. (Summer)
  Weekends Only (April – May)
- Admission: Begin at $14.00
  Children under 36" tall – FREE
- Miscellaneous: Picnic Area. Food Service. Swimming.

Old fashioned amusement park with the Screechin' Eagle wooden roller coaster, the Serpent steel roller coaster, log ride, train ride, pedal boats, and Kids World. They also have live shows with acts like the Fabulous Wallendas tightrope act, rock country musical acts and for the young, a Puppet Parade and Toy Tales.

OTHER SUGGESTIONS
(Look for local listings in your Yellow Pages)

- Fun Centers/Amusement Centers (ex. Discovery Zone, Chuck E. Cheese)
- Canoe Rides or Riding Stables

Chapter 2
ANIMALS & FARMS

AREA "C"

COLUMBUS ZOO

9990 Riverside Drive (Route 257, I-270 to Sawmill Road Exit), **Columbus**

- Area: **C**
- Telephone Number: (614) 645-3550
- Hours: Daily, 9:00 a.m. – 6:00 p.m. (Summer)
  9:00 a.m. – 5:00 p.m. (September – May)
  9:00 a.m. – 8:00 – p.m. (Wednesday Family Night)
  Open 365 days a year
- Admission: $5.00 Adult, $3.00 Children (2-11)
  Family Membership available
  Parking fee
- Miscellaneous: Gift Shops and Concessions

The famous Director Emeritus of the zoo, Jack Hanna, is a regular on "Late Night With David Letterman" and "Good Morning America". Highlights of the zoo include cheetahs, polar bears, lowland gorillas, children's petting zoo (a big hit!), North American Bald Eagles (named George and Barbara) and the Pet-A-Shark exhibit. The zoo is very active in the community and brings Zoofari Outreach and On Safari programs to many public functions. A 100,000-gallon coral reef exhibit and one of the largest reptile collections in the United States are also featured.

OHIO STATE UNIVERSITY ENTOMOLOGY DEPARTMENT

1735 Neil Avenue (State Route 315 to King Avenue – North on Neil Avenue), **Columbus**

- Area: **C**

ANIMALS & FARMS

- ❑ Telephone Number: (614) 292-9634
- ❑ Tours: Appointment Necessary (Be sure to ask about parking arrangements – street parking may not be available)
  15 or more persons, 4th grade and up
  Weekdays
- ❑ Admission: FREE

This is a great introduction to science. Learn how and why "bugs" are important to us. Even the mothers in our group found this tour interesting. Your group will see and maybe touch many interesting live insects. You can combine the tour with the Botany Department Tour.

OHIO STATE UNIVERSITY VETERINARY HOSPITAL

1935 Coffey Road – OSU Agricultural Campus (off State Route 315), **Columbus**

- ❑ Area: **C**
- ❑ Telephone Number: (614) 292-8831
- ❑ Tours: Saturday afternoons – Call for details
  Age: 13 years old +

Pre-veterinarian students take children on a tour of all the many rooms where animals are treated. The animals you will see depend on what "patients" are there when you arrive. However, there is a good chance you will see a horse, a cow, a pig, or sheep along with the cats and dogs. Because they treat larger animals, the equipment is "giant" sized (an awesome sight for kids). Many tour groups receive a souvenir of their trip at the end of the tour.

MALABAR FARM STATE PARK

4050 Bromfield Road (I-71 to Exit 169, follow signs),
Mansfield

- Area: **C**
- Telephone Number: (419) 892-2784
- Admission: Big House Tour, $3.00 Adult
  $1.00 Youth (6-18)
  Tractor Drawn Wagon Tour, $1.00 (12+)
- Miscellaneous: Malabar Inn. 1820's stagecoach stop restaurant.

A writer and lover of nature, Louis Bromfield, dreamed of this scenic land and home. It is still a working farm and the place where Bromfield discovered new farming techniques. The guides at the Big House tell captivating stories.

AREA "CE"

THE WILDS

14000 International Road (off State Route 284),
Cumberland

- Area: **CE**
- Telephone Number: (740) 638-5030
- Hours: Daily, 9:00 a.m. - 6:00 p.m. (Summer)
  Daily, 9:00 a.m. - 5:00 p.m. (Rest of the Year)
- Admission: $8.00 Adult, $5.00 Children (4-12)
- Tours: 1 hour tours in a shuttle bus

Once a strip mine (donated by American Electric Power) it is now home to the International Center for the preservation of wild animals. Over 9000 acres of forest and grassland with 150 lakes is home to animals in a protected open range habitat (no

ANIMALS & FARMS

pens, stables, and cages) designed to create an environment for reproduction. You'll see many animals you don't see in zoos like African gazelles, reticulated giraffes, mountain zebras, tundra swans and red wolves in herds. We saw an Indian rhinoceros that was born in captivity and had foot problems so severe he couldn't be displayed in zoos. With lots of "tender loving care" and adaptation exercises, he now roams free. You might also see real wild horses that look like a rhinoceros and a horse. They are very strong and tough (yet beautiful to watch) animals.

ROLLING RIDGE RANCH
County Road 168 (State Route 62 to CR 168), **Millersburg**

- Area: **CE**
- Telephone Number: (330) 893-3777
- Hours: Monday – Saturday, 9:00 a.m.–1 hour before sunset

Take a 2-mile safari ride in your own vehicle or a horse drawn wagon to see over 200 animals from 6 continents. Feed the animals from the vehicle and stop by the petting zoo before you leave.

AREA "CW"

CARRIAGE HILL FARM AND MUSEUM
7860 East Shull Road (I-70 to Exit 38 - State Route 201 north), **Huber Heights**

- Area: **CW**
- Telephone Number: (937) 879-0461
- Hours: Monday - Friday, 10:00 a.m. - 5:00 p.m.
  Saturday - Sunday, 1:00 - 5:00 p.m.
- Admission: Donation

❑ Miscellaneous: Visitor's Center - Exhibits, videos, picnic area, fishing, horseback riding, cross country skiing, hayrides and bobsled rides.

The self-guided tour of an 1880's working farm is a great benefit to the community. The farm includes a summer kitchen, workshop, black smith and barns. They are best to visit when workers are planting or harvesting gardens.

ST. MARY'S FISH FARM
State Route 364 (East Side of Grand Lake), **St. Mary's**

- ❑ Area: **CW**
- ❑ Telephone Number: (419) 394-5170
- ❑ Hours: Daily, 9:00 a.m. - 4:00 p.m.

After boating or swimming on Grand Lake (man-made), wander through 52 acres of ponds where pike, catfish, etc. are raised. The farm is one of the only three in Ohio and is the only farm with a large mouth bass hatchery.

FRESHWATER FARMS OF OHIO
2624 State Route 68, **Urbana**

- ❑ Area: **CW**
- ❑ Telephone Number: (937) 652-3701
- ❑ Hours: Monday - Friday, 1:00 - 6:00 p.m. Saturday, 10:00 a.m. - 6:00 p.m.
- ❑ Tours: By appointment
- ❑ Miscellaneous: Supplies for ponds at home - compatible fish, frogs. Produces several hundred thousand trout sold to premium restaurants.

ANIMALS & FARMS

Start your tour by petting a sturgeon fish. Why can you touch them, but not catfish? They raise rainbow trout that are bred in large water tanks. Farmer Smith, a marine biologist with a doctorate in nutrition, and his father (an engineer), developed a system of tracks and tanks using re-circulated pure cleaned water. The fish are really spoiled with a special diet and solar heated hatchery. View the spring water "ponds" with gravel bottoms (outside) and put a quarter in the machine to get fish food to feed the fish. These fish are really spoiled, aren't they?

YOUNG'S JERSEY DAIRY FARM
6880 Springfield-Xenia Road (On Route 68), **Yellow Springs**

- Area: **CW**
- Telephone Number: (937) 325-0629
- Hours: Daily, 10:00 a.m. – 10 p.m.
- Tours: Monday – Friday, (April – October)
  1 hour, $2.00 Children – FREE for Adults
  Short video follows the farming process
- Miscellaneous: Retail store began in 1960 and is still operated by members of the Young family. Meet the COW family - Barnabe, Cowtherine, Calfleen, and Cowvin. Udders and Putters Miniature Golf, Driving Range, Batting Cage, Corny Maze (a 3 acre corn field maze in late summer), Wagon Rides, Petting Area – Baby Jersey (pretty-faced calves), cows, pigs and sheep.

It is truly amazing at just how much food milk producing cows need! A daily average of 25 gallons of water plus 60 lbs. of silage (fermented hay or corn stalks), 30 lbs. of hay, and 20 lbs. of grain! Silage is stored and fermented in silos. Cows have 4 compartment stomachs. (Find out what "chewing her cud" means!) Cows produce milk after having their first calf and are then milked twice daily to produce 4-5 gallons of milk per day. When milk is fresh out of the cow it is cooled immediately to 35 degrees and then bottled. Raw milk has more nutrients and is more digestible (it still has a lot of enzymes). Learn the biggest secret to making GREAT home made ice cream. Go to the petting area and then the wagon ride with a treat at the end in the restaurant.

MARMON VALLEY FARM
5807 County Road 153, **Zanesfield**

- Area: **CW**
- Telephone Number: (937) 593-8051
- Hours: Call for details

Winter and summer activities are available at Marmon Valley Farm. They have live farm animals and a fun barn with rope bridges, rope swings and barn games. Hiking and horseback riding are available. If it's very cold, try ice-skating. When there's snow, you may want to take your sled along for some great sled riding hills. Horseback riding lessons are also available.

AREA "NC"

THE BUTTERFLY BOX
601 Division Street, **Kelley's Island**

- Area: **NC**
- Telephone Number: (419) 746-2454

Walk through a garden full of hundreds of North American butterflies. Beautiful colored butterflies in an exotic plant environment.

ANIMALS & FARMS

AFRICAN WILDLIFE SAFARI PARK
267 Lightner Road (Off State Route 2), **Port Clinton**

- Area: **NC**
- Telephone Number (419) 732-3606 or (800) 521-2660
- Hours: Daily, (May – September)
- Admission: $7.00 - $11.00
- Miscellaneous: Mombassa Café. Jungle Junction Playland. Safari Junction pony and camel rides, petting zoo.

See more than 400 animals (including llamas, alpacas, and zebras) as they wander freely around your vehicle as you drive through a 100-acre park. This is the only drive through safari park in the Midwest. The giraffe lean their long necks over to check you out through your car windows. Another favorite is the "Porkchop Downs" pig races. Boy, do they snort loud when they're trying to win!

THE ALASKAN BIRDHOUSE WILDLIFE AREA
Meechen Road, **Put-In-Bay**

- Area: **NC**
- Telephone Number (419) 285-9736
- Admission: $3.00 Adult, $2.00 Senior $1.50 Youth (6-12)

Narrated tours of North American Wildlife including grizzly bears, moose, geese, walleye fish, whales, cranes, quails, and ducks. Over 100 stuffed pelts of animals are displayed in their natural habitats.

LAGOON DEER PARK

State Route 269 (between State Route 2 and US 6), **Sandusky**

- Area: **NC**
- Telephone Number: (419) 684-5701
- Hours: Daily, 10:00 a.m. – 6:00 p.m.
  Mid April – Mid October
- Admission: $5.00 Adult, $3.00 Children (3-12)
  Pay Fishing available in stocked lake

Hand feed and pet hundreds of deer, llamas, miniature donkeys and other tame species. Altogether, they have 250 exotic animals from Europe, Japan, Asia, South and North America. Approximately 75 baby animals are born here each year.

CELERYVILLE VEGETABLE FARMS

4200 Broadway (Route 224 West to Route 103 South to Celeryville), **Willard**

- Area: **NC**
- Telephone Number: (419) 935-3633
- Hours: Weekdays, (June – September)

Judged one of the best industrial tours in the state, this is a 3000-acre organic "muck" vegetable garden. On tour you'll see greenhouses, celery and radish harvesting machines in action, and vegetable processing (cleaning, pruning) and packaging. Truly unique!

AREA "NE"

AKRON ZOOLOGICAL PARK

500 Edgewood Avenue, Perkins Woods Park, **Akron**

ANIMALS & FARMS 23

- Area: **NE**
- Telephone Number: (330) 375-2550
- Hours: Monday – Saturday, 10:00 a.m. – 5:00 p.m.
  Sunday – Holidays, 10:00 a.m. – 6:00 p.m.
  Mid April – Mid October
- Admission: $5.00 Adult, $4.00 Senior
  $4.00 Children (2-14)
  $1.00 Parking

A medium-sized zoo featuring Monkey Island, The River Otter Exhibit, and an Ohio Farmyard petting area.

SEA WORLD
1100 Sea World Drive (Off State Route 43 – Turnpike Exit 13), **Aurora**

- Area: **NE**
- Telephone Number: (800) 63-SHAMU
- Hours: Daily, 10:00 a.m. – Call for schedule of closing times. (May – September)
- Admission: $20.00 - $28.00, Under age 3 FREE
  $4.00 for Parking
- Miscellaneous: Picnic Areas, Food Service, Restaurants, Diaper Change and Nursing Facilities

A marine life theme park – home of the famous killer whale, Shamu. Also see shows with entertaining trained dolphins, sea lions, penguins, sea otters and walruses. There's lots of other sites to see like the Baywatch water ski show, Dolphin Cove (interactive dolphin habitat), Monster Marsh (life-sized dinosaurs moving in a "Jurrasic Park" setting), "Pirates" (silly 3D movie) and Shamus's Happy Harbor (3-acre pirate boat play ground). Another exhibit you won't want to miss, Shark Encounter is an arched tank that goes overhead making it look like sharks are surrounding you.

CLEVELAND METROPARKS ZOO
3900 Wildlife Way, **Cleveland**

- Area: **NE**
- Telephone Number: (216) 661-6500
- Hours: Daily, 9:00 a.m. – 5:00 p.m. (Summer)
  Until 7:00 p.m. Weekends (Summer)
  Rainforest, 10:00 a.m. – 5:00 p.m.
- Admission: $7.00 Adult (12+), $4.00 Children (2-11)
  Free Parking
- Miscellaneous: Outback railroad train ride. Concessions.

A rainforest with animal and plant settings like the jungles of Africa, Asia, and South America is the most popular exhibit to explore. The rainforest boasts a storm every 12 minutes, a 25-foot waterfall, and a walk-through aviary. Altogether, the whole zoo holds more 3300 animals from all continents including Africa and Australia.

LAKE FARM PARK
8800 Chardon Road (3 miles South on State Route 306 to State Route 6), **Kirtland**

- Area: **NE**
- Telephone Number: (800) 366-FARM
- Hours: Daily, 9:00 a.m. - 5:00 p.m.
- Admission: $5.00 Adult, $4.00 Senior (65+)
  $3.50 Children (2-11)
- Miscellaneous: Gift Shop. Restaurant. Comfortable walking or tennis shoes are best to wear on the farm. Wagon rides throughout the park are included. Wagon rentals are available.
  Barnyard - ostriches, poultry, sheep petting. Pony rides are $2.00.

ANIMALS & FARMS

Not really a farm - it's a park about farming (and the cleanest farm you'll ever visit!). Most of their focus is to discover where food and natural products come from. In the Dairy Parlor, you can milk a real cow and make ice cream from the cow's milk. Wander over to the Arena and watch the sheep show. What products can be made with the help of sheep? - How about feta cheese from their milk and yarn from their wool coats. Use special brushes to clean their wool and then spin some by hand. Exhibits are ready to be played with all day in the Great Tomato Works. A giant tomato plant (6 feet wide with 12-ft. leaves) greets you and once inside the greenhouse, you can go down below the earth in the dirt to see where plants get their start. Sneak up on a real honeybee comb, but mind the words on the sign, "*DO NOT DISTURB - HONEYBEES AT WORK*". This visit generates lots of questions about the food you eat. Great learning!

AREA "NW"

CULBERTSON'S MINI ZOO
(State Route 2 to Holland-Sylvania Road, North to Angola West), **Toledo**

- Area: **NW**
- Telephone Number: (419) 865-3470
- Hours: Monday – Saturday, 9:00 a.m. – 6:00 p.m.
- Admission: $2.00 Adult, $0.75 Children (3-14)
- Miscellaneous: Gift Shop

Specializes in the rescue and refuse of exotic animals like cougars, lions, tigers, baboons, buffaloes, deer, birds, and fish.

TOLEDO ZOO

2700 Broadway (I-75 to US 25 - 3 miles South of downtown),
Toledo

- Area: **NW**
- Telephone Number: (419) 385-5721
- Hours: Daily, 10:00 a.m. - 5:00 p.m. (April - Labor Day) Daily, 10:00 a.m. - 4:00 p.m. (Rest of the Year)
- Admission: $5.00 Adult $2.50 Senior (60+) and Children (2-11)
- Miscellaneous: Carnivore Cafe (dine in actual cages once used to house big cats!). Children's Zoo - petting zoo and hands on exhibits.

They have areas typical of a zoo but they are known for their Hippoquarium (the world's first underwater viewing of the hippopotamus) along with a well-defined interpretive center and hands- on exhibits. The Kingdom of Apes and African Savanna are other popular exhibits.

AREA "SC"

NOAH'S ARK ANIMAL FARM

1527 McGiffins Road (5 miles East on State Route 32),
Jackson

- Area: **SC**
- Telephone Number: (800) 282-2167
- Hours: Monday – Saturday, 10:00 a.m. – 6:00 p.m. Sunday, Noon – 6:00 p.m. (April – October).
- Admission: $5.00 Adult, $4.00 Children (3-12)

Exotic animals and birds (more than 150), miniature golf, Pay Fishing lake and ¼ mile train ride (additional $1.00).

BOB EVAN'S FARM
State Route 588 (off US 35 to State Route 325 South), **Rio Grande**

- Area: **SC**
- Telephone Number: (800) 944-FARM
- Hours: Daily, 8:30 a.m. - 5:00 p.m. (Summer)
  Weekends in September
- Tours: By wagon - 10:00 a.m., Noon, 2:00 and 4:00 p.m.
- Admission: FREE for tour - Activities additional

Begin or end your visit at the restaurant, once named "The Sausage Shop"-Bob's first restaurant. Then, wander round to visit the Farm Museum (implements of yesteryear farms and a pictorial history of the company). See a log cabin village with a one-room school house, small animal barn yard, hay rides, horseback riding, canoe trips, craft barn and demonstrations, plus the Homestead (an old stagecoach stop and former home of Bob and Jewel Evans). Nearby in Bedwell (State Route 50/35) is Jewel Evan's Mill where you can view millstones grinding flour.

AREA "SW"

CINCINNATI ZOO AND BOTANICAL GARDENS
3400 Vine Street (I-75 to Exit 6), **Cincinnati**

- Area: **SW**
- Telephone Number: (800) 944-4776
- Hours: Daily, 10:00 a.m. – 8:00 p.m. (Summer)
  9:00 a.m. – 6:00 p.m. (Rest of the Year)
  Children's Zoo – 10:00 a.m. 4:00 p.m.
- Admission: $8.00 Adult, $5.75 Senior (62+) $4.50 Children (2-12)

Children's Zoo additional $0.75
Parking Fee
- Miscellaneous: Safari Restaurant. Concessions. Camel, elephant and train rides.

Ranked one of the top 5 zoos in the United States, its highlights are the Bengal tigers and Kemodo dragons (10 feet long and 300 lbs.!). Their landscaped gardens duplicate the animals' world and the Jungle Trails exhibit even has a tropical rainforest. The first Insectarium (you guessed it!) in the nation is also here.

MISCELLANEOUS ACTIVITIES
(All entries are sorted by Region within Type)

ALPACA FARMS

TENDER SHEPHERD FARMS

C - 7434 Lafayette Road, **Lodi**. (330) 948-4218. Alpaca farm with over 40 acres to tour. Learn about their care and fiber products made from their fur.

MAGICAL FARMS

NE - 5280 Avon Lake Road, **Litchfield**. (330) 667-3233. Tours: Daylight hours. Second largest alpaca breeding farm in North America.

HUMANE SOCIETY / ANIMAL SHELTERS
- Columbus: (614) 777-7387
- Richland County: (419) 747-4174
- Cincinnati: (513) 541-6100

This is a great tour for a new pet owner or a child who is anxiously waiting for their first pet. Not only will you see many cats and dogs available for adoption, but a knowledgeable guide also shows you the Humane Society clinic and surgery rooms and explain the needs of your pet and how to be a good pet

ANIMALS & FARMS

owner. Be prepared to have the children fall in love with one of the animals while they are there!

ORCHARD / CROP FARMS

MILLER'S COUNTRY GARDEN

C - 2488 West State Route 37, **Delaware**. (740) 363-5229. Pick fresh tomatoes, peas, apples, peaches and beans.

CIRCLE "S" FARMS

C - 9015 London-Groveport Road, **Grove City**. (614) 878-7980. Hours: Daily (June – October). Vegetable and fruit picking. Farm produce, jams, and baked goods. Farm animals. Entertainment on weekends.

THE APPLE CABIN

C - 7665 Lafayette Road, **Lodi**. (330) 948-1476. Pick your own apples. Hayrides, fruit for sale.

APPLE HILL ORCHARDS

C - 1175 Lexington – Ontario Road (US 30 to Route 309), **Mansfield**. (419) 884-1500. Hours: Monday, 9:00 a.m. – 6:00 p.m., Sunday, 10:00 a.m. – 6:00 p.m. Pick your own apples.

LAWRENCE ORCHARDS

C - 2634 Smeltzer Road, **Marion**. (740) 389-3019. Apples, Festivals.

LYND FRUIT FARM

C -9090 Morse Road, **Pataskala**. (740) 927-7113. Pick red or golden delicious apples.

PINE CREST FARMS

C - 7586 River Corners, **Spencer**. (330) 667-2968. Pick your own strawberries (April – October). Pumpkin town (October).

ROCKWELL ORCHARDS

CE - Sandy Ridge Road (Off Route 147 East), **Barnesville**. (740) 425-2710. Hours: Monday – Saturday, 8:00 a.m. – 6:00 p.m. Processing and cider mill.

EBBERT'S FARM MARKET

CE - Ebbert Road (I-70 to Exit 218/220 off Route 40), **St. Clairsville**. (740) 695-5619. Vegetables and fruits by the season.

THE APPLE BARN

CW - 5842 State Route 571 East, **Greenville**. (937) 548-1223. Apples and peaches. Amish Room, Angel Room, Apple Room, Candy Room and Christmas Room.

FULTON FARMS

CW - State Route 202, **Troy**. (937) 339-2077. Strawberries, vegetables, melons, apples. Gift Loft. Market Café.

ROTHSCHILD BERRY FARM

CW - 3143 East State Route 36, **Urbana**. (937) 653-7397. Hours: Daily (call for details). Famous raspberry and herb picking. Gourmet market.

HILLSIDE ORCHARD

NE - 2397 Center Road (Route 303 and I-71), **Hinckley**. (330) 225-4748. Hours: Open Spring, Summer, and early Winter – Call for details. Fruits and vegetables.

PARKY'S FARM

SW - 10245 Winton Road, **Cincinnati**. (513) 521-PARK. Explore orchards and crops plus farm animals. Pony rides and play barn (farm theme play pits with plastic apples and eggs to jump in).

MINGES FARM

SW - 10109 New Haven Road, **Harrison**. (513) 367-2035. Strawberries (Summer).

ANIMALS & FARMS

HIDDEN VALLEY FRUIT FARM

SW - 5474 North State Route 48, **Lebanon**. (513) 932-1869. Strawberry Festival (June), Apple Days (September), Ohio Cider (October). Hayrides, crafts, cloggers, and pig roast.

IRONS FRUIT FARM

SW - 1640 Stubbs Mills Road, **Lebanon**. (513) 932-2853. Pick strawberries, cherries, red raspberries, blackberries, and blueberries. Corn, squash, apples, etc. are also sold. Petting zoo.

ROUSTERS APPLE HOUSE

SW - 1980 State Route 131, **Milford**. (513) 625-5504. Blueberries, blackberries, raspberries. Farmers market.

WINDMILL FARM MARKET

SW - State Route 73 and State Route 48, **Springboro**. (513) 885-3965. Pick your own fruits. Vegetables, herbs and plants for sale.

Chapter 3

FUN INTERACTIVE LEARNING

AREA "C"

OHIO'S CENTER OF SCIENCE AND INDUSTRY (COSI)
280 East Broad Street, Downtown, **Columbus**

- Area: **C**
- Telephone Number: (614) 228-COSI
- Hours: Monday – Saturday 10:00 a.m. – 5:00 p.m. Sunday, Noon – 5:30 p.m.
- Admission: $20.00 per family, $6.00 Adult $5.00 Youth (13-18), $4.00 Children (2-12)

Children and adults of every age love COSI. It is a place you can go again and again to be educated in a fun, challenging atmosphere. Explore four floors of hands-on exhibits focusing on science, technology, health and history. Take your preschool-aged children upstairs to Kid-Space. They will pet live animals (mice, chickens, turtles), paint their faces, do a puppet show, water play, ride in a boat, and just have a good active time there. Other favorite areas are the Animal Lab (rodents play games), Jeffrey Simulated Coal Mine, the planetarium shows and the Streets of Yesteryear (with old time movie theater). Older kids conquer their fears and ride the high wire cycle 20 feet above to ground or have their hair stand on end at a rechostatic generator. In Kid-Space they can star in their own news or rock video and purchase a copy as a souvenir.

PERKINS OBSERVATORY
State Route 23, 1 mile south of Delaware, **Columbus**

- Area: **C**
- Telephone Number: (740) 363-1257
- Schedule: Friday night Open House held once a month

FUN INTERACTIVE LEARNING

- Admission: FREE (must be ordered in advance – 6 ticket limit). Send self-addressed stamped envelope to:
  Perkins Program
  P.O. Box 16209
  Columbus, Ohio 43216

Children who have studied astronomy will especially enjoy this. The stars naturally fascinate them at night so this is a real treat to see them this close. The program includes a tour of the observatory, a talk on astronomy, and then telescope observation if it is a clear night.

INSTITUTE OF INDUSTRIAL TECHNOLOGY
55 South First Street, Newark

- Area: **C**
- Telephone Number: (740) 349-9277
- Hours: Wednesday – Sunday, Noon – 4:00 p.m.

History of Licking County including the Heisey Glass Studio where artisans create beautiful blown glass. Also displays of molds and tools used to make pressed glass.

Transportation Area – Methods of travel including the shipping canals, railroads, and roads.

Process and Products Area – Turn a real line shaft. See products made in Licking Country such as Mason jars and engines for farm machines.

Materials Area – See where local raw materials are used in manufacturing, farming and fuel production. Interactive touch displays educate kids on what, where, and how materials are extracted (raw and finished forms).

AREA "CE"

McKINLEY MUSEUM & DISCOVER WORLD

800 McKinley Monument Drive, NW (I-77 south to exit 106, I-77 north to exit 105, follow signs), **Canton**

- Area: **CE**
- Telephone Number: (330) 455-7043
- Hours: Monday – Saturday, 9:00 a.m. – 5:00 p.m. (until 6:00 p.m. Summer)
  Sunday, Noon – 5:00 p.m. (until 6:00 p.m. Summer)
- Admission: $6.00 Adult, $5.00 Senior $4.00 Children, $18.00 Family Rate
- Miscellaneous: Planetarium, Research stations with topics like Dinosaurs, Geology, Archaeology, Beavers Life, Baby Shamu, Tornadoes, and a Human Heart

After you park, take the 108 steps leading up to the bronze doors of the stunning McKinley Memorial where President William McKinley and his wife and children were laid to rest. A few steps away is the McKinley Museum where you can visit McKinley Hall, Historical Hall and the Street of Shops. Walk along the 19th Century Street of homes, general store, print shop, and doctor's office – all indoors on exhibit. Kid's eyes sparkle at the model trains and pioneer toys such as paper dolls and cast iron mini kitchen appliances. Last, but even more exciting for kids, is Discover World. A large dinosaur robot named Alice greets you and a real Stark County mastodon Bondo Betty is around the corner. Find hidden fossil drawers, make a fossil, look for the queen bee in a living beehive, touch a chinchilla, play a tune on tone pipes, or be a weather forecaster – All in one afternoon!

PRO FOOTBALL HALL OF FAME
2121 George Halas Drive NW (I-77 and US 62), **Canton**

- Area: **CE**
- Telephone Number: (330) 456-8207
- Hours: Daily, 9:00 a.m. – 8:00 p.m., Memorial Day – Labor Day
  Daily, 9:00 a.m. – 5:00 p.m., Rest of Year (Closed Christmas Only)
- Admission: $9.00 Adult, $6.00 Senior (62+)
  4.00 Youth, $22.00 Family
- Miscellaneous: Tailgating Snack Bar – over the counter / vending with Top Twenty Tele-trivia and QBI Call-the-Play Game.
  Special video presentations in the center of each room (our favorite – <u>16 Fantastic Finishes</u>)

If you're an NFL Football Fan, the anticipation builds as you enter the grounds of the sprawling Hall of Fame. At the top of the curving ramp upstairs you view the first 100 years of football with Pro Football's Birth Certificate and the oldest football (1895) available for display. Then hit some Astroturf and browse through Pro Football today and Photo Art Gallery (award winning, some amazing, photographs of football heroes in action). Older children look forward to the Enshrinement Galleries and Super Bowl Room. The newest addition to the Hall is Game Day Stadium. A 100-Yard film is shown in a two-sided rotating theater. Start at the Locker Room Show. Then the entire seating area rotates 180 degrees to the Stadium Show where you become part of a NFL game with a 2 story Cinemascope presentation. You see, hear and almost make contact with the players! What a rush!

AREA "CW"

DAYTON MUSEUM OF DISCOVERY
2600 DeWeese Parkway (North of downtown I-75 to exit 57B, follow signs), **Dayton**

- Area: **CW**
- Telephone Number: (937) 275-7431
- Hours: Monday – Saturday, 9:00 a.m. – 5:00 p.m. Sunday, Noon – 5:00 p.m.
- Admission: $4.00 Adult, $2.50 Senior $1.50 Children (3-16) $1.00 additional for Space Theater

Includes Museum of Natural History, Children's Museum plus Lasersphere (computer animated planetarium).

Wild Ohio – An indoor zoo with small animals in natural surroundings. Visit the den of bobcat Van Cleve.

Ancient World – Egyptian artifacts with 3000 year old mummy.

Science Center – Inventions stations, preschool area, chemistry lab, and discovery tower provides hands on adventures.

UNITED STATES AIR FORCE MUSEUM
Wright Patterson Air Force Base, I-75 to State Route 4 East to Harshman Road Exit, **Fairborn**

- Area: **CW**
- Telephone Number: (937) 255-3286
- Hours: Daily, 9:00 a.m. - 5:00 p.m.
- Admission: FREE
- Miscellaneous: Largest Gift Shop imaginable IMAX Theater - 6 story with hourly 40 minute

space/aviation films - feel like you're flying with the pilots. (Fee $2.00 - $5.00)
Huffman Prairie Field - See where The Wright Brothers first attempted flight. Continuous films played at stations throughout the complex.

Anyone close to Dayton has to visit the world's oldest and largest military aviation museum with 50 vintage WWII aircraft and 300 other aircraft and rockets. See everything from presidential planes, to Persian Gulf advanced missiles and bombs, to the original Wright Brothers wind tunnel, to the original Apollo 15 command module. Look for the observation balloon (easy to find--just look up ever so slightly), Rosie the Rivetor and "Little Vittles" parachuted goodies. Discovery Hangar Five follows a common museum trend and focuses on interactive learning of why things fly and different parts of airplanes.

NEIL ARMSTRONG AIR AND SPACE MUSEUM

500 South Apollo Drive (I-75 to Exit 111), **Wapakoneta**

- Area: **CW**
- Telephone Number: (419) 738-8811 or (800) 860-0142
- Hours: Monday – Saturday, 9:30 a.m. – 5:00 p.m.
  Sunday, Noon – 5:00 p.m.(March – November)
- Admission: $4.00 Adult, $1.00 Youth (6-12)

The museum honors Neil Armstrong (a Wapakoneta native) and other area aeronauts (like the Wright Brothers) and their flying machines. After greeted by a NASA Skylaneer flown by Armstrong in the early 1960's, trace the history of flights from balloons to space travel. Look at the Apollo crew spacesuits or watch a video of lunar space walks. In the Astro Theater, pretend you're on a trip to the moon. Another favorite is the Infinity Cube

– 18 square feet covered with mirrors that make you feel like you've been projected into space. Blast OFF!

AREA "NE"

INVENTURE PLACE

221 South Broadway Street (off State Route 18, Downtown),
Akron

- Area: **NE**
- Telephone Number: (800) 968-IDEA
- Hours: Wednesday – Saturday, 9:00 a.m. – 5:00 p.m. Sunday, Noon – 5:00 p.m.
  Summer extended hours
- Admission: $7.50 Adult
  $6.00 Senior (55+) and Children (3-13)
  FREE admission 1st Sunday of every month
- Miscellaneous: National Inventors Hall of Fame (4 floors of exhibits). Open architecture with 5 tiers of steel and windows.

Start with the Inventor's Workshop. The sign that greets you says it all - "This is a place to mess around. No rights. No wrongs. Only experiments and surprises!" This is honestly the most hands-on, exploring creativity area we've ever visited in Ohio. Kids (and adults) minds open before your eyes. Therefore, plan to spend at least 2 hours exploring. In the wood shop you can actually work with a hammer, nails, and saws (all real) to build a mini boat, house, or new instrument. The swap shop is an area where regular visitors can bring broken appliances, give a description of the problem, then swap for another item to fix or take apart. A favorite exhibit was the "untitled" (metal grasses) which was sculpted of iron powder and danced to music in a magnetic field. Also the animation area where we each made our own "Toy Story" type movies.

CLEVELAND CHILDREN'S MUSEUM
10730 Euclid Avenue, University Circle (I-90 to Chester Avenue Exit), **Cleveland**

- Area: **NE**
- Telephone Number: (216) 791-7114
- Hours: Tuesday - Friday, 1:00 p.m. - 5:00 p.m. (Summers open at 11:00 a.m.)
Saturday, 10:00 a.m. - 5:00 p.m.; Sunday, Noon - 5:00p.m.
Monday - Toddler Time 1:00 - 5:00 p.m. (Pre-school only)
- Admission: $5.00 Adult, $4.50 Senior
2nd Wednesday 5:00 - 8:00 p.m. (Only $1.00 everyone)

Our favorites was the "Little House Under Construction" where you pretend to paint and fix a home with roller brushes, roof slats, and pretend tools. Work a wrecking ball or bulldozer too. Also, wander through over 100 interactive displays like Weathernet, Circus of Circles, Over and Under Bridges, and People Puzzle. "Water-Go-Round" has a kid's pump, river tanks and boat races on a replica of Lake Erie.

THE CLEVELAND MUSEUM OF NATURAL HISTORY
1 Wade Oval Drive, University Circle, **Cleveland**

- Area: **NE**
- Telephone Number: (216) 231-4600
- Hours: Daily, 10:00 a.m. – 5:00 p.m. Sundays, Noon – 5:00 p.m., Wednesday until 10:00 p.m. (September – May)
- Admission: $6.00 Adult, $4.00 Children (5-17) / Senior
- Miscellaneous: Gift shop. Planetarium $1.50 extra

Meet "Happy" the 70 foot long dinosaur or "Lucy" the oldest human fossil. Birds and Botany outdoors and a Gem Room and Hall of Man (human skeletons) highlight your visit.

GREAT LAKES SCIENCE CENTER
601 Erieside Avenue (E 9th Street and I-90, North Coast Harbor, Downtown), **Cleveland**

- Area: **NE**
- Telephone Number: (216) 694-2000
- Hours: Monday – Sunday, 9:30 a.m. – 5:30 p.m., Wednesday and Thursday until 9:00 p.m.
- Admission: $9.95 Adult, $7.00 Children (3-17) Memberships Available
- Miscellaneous: Gift Shop – We picked up Astro Food (freeze dried ice cream and french fries). OmniMax Theater – 6 story domed screen image and sound.

Over 300 interactive exhibits – especially fun on the second floor. Pilot a blimp, test your batting skills, or bounce off the walls in the Polymer Funhouse. The science playground museum focuses on the Great Lakes region and its environment. Young lab scientists (guests) can create a tornado or create light.

THE HEATH MUSEUM
8911 Euclid Avenue, University Circle, (I-90 Exit on Chester), **Cleveland**

- Area: **NE**
- Telephone Number: (216) 231-5010
- Hours: Monday – Friday. 9:00 a.m. – 5:00 p.m. Saturday, 10:00 a.m. – 5:00 p.m. Sunday, Noon – 5:00 p.m.
- Admission: $4.50 Adult
- $3.00 Senior and Youth (6-17)

FUN INTERACTIVE LEARNING   43

- ❑ Miscellaneous: Heath related books and games.
    Group tours suggested as they present specially designed age specific topics for your group.

Learn from Stuffie, the stuffed doll, with a zippered window to his organs that can be removed and played with. Have you met "Juno" the transparent talking woman or seen the world's largest tooth (an 18 foot walk-through). Touch Island is interactive and the Children's Health Fair features "Stop That Germ", Food Guide Pyramid and Cardiovascular Fitness.

WILLIAM G. MATHER MUSEUM
Docked at 1001 East 90th Street Pier. Northcoast Harbor,
Cleveland

- ❑ Area: **NE**
- ❑ Telephone Number: (216) 574-6262
- ❑ Hours: Daily, 10:00 a.m. - 5:00 p.m., except Sunday, Noon - 5:00 p.m. (Summer)
    Weekends Only (May/September/October)
- ❑ Admission: $5.00 Adult, $4.00 Senior, $3.00 Youth (5-18)
- ❑ Miscellaneous: Best for preschoolers and older because of dangerous spots while walking. Films play continuously.

The floating Mather is an iron boat once used to carry ore, coal and grain along the Great Lakes. Little eyes will open wide in the 4 story engine room and they will have fun pretending to be the crew (or maybe guests) in the cozy sleeping quarters or the elegant dining room. Group tours are treated to programmed learning fun in the Interactive Cargo Hold area. Make a sailor hat or a boat made from silly putty (why does a boat float?). Learn to tie sailors' knots with real rope or pretend you're at sea as you move the ship's wheel. In the pilothouse area, kids use navigation charts, working radar, and a marine radio to plan a trip.

AREA "NW"

COSI TOLEDO
One Discovery Way, Downtown, **Toledo**

- Area: **NW**
- Telephone Number: (419) 244-COSI
- Hours: Monday - Saturday, 10:00 a.m. - 5:00 p.m. Sunday, Noon - 5:30 p.m.
- Admission: $6.50 Adult (19-64)
  $5.00 Senior (65+) and Children (2-18)
  $25.00 Family
- Miscellaneous: Science 2 Go Gift Shop. Einstein's Diner - restaurant of food, "Science where you're encouraged to play with your food".

Seven learning worlds including Mind Zone (distorted Gravity Room, Animation, T-Rex), Sports (improve your game using science), Life Force (secrets of parts of the body like your skin, brain, and stomach), Water Works (water arcade, water travel, rainstorms), KidSpace, and BabySpace (18 months and under). The older kids will love Whiz-Bang Engineering and Science Park (greeted by Ed the animatronic security guard, feel hydraulics with motion simulator, take the Science on the Go Challenge!).

AREA "SW"

CINCINNATI FIRE MUSEUM
315 West Court Street, Downtown **Cincinnati**

- Area: **SW**
- Telephone Number (513) 621-5553
- Hours: Tuesday – Friday, 10:00 a.m. – 4:00 p.m.

Weekends, Noon – 4:00 p.m.
- Admission: $3.00 Adult, $2.50 Senior (55+) $2.00 Children (2-12)

From the minute you walk in the restored fire station, the kids will be intrigued by the nation's first professional fire department exhibits. Displays chronicle fire fighting history from antique equipment to the cab of a newer fire truck where you can actually pull levers, push buttons, ring the siren and flash emergency lights. The museum has an emphasis on fire safety with "Safe House" models and a video about fire fighting dangers. Before you leave be sure your guide has let you slide down the 5-foot fire pole or push the hand pump engine.

CINCINNATI HISTORY MUSEUM
1301 Western Avenue (I-75 North to Exit 1), **Cincinnati**

- Area: **SW**
- Telephone Number: (800) 733-2077
  Hours: Monday - Saturday (& Holidays), 9:00 a.m. - 5:00 p.m.; Sunday, 11:00 a.m. - 6:00 p.m.
- Admission: $5.50 Adult, $3.50 Children (3-12)
- Miscellaneous: Gift Shops - Worth a good look!

Walk through re-created streets of Cincinnati. Visit the Fifth Street Market and Millcreek Millery - try on hats of the early 1900's and then shop next door at the pretend open air market. Next, walk through a life-like forest with shadows and birds wrestling and singing. The kids can play on a miniature cabin and flat boat. Probably first, you'll visit with The Flynns (ring the doorbell first) family talking about life at home during World War II. Hop on board a streetcar with the conductor telling news of the war. Pre-schoolers can play in the "Garden for Victory" where they pretend to plant and harvest a garden (in a sandbox with plastic vegetables and utensils). The produce from Victory Gardens was canned for soldiers. Moms and grandmothers will have to check out the "Leg Makeup Bar" (clue: there was a stocking shortage during the war). Very authentically presented, clever displays throughout the whole museum. Cincinnati folks should be proud.

CINCINNATI MUSEUM OF NATURAL HISTORY AND SCIENCE

1301 Western Avenue (I-75 North to Exit 1), **Cincinnati**

- Area: **SW**
- Telephone Number: (800) 733-2077
- Hours: Monday - Saturday, 9:00 a.m. - 5:00 p.m. Sunday, 11:00 a.m. - 6:00 p.m.
- Admission: $5.50 Adult, $3.50 Children (3-12)
- Miscellaneous: Gift shops. All are worth a visit. Many science projects to do at home.

Want to know a lot about the Ohio Valley's Natural and Geological history? Start at the Ice Age of fossils and re-created walk-through glaciers. (There are two routes - one that is challenging and involves much climbing and navigating, and the other that is wheelchair or stroller accessible). On to the simulated Limestone Cavern with underground waterfalls and a live bat colony (behind glass!). You can pretend you're an archeologist digging up dinosaur bones in a sandbox with tools and brushes in Dinosaur Hall. In the recycling center take a look at the garbage used by an average family and ways to reduce it. When you see a pile of garbage bags stacked on end and towering to the ceiling, your family will want to consider ways to sort recyclables and reduce unnecessary waste. Find out "All About You" as you explore inside, outside and beneath your great body. Brush a huge tooth, see under the skin of your hand, pretend in the office of doctors and dentists, or maybe play pinball as your "food ball" goes through the digestive system. Plan a day at this extremely well done exhibit!

Chapter 4

MUSEUMS

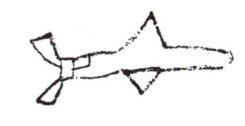

AREA "C"

BARBER'S MUSEUM AND HALL OF FAME
2 ½ South High Street, **Canal Winchester**

- Area: **C**
- Telephone Number: (740) 833-9931 or (740) 466-HAIR
- Admission: FREE

See a collection of shaving mugs and old barber chairs, some over 150 years old. Reflections of other trades related to barbering (surgery, dentistry, and medicine) are also displayed because early barbers dabbled in many of these areas. You will see 6 rooms set up depicting different eras of barbering.

MID-OHIO HISTORICAL MUSEUM
700 Winchester Pike, **Canal Winchester**

- Area: **C**
- Telephone Number: (740) 837-5573
- Hours: Wednesday - Saturday, 11:00 a.m. - 5:00 p.m. Spring - Mid December
- Admission: $2.00 (6 and under FREE)
- Miscellaneous: Gift Shop, Old and New Collectibles

As you step in the door, you will see a train display in the lobby. To your left, you will go through a door into the magical world of dolls. The collection includes rare antique dolls and toys dating from the 1700's to contemporary. Barbie fans of all ages will love the extensive Barbie collection.

TED LEWIS MUSEUM
133 West Main Street (Route 23 – follow signs), **Circleville**

- Area: **C**
- Telephone Number: (740) 474-3231 or (740) 474-3834
- Hours: Friday and Saturday, 1:00 – 5:00 p.m.
- Tours: By Appointment
- Admission: $1.00 per person

Ted Lewis was a famous songwriter and dance man with hit songs such as "Me and My Shadow" and "When My Baby Smiles at Me". Kids love the story about Lewis' famous top hat. Hear his syncopated jazz music while you tour the museum. At the end of your visit, be sure to sit for a while in the Ted Lewis Theatre where you can watch videos of Ted's performances and movie and TV appearances. Be sure to bring the grandparents for this walk down memory lane!

KELTON HOUSE MUSEUM AND GARDENS
586 East Town Street (Downtown), **Columbus**

- Area: **C**
- Telephone Number: (614) 464-2022
- Hours: Sundays, 1:00 – 4:00 p.m.
- Tours: Available by Reservation
- Admission: $1.50 Adult, $1.00 Children and Seniors

The Kelton House was once a stop on the Underground Railroad and home of a prominent Columbus merchant family from 1852 to 1975. The Victorian home has large music boxes playing the tune "A Bicycle Built for Two", tin bathing tubs and authentic wardrobes. While you are outside, you will walk through the Victorian gardens and learn the meaning of different flowers (tulip means charity). The museum has many Kelton family momentos and Victorian furnishings. Your tour guide may slip in a few words about the Kelton House ghost if you are interested! The Columbus Junior League is responsible for the Kelton House tours.

MUSIQUE MECHANIQUE
2960 North High Street, **Columbus**

- Area: **C**
- Telephone Number: (614) 263-2636
- Tours: Wednesday - Sunday, 12:00 - 5:30 p.m. (Spring - Fall)
- Admission: $2.50 per person

This is a place very few people know about (except for the music box shop downstairs). Musique Mechanique is an Old World handcrafted musical show museum. The kids find the music and movement exciting.

THURBER HOUSE
77 Jefferson Avenue (Downtown), **Columbus**

- Area: **C**
- Telephone Number: (614) 464-1032
- Hours: Daily, Noon – 4:00 p.m.
- Tours: Guided tours Sundays, 2:00 p.m. or by appointment Group Tours: 8 – 18 (or larger), Appointment only
- Admission: $2.00 Adult , $1.50 Children (12+)

Only the very new to Columbus have not heard of James Thurber, the well-known humorist and cartoonist who grew up in Columbus. The restored home is where James lived during his college years. The house is featured in several of Thurber's stories. Be sure to read some of Thurber's works before you visit or purchase some of his books at the bookstore in Thurber House. The bookstore sells books by other Ohioians also.

THE LIVING BIBLE MUSEUM
500 Tingley Avenue, (I-71 to US 30 West to State Route 545 North), **Mansfield**

- Area: **C**
- Telephone Number: (419) 524-0139
- Hours: Monday – Friday, 10:00 a.m. – 5:00 p.m. (April – December)
- Weekends & Holidays, 10:00 a.m. – 7:00 p.m. (January – December)
- Admission: $4.50 Adult, $4.25 Senior, $3.50 Youth (6-18)
- Miscellaneous: Gift Shop. Collection of rare bibles and religious woodcarvings.

The only life-size wax museum in Ohio – it features figures from the Old and New Testaments. Featured stories include the Life of Christ, Jonah and the whale, and Adam and Eve. The tour guide takes you through dimly lit hallways that add a theatrical, dramatic effect. At the end of the tour you will be left emotional (a small chapel is available to reflect).

WYANDOT POPCORN MUSEUM
169 East Church Street, (Heritage Hall – Marion County Museum of History), **Marion**

- Area: **C**
- Telephone Number: (740) 387-HALL
- Hours: Wednesday – Sunday, 1:00 – 4:00 p.m. (May – October)
  Weekends Only (November – April)
- Group tours of 20+ people by appointment

Before you enter the Popcorn Museum, see the hand-made miniature, working carousel and Prince Imperial (a stuffed 25 year old horse from France). You won't believe how they braided his mane! As you enter the large, colorful tent, you'll be enchanted by the antique popcorn poppers and concession wagons. See the first automated popper and the first all electric popper – all in pristine condition. It's the only museum like it in the world and is popular with stars like Paul Newman, who borrowed a Wyandot Concession Wagon to promote his popcorn, "Old Time Style", in Central Park.

MOTORCYCLE HERITAGE MUSEUM

33 Collegeview Road, **Westerville**

- Area: **C**
- Telephone Number: (614) 891-2425
- Hours: Monday - Friday, 9:00 a.m. - 5:00 p.m.
  Saturday, 10:00 a.m. - 4:00 p.m.
  Sunday & Holidays, 1:00 - 4:00 p.m.
- Admission: Donation

A self-guided tour featuring a wall mural, the history of motorcycles, and the Glory Days. Kids are most attracted to the 50 motorcycles on display.

YE OLDE MILL ICE CREAM MUSEUM

Velvet Ice Cream (State Route 13), **Utica**

- Area: **C**
- Telephone Number: (740) 892-3921
- Hours: Daily, 11:00 a.m. – 9:00 p.m. (Summer)
  Daily, 11:00 a.m. – 8:00 p.m. (September)

Daily, 11:00 a.m. – 7:00 p.m. (October)
- Admission: FREE

Did you know that the ice cream cone originated by mistake at the St. Louis World's Fair when a waffle vendor rolled waffles into cones for an ice cream vendor who ran out of serving cups? Learn all sorts of ice cream trivia at the Ice Cream Museum located in the restored 1817 mill and water wheel which is surrounded by 20 acres of wooded parklands with ducks and picnic areas. While you are at the mill, stop by the viewing gallery to watch ice cream being made and packaged. Then, catch a light meal and ice cream or yogurt dessert at the 1800's Ice Cream Parlor and gift shop.

AREA "CE"

BARBARA BARBE DOLL MUSEUM
211 Chestnut Street (State Route 147 and State Route 800),
Barnesville

- Area: **CE**
- Telephone Number: (740) 425-1760
- Hours: Wednesday – Sunday, 1:00 – 4:00 p.m.
  May – September
- Admission: $2.00 Adult, $1.00 Youth (6-12)

Five rooms of a former 1836 women's seminary display 3000 dolls of the late Barbara Barbe's (noted designer and collector) collection. The museum includes dolls made of bisque, wax, tin and plastic. See recent models by Ideal and old European dolls dressed in original costumes.

NATIONAL ROAD ZANE GREY MUSEUM
U.S. 40 / I-70 Norwich Exit

- Area: **CE**
- Telephone Number: (740) 872-3143
- Hours: Monday – Saturday, 9:30 a.m. – 5:30 p.m. Sunday, Noon – 5:00 p.m. (May – September) Daily, Except Monday & Tuesday (March, April, October and November)
- Admission: $5.00 Adult, $1.25 Youth (6 – 12)

"Head West Young Man" in a Conestoga wagon as you explore the history of US 40 National Road. Built based on a concept of George Washington, it stretches between western territories in Illinois to the eastern state of Maryland. It was vital to the development of the frontier heading west and later called "America's Main Street". Play a game where children locate all the different types of bridges on this route (examples: the "Y" and "S" Bridge). The facility also commemorates author Zane Grey and his western novels.

TOY & HOBBY MUSEUM
531 West Smithville Road (off State Route 57 by Smith Dairy), **Orrville**

- Area: **CE**
- Telephone Number: (330) 683-TOYS
- Hours: Monday and Friday, 6:30 – 9:00 p.m.
- Saturday, Noon – 6:00 p.m.
- Admission: $3.00 General, $10.00 Family
- Miscellaneous: More than 2000 toy trucks, miniature toy farm equipment and oodles of pencils.

DAVID WARTHER MUSEUM
1387 State Route 39 (In the Dutch Valley Complex), **Sugarcreek**

- Area: **CE**
- Telephone Number: (330) 852-3455

David Warther II is the grandson of Ernest Warther. He continues the legacy of carvings with a special emphasis on carving the theme "The History of the Ship" – solid legal ivory model ships. Even the rig lines are carved of ivory (one strand measures $1/10,000^{th}$ of an inch in diameter). David's workshop is on location.

AREA "CW"

PAUL LAWRENCE DUNBAR STATE MEMORIAL
219 North Paul Lawrence Dunbar Street, **Dayton**

- Area: **CW**
- Telephone Number: (800) 860-0148
- Hours: Wednesday – Saturday, 9:30 a.m. – 5:00 p.m.
  Sunday & Holidays, Noon – 5:00 p.m.
  Memorial Day – Labor Day
  Weekends Only (September, October)
- Admission: $2.50 Adult, $2.00 Senior (60+)
  $2.00 Youth (6-12)

The restored home of the first African American to achieve acclaim in American literature. From a young poet at age 6 to a nationally known figure (until his death at age 33 of tuberculosis), the guide helps you understand his inspiration especially from his mother and her stories of slavery. Personal belongings like his bicycle built by the Wright Brothers and a sword presented to him by President Roosevelt lead you to his bedroom where he wrote 100 novels, poems and short stories.

MUSEUM OF POSTAL HISTORY

131 North Main Street (Lower Level of Post Office), **Delphos**

- ❑ Area: **CW**
- ❑ Telephone Number: (419) 695-2811
- ❑ Hours: Monday, Wednesday, Friday, 1:30 – 3:30 p.m.

7000 square feet of displays plus media presentations that show development of American history and the influences of the U.S. Mail. See the progress of mail processing, development of the letter, stamps, postmarks and the idea of a post office. You can actually sit in a 1906 rural mail coach.

AREA "NC"

MERRY-GO-ROUND MUSEUM

West Washington and Jackson Streets (State Route 6), **Sandusky**

- ❑ Area: **NC**
- ❑ Telephone Number: (419) 626-6111
- ❑ Hours: Monday - Saturday, 11:00 a.m. - 5:00 p.m.
    Sunday, Noon - 5:00 p.m. (Summer)
    Weekends Only, (January & February)
    Wednesday - Sunday (Rest of the Year)
- ❑ Admission: $4.00 Adult, $3.00 Senior (60+) $2.00 Children (4-14)
- ❑ Miscellaneous: Gift Shop

MUSEUMS

This colorful, bright, big museum was the former Post Office. Once inside, you'll see all sorts of carousel memorabilia and history. Next, tour the workshop to watch craftsman make carousel horses with authentic "old world" tools. Finally, ride the Herschel 1930's indoor merry-go-round.

AREA "NE"

STAN HYWET HALL
714 North Portage Path, (I-77 to State Route 18 to North Portage), **Akron**

- Area: **NE**
- Telephone Number: (330) 836-5533
  Hours: Tuesday – Saturday, 10:00 a.m. – 4:00 p.m.
    Sunday, 1:00 – 4:00 p.m. (Year Round)
  Monday, 10:00 a.m. – 4:00 p.m. (April – December)
- Admission: $7.00 Adult, $6.50 Senior
  $3.50 Children (6-12)
- Miscellaneous: Museum Store, Carriage House Café

Want to pretend you're visiting old rich relatives for tea – this is the place. The long driveway up to the home is beautifully landscaped. You can park right next to the home and carriage house (vs. a block away) and are greeted as an invited guest. The actual family photographs of the Seiberling Family (Frank was the co-founder of the Goodyear Tire and Rubber Company) scattered throughout the home make you feel as if you know them. Stan Hywet means "stone quarry" referring to the stone quarry the house was built on and the stone that was supplied for building. Being an English Tudor, it is rather dark inside with an almost "castle-like" feeling (the detailed wood panels and crown molding are magnificent). Try to count the fireplaces (23) and discover concealed telephones behind the paneled walls.

VICTORIAN PERAMBULATOR MUSEUM
26 East Cedar Street (off State Route 46), **Jefferson**

- Area: **NE**
- Telephone Number: (440) 575-9588
- Hours: Saturday, 11:00 a.m. – 5:00 p.m.
  Wednesday, 11:00 a.m. – 5:00 p.m. (Summer Only)
- Admission: $3.00 Adult, $2.50 Youth (6-11)

First of all, do you know what a perambulator is? If you were like us, we just had to know! Answer...a baby carriage. Two sisters have collected and displayed almost 140 carriages dating from the mid- 1800's to the early 1900's. Some are shaped like swans, gondolas, seahorses, and antique cars (made from wicker, which was the Victorian style). This is supposedly the nation's only baby carriage museum.

YOUNGSTOWN HISTORICAL CENTER OF INDUSTRY & LABOR
151 West Wood Street, **Youngstown**

- Area: **NE**
- Telephone Number: (800) 262-6137 or (330) 743-5934
- Hours: Wednesday – Saturday, 9:00 a.m. – 5:00 p.m.
  Sunday, Noon – 5:00 p.m.
- Admission: $4.00 Adult, $3.50 Senior
  $1.00 Youth (6-12)

If your family has a heritage of steelworkers in the family, then this is the place to explain their hard work. The history of the iron and steel industry in the Mahoning Valley area can be viewed easily looking at the life-sized dioramas titled, "By the Sweat of Their Brow". Rooms are set up like typical steel mill locker rooms, company houses, and a blooming room. They certainly give you the "feel" of the treacherous work at the mill.

AREA "NW"

TOLEDO FIREFIGHTERS MUSEUM
918 Sylvania Avenue, **Toledo**

- Area: **NW**
- Telephone Number: (419) 478-FIRE
- Hours: Saturday, Noon – 4:00 p.m. (Summer)
  Saturday and Sunday, Noon – 4:00 p.m. (Winter)

Feel what 150 years of history of firefighting must have meant to the fireman. Learn fire safety tips. See actual vintage pumpers, uniforms, and equipment used that trace the growth of the Toledo Fire Department. Located in the former No. 18 Fire Station.

AREA "SC"

JAMES M. THOMAS TELEPHONE MUSEUM
68 East Main Street, **Chillicothe**

- Area: **SC**
- Telephone Number: (740) 772-8200
- Hours: Monday – Friday, 8:30 a.m. – 4:30 p.m.
- Admission: FREE

Run by the Chillicothe Telephone Company, it shows the telephone from its' invention stages to modern times. Especially note the display of early telephone sets.

BUCKEYE FURNACE MUSEUM
123 Buckeye Park Road (Off Route 124), **Wellston**

- Area: **SC**
- Telephone Number: (740) 384-3537
- Hours: Wednesday – Saturday, 9:30 a.m. – 5:00 p.m. (Summer)
  Sundays and Holidays, Noon – 5:00 p.m.
  Weekends Only, (Labor Day – October)
- Admission: $2.50 Adult, $1.00 Youth (6-12)

Visit Ohio's only restored charcoal furnace which remains from the original 80 furnaces in Ohio. In the mid – 1800's this industry took root as a large stone converted trees into charcoal to make iron for railroads and ammunition. The self-guided tour of the furnace shows you where raw materials (charcoal, iron ore, etc.) were brought to the top of the hill and poured into the furnace to be heated to 600 degrees F. Impurities (slag) stayed on the top while liquid iron (which is heavier) flowed to the base.

Area "SE"

BUTCH'S COCA-COLA MUSEUM
118 Maple Street, Harmar Village, **Marietta**

- Area: **SE**
- Telephone Number: (740) 376-COKE
- Hours: Tuesday – Saturday, 10:00 a.m. – 5:00 p.m. (Spring – Fall)
  Friday and Saturday, 10:00 a.m. – 5:00 p.m. (Winter)
- Admission: Donation

MUSEUMS 61

Memorabilia from 1900 to the present traces the history of this beverage and its marketing. Buy a bottle of COKE or Sarsaparilla (vanilla Root Beer) and sip it while you browse. The Icy-O-Cooler (1900) looks like a top-loading washing machine and was the 1st style of COKE coolers (one of only 6 left in the country). Although it's rusted, you can still see the COCA-COLA logo on the front. Of special interest to us was the 2 Liter glass bottle and all of the single serving bottles from foreign countries. We asked about a plastic can of COKE and Butch told us it was test marketed in Atlanta, GA for 3 weeks. The idea was "trashed" when the recyclers became upset because the can would not recycle effectively (the top was aluminum and the can, plastic).

AREA "SW"

U.S. PLAYING CARD COLLECTION MUSEUM

4590 Beech Street (Norwood), **Cincinnati**

- Area: **SW**
- Telephone Number: (513) 396-5731
- Hours: Tuesday and Thursday, Noon – 4:00 p.m.
- Miscellaneous: Factory Gift Shop and Museum. Watch a video explaining the history of card games or view playing cards dating back to the 16th century.

(The following listings are sorted by area/city within each category)

CLASSIC CAR MUSEUMS

CANTON CLASSIC CAR MUSEUM

555 Market Avenue (South at 6th Street SW – I-77 to Tuscarawas Exit), **Canton**

- Area: **CE**
- Telephone Number: (330) 455-3603
- Hours: Daily, 10:00 a.m. – 5:00 p.m.
- Admission: $5.00 Adult, $3.00 Senior (65+) $2.50 Youth (6-18)

Housed in Ohio's earliest Ford-Lincoln dealership, this museum offers over 35 antique, classic and special interest cars displayed in the motif of flapper era Roaring 20's. Favorite exhibits are the Rolls Royce and celebrity cars including Queen Elizabeth's tour car, famous movie cars and Amelia Earhart's 1916 Pierce Arrow.

CITIZEN'S MOTORCAR PACKARD MUSEUM

420 South Ludlow Street - Downtown, **Dayton**

- Area: **CW**
- Telephone Number: (937) 226-1917
- Hours: Tuesday – Friday, Noon – 5:00 p.m. Saturday and Sunday, 1:00 – 5:00 p.m.

See the world's largest collection of Packard automobiles in an authentic showroom. The art deco Packard dealership interior exhibits are spread through 6 settings, Included are the service area and a salesman's office with an old fan blowing and a radio playing early 1900's music.

THE PACKARD MUSEUM

197 West Market Street, **Warren**

- Area: **NE**
- Telephone Number: (330) 394-8484
- Hours: Wednesday, Friday, Saturday, 11:00 a.m.– 3:00p.m. Sunday, 1:00 – 4:00 p.m.
  Weekends Only (December – April)
- Admission: $2.00 Adult, $1.00 Senior and Student

Watch a video about Packard's family of vehicles and personal family stories. See memorabilia about the manufacturer's history from 1899 – 1958. Also Packard Electric history display.

OBERHAUS ENTERPRISES

State Route 66, **Archbold**

- Area: **NW**
- Telephone Number: (419) 446-2773
- Hours: Monday – Friday, 8:30 a.m. – 3:00 p.m.
  Admission: $3.00 Adult, $2.50 Senior
- Miscellaneous: Antique cars, furniture and other collectibles. See Pierce Arrows, Cadillacs, and a 1918 Milburn Electric.

FLIGHT MUSEUMS

OHIO HISTORY OF FLIGHT MUSEUM

4275 Sawyer Road (at Port Columbus Airport), **Columbus**

- Area: **C**
- Telephone Number: (614) 231-1300
- Hours: Monday – Friday, 9:00 a.m. – 4:00 p.m.
  Weekends, (By Appointment)
- Tours: Call for appointment
- Admission: $2.00 Adult, $1.50 Children (5-15)

There's much to see and it is a great way to teach children the flight history of Ohio. The museum features a Curtiss Model D built on 1911-1912 in Wilbur Curtiss' attic, a 1927 WACO 9 and Foster Lane's first airplane. There's much to learn about Ohio's inventor pilots and aircraft. Most children spend a lot of time looking over the prototype of a rubber-like inflat-a-plane, sitting in a flight simulator, pushing buttons on a working model of an old airplane engine, or playing on the space shuttle and rocket outside. Before you leave, ask a guide for a look at one of their flight videos. We saw "The Thunderbirds".

MAPS AIR MUSEUM

5359 Massillon Road (I-77 to Exit 113), Akron-Canton Airport, **North Canton**

- Area: **CE**
- Telephone Number: (330) 896-6332
- Hours: Monday, 9:00 a.m. – 4:00 p.m.
  Wednesday, 6:00 – 9:00 p.m.
  Saturday, 8:00 a.m. – 4:00 p.m.
- Admission: Yes
- Miscellaneous: Gift shop

The staff here are pilots, mechanics, officers, and crew who desire to preserve the legacy of America's aviation heritage. Their slogan "Rebuilding History – One Rivet At a Time" really describes their dedication to acquire and renovate some of the world's greatest military aircraft. MAPS offers not just displays of mint condition aircraft, but also a truly unique "hands on" view of the restoration of some of the world's greatest aircraft by people who may have flown them years ago.

INTERNATIONAL WOMEN'S AIR AND SPACE MUSEUM

26 North Main Street (Off I-675), **Centerville**

- Area: **CW**
- Telephone Number: (937) 433-6766
- Hours: Saturday, 10:00 a.m. – 4:00 p.m.
- Admission: FREE

See women in aviation history. Special display honors Katharine Wright, the Wright Brother's sister. Orville once said, "When the world speaks of the Wrights, it must include my sister, for much of our effort has been inspired by her". Equal time to Amelia Earhart, women astronauts and Desert Storm pilots.

WRIGHT CYCLE COMPANY

22 South Williams Street (off West 3rd Street), **Dayton**

- Area: **CW**
- Telephone Number: (937) 443-0793
- Hours: Summer, Daily, 10:00 a.m. – 4:00 p.m.
  Saturday, 10:00 a.m. – 4:00 p.m.
  Sunday, Noon – 4:00 p.m.
  Weekends Only (Winter)
- Admission: Donation

Actual site where the Wright Brothers had a bicycle business from 1895-1897 and developed their own brand of bicycles. On this site, they also developed ideas that led to the invention of flight almost 7 years later. We walked on the same floorboards that the brothers did and saw actual plans for a flying bicycle!

WRIGHT B. FLYER

10550 Springboro Pike (State Route 741 – Dayton International Airport), **Miamisburg**

- Area: **CW**
- Telephone Number: (937) 885-2327
- Hours: Tuesday, Thursday, and Saturday, 9:00 a.m. – 2:00 p.m.
- Admission: Periodical flights on Wright B available for a charge.

This hangar houses a flyable replica of the 1911 plane built by Wilbur and Orville Wright. They also have a half scale model of the plane and other aviation exhibits and souvenirs.

NASA LEWIS RESEARCH VISITOR CENTER

21000 Brookpark Road. (I-480 to Exit 9, next to Cleveland Hopkins Airport), **Cleveland**

- Area: **NE**
- Telephone Number: (216) 433-2001
- Hours: Weekdays, 9:00 a.m. – 4:00 p.m.
  Saturday, 10:00 a.m. – 3:00 p.m.
  Sunday and Holidays, 1:00 – 5:00 p.m.
- Tours: Available, call for details
- Admission: FREE

The main exhibit space called the Microgravity Materials Science Laboratory houses a space shuttle, satellites, zero gravity chamber, wind tunnels, and space environmental tanks. Look for the moon rock and space suit used by astronauts (audio explanation). A fun treat is to watch the "Astrosmiles" video – you'll learn clever space jokes told by astronauts.

MARINE MUSEUMS

INLAND SEAS MARITIME MUSEUM & LIGHTHOUSE

480 Main Street (3 blocks North of State Route 60 / US 6), **Vermillion**

- Area: **NC**
- Telephone Number: (800) 893-1485
- Hours: Daily, 10:00 a.m. – 5:00 p.m.
- Admission: $5.00 Adult, $4.00 Senior, $3.00 Youth (6-15) $10.00 Family Rate
- Miscellaneous: Gift Shop. Video to watch of the wreck of the Edmund Fitzgerald iron ore boat.

The museum celebrates adventures of the Great Lakes including models, photographs, instruments, a steam tug engine, and a 1905 pilothouse. Special artifacts are the timbers from the Niagara (Admiral Perry's 1812 ship) and an 1847 lighthouse built with a 400 foot catwalk to the mainland. The lighthouse began tilting toward the harbor in 1928, so it was dismantled. In 1992, it was rebuilt and the 1891 (leaded glass) lens shines once again!

GREAT LAKES MARINE AND U.S. COAST GUARD MEMORIAL MUSEUM

1071 Walnut Boulevard, (Off Hulbert Street, Downtown), **Ashtabula Harbor**

- Area: **NE**
- Telephone Number: (440) 964-6847
- Hours: Friday – Sunday, Noon – 6:00 p.m. (Summer)
  Friday – Sunday, 1:00 – 5:00 p.m. (September, October)
- Admission: Donation
- Miscellaneous: Gift Shop

From the front lawn, you can watch the working giant drawbridge down in the harbor. This harbor is still busy and the view from the hill enables you to take in many industrial activities. The museum is an old lighthouse keeper's home built in 1898. The seven rooms are packed with momentos of a sailor's life. Kids like the pilothouse with a real stern and whistle and working radar. There is also a scale model of a hulett (unloading machine for iron ore).

U.S.S. COD

1809 East 9th Street. (North Marginal Road next to Burke Lakefront), **Cleveland**

- Area: **NE**
- Telephone Number: (216) 566-8770
- Hours: Daily, 10:00 a.m. - 5:00 p.m. (May - September)

- Admission: $4.00 Adult
  $2.00 Student (under 5 FREE)

We started our visit at the Aristotle periscope on shore that gives you a view of Lake Erie and puts you in the mood to explore the WW II submarine that sank enemy shipping boats. The ninety-man crew lived in cramped quarters--an amazing reminder of the price of freedom. The eight separate compartments, tight quarters, ladders to climb and plenty of knobs to play with give an authentic feeling of submarine life.

FAIRPORT MARINE MUSEUM

129 Second Street (State Route 2 and County Route 538), **Fairport Harbor**

- Area: **NE**
- Telephone Number: (440) 351-4825
- Hours: Wednesday, Saturday, Sunday and Holidays 1:00 – 6:00 p.m. (Memorial Weekend – Labor Day)
- Admission: $2.00 Adult, $1.00 Senior and Student Under 6 – FREE

Pretend you're on a sea voyage as you explore an old pilothouse with navigation instruments, maps and charts and a large ship's wheel. Find out what number of whistles you use to indicate the ship's direction. This room was large enough to really romp around. The highlight of this museum has to be the real lighthouse (although it's a steep, tough climb up and out to the deck). After you proudly climb the 69 steps, catch your breath with a beautiful view of Lake Erie.

SS WILLIS B BOYER MARITIME MUSEUM

26 Main Street, International Park, (East side of Maumee River – Downtown), **Toledo**

- Area: **NW**

- Telephone Number: (419) 936-3070
- Hours: Daily, 10:00 a.m. – 5:00 p.m. (May – October)
  Tuesday – Saturday, 10:00 a.m. – 5:00 p.m. (November – April)
- Admission: $4.00 Adult, $3.00 Student

The 617-foot freighter depicts how ships of the Great Lakes worked in the early to mid 1900's. It was the biggest, most modern ship on the Great Lakes (in its day) and as you drive up, it takes up your whole panoramic view. A nautical museum of Lake Erie resides inside with photographs, artifacts and best of all for kids, hands-on exhibits.

OHIO RIVER MUSEUM
Washington & Front Street, (Downtown), **Marietta**
- Area: **SE**
- Telephone Number: (740) 373-3750
- Hours: Wednesday – Saturday, 9:30 a.m. – 5:00 p.m. (October – November)
  Daily, 9:30 a.m. – 5:00 p.m., Sunday, Noon – 5:00 p.m. (May – September)
- Admission: $4.00 Adult, $3.20 Senior (65+)
  $1.00 Children (6-12)

The *WP Snyder, Jr.* moored along the museum is the last surviving stern-wheeled towboat in America. Also, see a model of a flat boat and other scale models of many riverboats. A video titled, "Fire on the Water" describes dangerous early times when boilers might explode, killing many. Diorama (full scale) of wildlife along the Ohio River.

McGUFFEY MUSEUM

Spring and Oak Streets, **Oxford**

- Area: **SW**
- Telephone Number: (513) 529-2232
- Hours: Weekends, 2:00 - 4:00 p.m. (Except August and Holidays)
- Admission: FREE

See an original collection of McGuffey Reader (lesson books on the three R's and morality, i.e. brotherly love, honesty and hard work). The home, built in the early 1830's is where William Holmes McGuffey wrote his readers while preparing classwork for children. Check out the eight-sided desk!

RAILROAD MUSEUMS

OHIO RAILWAY MUSEUM

Proprietors Road, (Off State Route 161), **Worthington**

- Area: **C**
- Hours: Sunday, 1:00 – 5:00 p.m. (Mid-May – Mid-October)
- Admission: Yes

They have displayed approximately 30 pieces of Ohio Railway History dating from 1897 – 1950. The guide explains that steam engines have their own personality. Get close to one under steam and hear it talk!

UNION DEPOT RAILROAD MUSEUM

145 South Depot Street, (Off State Route 57 – follow signs), **Orrville**

- Area: **CE**
- Telephone Number: (330) 683-2426

MUSEUMS

- ❑ Hours: Saturday, 10:00 a.m. – 4:00 p.m. (May – October)
- ❑ Former Pennsylvania Railroad Station. They hold a few festivals in the summer.

MAD RIVER & NKP RAILROAD SOCIETY MUSEUM

253 South West Street (Just South of US 20), **Bellevue**

- ❑ Area: **NC**
- ❑ Telephone Number: (419) 483-2222
- ❑ Hours: Daily, 1:00 – 5:00 p.m. (Memorial Day - Labor Day)
  Weekends Only, 1:00 – 5:00 p.m. (May, September, October)
- ❑ Admission: $2.00 Adult (NKP), $1.00 Children (3-12) $5.00 Adult (Mad River)

Look for "Thomas the Tank Engine", "Diesel", or the huge snow plow. Once you find them, browse through their collections of full-scale locomotives, cabooses, and mail cars – many that you can climb aboard. Tour guide volunteers are usually retired railway personnel who are knowledgeable and excited to tell you stories about the old railway days.

TRAIN – O – RAMA

Route 161 East, **Marblehead**

- ❑ Area: **NC**
- ❑ Telephone Number: (419) 734-5856
- ❑ Hours: Monday – Saturday, 11:00 a.m. – 5:00 p.m.
  Sunday, 1:00 – 5:00 p.m. (until 6:00 p.m. in summer).
- ❑ Admission.
- ❑ Miscellaneous: Gift Shop.

CONNEAUT HISTORICAL RAILROAD MUSEUM
Depot Street and Mill Street (East of Route 7), **Conneaut**
- Area: **NE**
- Telephone Number: (440) 599-7878
- Hours: Daily, Noon – 5:00 p.m. (Memorial – Labor Day)
- Admission: Donation
- Miscellaneous: Old New York Central depot with an old steam engine and railroad cars.

HISTORICAL HARMAR MODEL RAILROAD STATION MUSEUM
220 Gilman Street, Harmar Village, **Marietta**
- Area: **SE**
- Telephone Number: (800) 288-2577
- Hours: Daily, 11:00 a.m. – 5:00 p.m.
- Admission: $5.00 General (4th grade and older) $15.00 Family

More than 1500 linear feet of authentic toy electric trains on several levels of track. Up to 15 trains operate simultaneously and over 200 vintage locomotives are on display. The museum is housed in the original town station depot. Operating electric train exhibit with different sized trains. Museum with antique railroads and memorabilia.

Chapter 5

OHIO HISTORY & GOVERNMENT

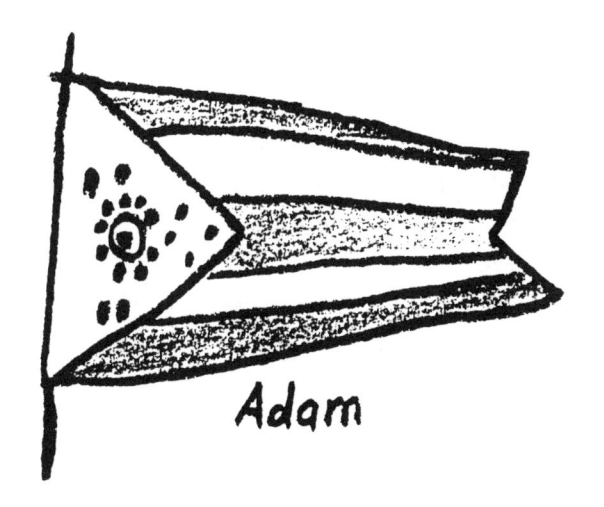

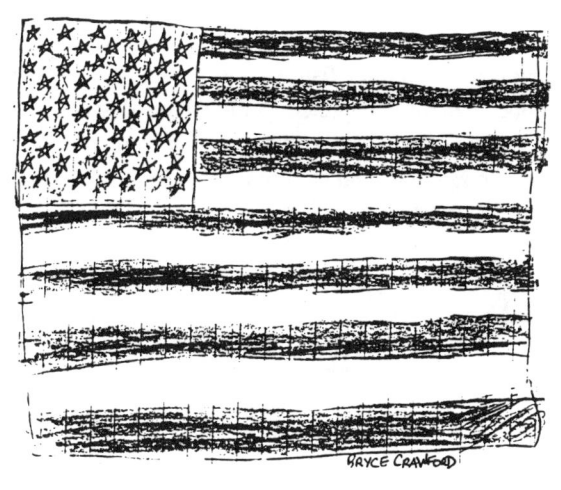

AREA "C"

SLATE RUN HISTORICAL FARM
9130 Marcy Road, **Ashville**

- Area: **C**
- Telephone Number: (740) 891-0700 or (740) 833-1880
- Hours: Tuesday, Wednesday, Thursday, 9:00 a.m. – 4:00 p.m. (June – August)
  Friday and Saturday, 9:00 a.m. – 6:00 p.m. (June – August), Sunday, 11:00 a.m. – 6:00 p.m.(June – August)
  Wednesday – Saturday, 9:00 a.m. – 4:00 p.m. (September – May),Sunday, 11:00 a.m. – 4:00 p.m. (September – May)
  Memorial and Labor Day, Noon – 6:00 p.m.
- Tours: Available by appointment (special prices)
- Admission: FREE

This historic farm depicts life on a working family farm of the 1880's. Visitors may join in with the barnyard and household chores. All the work is done using equipment and methods of the time (some horse-powered machinery). Some of the specially scheduled programs have been: maple syrup demonstrations and production, toy making, fishing, ice cream socials, making root beer, rope making and pretend old-fashioned school. Kids love getting involved and doing chores at Slate Run. They offer nature trails, picnic grounds, and children's play facilities at the adjoining Slate Run Metro Park.

FLINT RIDGE STATE MEMORIAL MUSEUM
7091 Brownsville Road SE, (3 miles North of US 40 and State Route 68), **Brownsville**

- Area: **C**

- Telephone Number: (740) 787-2476
- Hours: Wednesday - Saturday, 9:30 a.m. - 5:00 p.m.
  Sunday, Noon - 5:00 p.m.
  Memorial Day - Labor Day
  Weekends Only (September and October)
- Admission: $3.00 Adult, $1.60 Senior (60+)
  $1.25 Youth (6-12)
- Miscellaneous: Flint Preserve open April - October, 9:30 a.m. to Dusk for further exploration.

Indians came to see this stretch of hills for flint stone (our official gem of the State of Ohio) to use for tools and weapons. Displays show how flint is formed from silica and what objects can be made today with flint (like sparks that start flames when flint is rubbed against steel). How else can we use flint?

OHIO HISTORICAL CENTER
1982 Velma Avenue (I-71 to 17th Avenue Exit), **Columbus**

- Area: C
- Telephone Number: (614) 297-2300 or (614) 297-2606 (Group Reservation)
- Hours: Monday - Saturday, 9:00 a.m. - 5:00 p.m.
  Sunday and Holidays, 10:00 a.m. - 5:00 p.m.
- Admission: Adult $4.00, $3.20 Senior (62+)
  $1.00 Children
  ** Half Price on Monday and Tuesday **
- Miscellaneous: Gift Shop, food and picnic tables

This is a museum and a whole lot more. There are exhibits and artifacts covering the history of Ohio from archaeology to natural history and the history of Ohio. There are many historical collections from early fossils and Indian tribes, original accounts from early explorers, and papers from political leaders such as General Meigs and Thomas Worthington. The building is recognized as an architectural landmark. "The Nature of Ohio" exhibit is guarded by a huge mastodon found in a swamp in Clark County. See the quirky 2-headed calf and Egyptian mummy.

OHIO STATEHOUSE

Broad and High Streets (10 acre square in downtown), **Columbus**

- Area: **C**
- Telephone Number: (614) 466-2125
- Tours: Monday - Friday, 9:00 a.m. - 2:00 p.m.
  Saturday and Sunday, 9:00 a.m. - 3:00 p.m.
  20 or more people, 45 minutes long
  Appointment necessary
- Admission: FREE

Visit the place where Abraham Lincoln made speeches in 1859 and 1861. The Statehouse is a Greek Revival building with Doric columns. Inside you'll see the rotunda with the state seal and historic paintings and documents. If the Ohio House or Senate is in session, you'll be able to listen to the debates. Outside is home to several war memorials and statues including Christopher Columbus. Did you know inmates from the former state penitentiary (that was located near downtown Columbus) built it?

OHIO VILLAGE

1982 Velma Avenue (I-71 and 17th Avenue Exit), **Columbus**

- Area: **C**
- Telephone Number: (614) 297-2300
- Hours: Wednesday - Saturday, 9:00 a.m. - 5:00 p.m. (April - November)
  Sunday, 10:00 a.m. - 5:00 p.m. (April - November)
  12:30 - 9:00 p.m. (December)
- Admission: Adult $4.00

$3.20 Senior (62+), $1.00 Children
** Half Price on Monday and Tuesday **

See an 1800's village that is a must for all ages. Authentic with unpaved and dusty roads. Be sure to get some postcards stamped with the official Ohio Village postmark at the village post office. Your children will see how doctors, blacksmiths, printers and many others practiced their trades in the America of the 1860's. Baseball fans can catch the Ohio Village Muffins in a real game played according to 19th Century rules. The Ohio Village has a general store offering hand-crafted goods and 1860's reproduction items. Colonel Crawford Inn serves an assortment of tempting traditional dishes. The Ohio Historical Center is next door, so plan your day for both of these.

RHODES STATE OFFICE TOWER
30 East Broad Street, Downtown, **Columbus**

- Area: **C**
- Telephone Number: (614) 466-7077 Security
- Hours: Monday – Friday, 8:00 a.m. – 5:00 p.m.
- Tours: Tuesday and Wednesday preferred
  10 – 40 people
  Appointment Only
- Admission: FREE

A 41 story Cornelian red granite building (the world's largest granite structure) with a five story lobby and 40th floor observation deck. As you enter the lobby you will see the Great Seal of the State of Ohio on the back wall and a gallery featuring the work of Ohio artists. The most fascinating part of the tour is sitting in on a session of the Ohio Supreme Court. If the court is not in session, a guide will come and explain the normal proceedings that take place.

SANTA MARIA

Scioto River (Downtown – Northeast of Broad Street Bridge),
Battelle Park, **Columbus**

- Area: **C**
- Telephone Number: (614) 645-8760
- Hours: Daily, 10:00 a.m. – 5:00 p.m. (April – October)
  Early evenings in Summer
- Admission: $3.50 Adult, $3.00 Senior (60+)
  $1.50 Student (5-17)

The Columbus Santa Maria is the world's most authentic, museum quality representation of Christopher Columbus' flagship. Climb aboard and return to 1492 as costumed guides share facts about the ship and the famous voyage. Feel the challenges and hardships faced by Columbus and his crew. You better be on your best behavior or you'll have to "walk the gang plank"! Sleeping quarters available for campouts.

HARDING MEMORIAL AND HOME

380 Mount Vernon Avenue (1.5 miles West of State Route 23 on State Route 95), **Marion**

- Area: **C**
- Telephone Number: (740) 387-9630
- Hours: Wednesday - Saturday, 9:30 a.m. - 5:00 p.m.
  (Summer) Sunday, Noon - 5:00 p.m. (Summer)
  Weekends Only (September and October)
  By appointment in Spring
- Admission: $3.00 Adult, $2.00 Senior
  $1.00 Youth
- Miscellaneous: Memorial is a circular monument (with columns of white marble) containing the tombs of Mr. and Mrs. Harding. Delaware Avenue.

A great way to learn Presidential history without a fuss from the kids. Do you know what the fancy pot is in the guestroom - the one lying on the floor? They have displayed a podium used at Harding's inauguration in 1920 as our 29th President. See the porch where Harding campaigned what was later called the "Front Porch Campaign", speaking to over 600,000 people overall. The original porch collapsed and a new one had to be built during the campaign. A special small house was built behind the main house for the press associates visiting the area to cover the campaign. Look for the ornate collar worn by their dog "Laddie Boy".

NEWARK EARTHWORKS
I-70 (9 miles North on State Route 79), **Newark**

- Area: **C**
- Telephone Number: (740) 344-1920
- Hours: Daily (April - October)
  Museum: Ohio Indian Art Museum, Wednesday –
  Saturday, 9:30 a.m. - 5:00 p.m.
  Sunday, Noon - 5:00 p.m. (Summer)
  Weekends Only (September and October)
- Admission: $3.00 Adult, $1.25 Children (6-12)
- Miscellaneous: Octagon State Memorial - Small mounds, Wright Earthworks State Memorial

The Moundbuilders is a circular mound 1200 feet in diameter with walls 8 to 14 feet high. In the museum, we found the primitive stamps most interesting. The engraved tablets were probably used for clothing decorations or tattoos. They feel the tablets were used as stamps because they found colored pigment on them. As you walk outside the museum, you walk right into the mouth opening of a circular mound. Once inside, just imagine the Hopewell Indian ceremonies that occurred many years ago.

HANBY HOUSE

160 West Main Street (across from Otterbein College), **Westerville**

- Area: **C**
- Telephone Number: (614) 882-4291 or (614) 891-6289
- Tours and Hours: Open to the public during specified hours and special events or by appointment. Tours can be arranged May - October.
- Admission: Adult $1.50, Children $0.50 (6-12)

Benjamin Hanby was the composer of over 80 folk songs and hymns including "Sweet Nelly Gray" and "Up On the Rooftop". Children will enjoy seeing Ben's original instruments and musical scores. This home was part of the Underground Railroad. Be sure to notice and ask about the roses in a vase by the front window. The tour also includes viewing a short introduction movie called "The Gift of Song".

ORANGE JOHNSON HOUSE

956 North High Street (just north of State Route 161), **Worthington**

- Area: **C**
- Telephone Number: (614) 885-6400
- Hours: (Open House) Sunday, 2:00 - 5:00 p.m. except January
- Tours: Weekdays by Appointment
- Admission: Small donation

The Orange Johnson House is a restored early 1800's home. There are many authentic objects and toys that children can pick up and pretend to use. The guide will describe chores children were given in those days (your own children will think they have it made!). Before you leave, you will learn how "Pop

Goes the Weasel" originated. A good time to visit is when they have cooking demonstrations.

AREA "CE"

FORT LAURENS STATE MEMORIAL AND MUSEUM
I-77 and State Route 212 - Follow Signs, **Bolivar**

- Area: **CE**
- Telephone Number: (800) 283-8914
- Hours: Wednesday - Saturday, 9:30 a.m. - 5:00 p.m.
  Sunday and Holidays, Noon - 5:00 p.m.
  Weekends Only (September and October)
- Admission: $2.00 Adult, $1.60 Senior
  $1.00 Youth (6-12)

Visit the site of the only U.S. Military fort in Ohio during the American Revolution. Also included is a museum (with visual and action packed audiovisual displays), that sits on what was once the fort's west gate. Re-enactment weekends are the best time to visit.

ROSCOE VILLAGE
311 Hill Street (State Route 16 and 83), **Coshocton**

- Area: **CE**
- Telephone Number: (800) 877-1830
- Hours: Daily, Most village shops open at 10:00 a.m.
  Special events May – December.
- Admission: "Living History Tour" $8.95 Adult
  $3.95 Children (5-12)
  Just Browsing is FREE!

Listed as "One of the 20 best sites to discover historic America", - it truly is a place that meets or exceeds your expectations. Experience life in a canal town with canal boat rides (for an additional fee) May through October. Watch craftsmen make brooms, weave or print. In the print shop we pressed our own bookmarks and postcards. Spend gobs of time in the General Store where you can play with and buy old-fashioned toys like harmonicas, paper dolls and wooden toys. Plan to have the kids bring their allowance (and you can too) because you won't be able to resist! During the summer, visit the Hillside where demonstrations of brick-making and woodworking take place. A family style restaurant, the rustic "Warehouse", was once a busy holding house for transport of goods.

OHIO SOCIETY OF MILITARY HISTORY

316 Lincoln Way East (US 30 to County Road 172), **Massillon**

- Area: **CE**
- Telephone Number: (330) 832-5553
- Hours: Tuesday - Friday, 10:00 a.m. - 5:00 p.m. Saturday, 10:00 a.m. - 3:00 p.m.
- Admission: Donations

The museum honors people from Ohio who have fought for the United States. A collection of photographs, clothing and medals dating from the recent "Operation Desert Storm" back to the Civil War.

SHOENBRUNN VILLAGE STATE MEMORIAL

State Route 259 (4 miles East of I-77 exit 81), **New Philadelphia**

- Area: **CE**
- Telephone Number: (800) 752-2711
- Hours: Monday – Saturday, 9:30 a.m. – 5:00 p.m. (Summer)
  Sunday, Noon – 5:00 p.m. (Summer)
  Weekends Only (September and October)
- Admission: $5.00 Adult, $1.25 Youth (6-12)
- Miscellaneous: Museum. Video orientation. Gift Shop.

Take a self-guided tour of the reconstructed log building village founded by a Moravian missionary in 1772. Church members tried to convert Delaware Indians to Christianity, but, after 5 years of Indian hostility, they were forced (300) to abandon the area and the village was destroyed. Being the first settlement in Ohio, Shoenbrunn claims the first civil code, the first church, and the first school.

ZOAR VILLAGE
198 Main Street (State Route 212 – I-77 to Exit 93), **Zoar**

- Area: **CE**
- Telephone Number (800) 262-6194 or (330) 874-4336
- Hours: Wednesday – Saturday, 9:30 a.m. – 5:00 p.m. (Summer)
  Sunday – Holidays, Noon – 5:00 p.m. (Summer)
  Weekends Only, (April, May, September, October)
- Admission: $5.00 Adult, $4.00 Seniors
  $1.25 Youth (6-12)
- Miscellaneous: Video presentation first explains Zoar history.

Zoar means "a sanctuary from evil". They, as a society of Separatists (separation between church and state), were known for their bountiful gardening designs based on the bible. The 12 block district of 1800's homes and shops include a dairy, bakery, museum, gardens, storehouse, tin shops, wagon shops, and blacksmith. They are actual original buildings in a real town of 75 families. Walk along streets dispersed with restored residences and shops for modern clients.

AREA "CW"

CARILLON HISTORICAL PARK

2001 South Patterson Boulevard (I-75 to Exit 51), **Dayton**

- Area: **CW**
- Telephone Number: (937) 293-2841
- Hours: Tuesday - Saturday, 10:00 a.m. - 6:00 p.m. (May - August)
  Sunday and Holidays, 1:00 - 6:00 p.m. (May - August)
  (Until 5:00 p.m. in September and October)
  (Until 4:00 p.m., November 1 - 14)
- Admission: $2.00 Adult, $1.00 Youth (6-17)
- Miscellaneous: Museum Store. Wooded park with Ohio's largest bell tower, the Carillon Bell Tower (57 bells)

A must see - very comfortable and educational - over 65 acres of historical buildings and outdoor exhibits of history, invention and transportation. Called the "Little Greenfield Village" in Miami Valley and we definitely agree! Our favorites are the Deed's Barn (learn about the Barn Gang and the big companies they started) and the rail cars that you can actually board - the Barney & Smith is ritzy!

SUNWATCH

2301 West River Road (I-75 to Exit 51), **Dayton**

- Area: **CW**
- Telephone Number (937) 268-8199

- Hours: Tuesday – Saturday, 9:00 – 5:00 p.m.
  Sunday and Holidays, Noon – 5:00 p.m.
  Mid-March – November
- Tours: Guided tours daily at 1:30 p.m. (Summer)
- Admission: $4.00 Adult, $3.00 Youth (6-17)

An 800 year old reconstructed 12th Century Indian Village with self guided tours of the thatched huts, gardens and artifacts of the lifestyle of a unique culture. Some activities include story telling, archery, multi-media presentation, and best of all, learn to tell time by charting the sun. See how the Indians used flint and bone to create jewelry and tools - then buy some as souvenirs.

FORT RECOVERY STATE MEMORIAL

State Route 49 and State Route 119, **Fort Recovery**

- Area: **CW**
- Telephone Number: (419) 375-4649
  Hours: Daily, Noon - 5:00 p.m. (Summer)
  Weekends Only (May and September)
- Admission: $1.00 Adult, $0.50 Youth (6-12)

The remaining blockhouses with connecting stockade wall are where General Arthur St. Clair was defeated by Indians in 1791. A museum with Indian War artifacts and dressed mannequins is also displayed on the property.

LOCKINGTON LOCKS STATE MEMORIAL

I-75 to exit 83 West on State Route 25A, 5 miles North of Piqua-Lockington Road, **Lockington**

- Area: **CW**
- Telephone Number: (937) 773-2522
- Hours: Daily, Dawn to Dusk
- Admission: FREE

View portions of six original locks (elevation adjusters for canal boats) and the aqueduct that lowered boats 67 feet into the Miami-Erie Canal.

PIQUA HISTORICAL AREA TOUR

I-75 to exit 83 (County Road 25A West to State Route 66 North), **Piqua**

- Area: **CW**
- Telephone Number: (937) 773-2522 or (800) 752-2619
- Hours: Wednesday – Saturday, 9:30 a.m. – 5:00 p.m. Sunday and Holidays, Noon – 5:00 p.m. (Summer) Weekends Only (September and October)
- Admission: $5.00 Adult, $1.25 Youth (6-12) Includes canal boat ride
- Miscellaneous: Rides at 12:30, 2:30, and 4:00 p.m.

Tour the Johnston Farm which includes a 1808 massive log barn which is probably the oldest such barn in Ohio. In the farmhouse, the kids will probably be most interested in the beds made of rope and hay filled sacks. Eight girls slept in one room (ages 2-20) and three boys in another. Many youth games of that time period are displayed. The Winter Kitchen is also very interesting – especially the size of the walk-in fireplace. The General Harrison canal boat is powered by Cindy and Sammy, two mules, which pull the boat down and back on a section of the Old Miami-Erie Canal (Cincinnati to Toledo). The cargo boat was once used to transport produce and meat at a speed limit of 4 MPH. The boats were fined $10.00 for speeding although many paid the fine and continued going 10 MPH. Once the railroads came, canals became obsolete.

NATIONAL AFRO-AMERICAN MUSEUM AND CULTURAL CENTER
1350 Brush Row Road (off US 42 - Next to Central State College), **Wilberforce**

- Area: **CW**
- Telephone Number: (800) BLK-HIST
- Hours: Tuesday - Saturday, 9:00 a.m. - 5:00 p.m. Sunday, 1:00 - 5:00 p.m.
- Admission: $4.00 Adult, $1.50 Children

Wilberforce was a famous stop on the Underground Railroad and became the center (Wilberforce University) for black education and achievements. The University was the first owned and operated by Afro-Americans. Best feature is the "From Victory to Freedom - the Afro-American Experience of 1950 - 1960's".

AREA "NC"

LYME VILLAGE
State Route 113, West of State Route 4, **Bellevue**

- Area: **NC**
- Telephone Number: (419) 483-4949 or (419) 483-6052
- Hours: Tuesday - Sunday, 1:00 - 5:00 p.m. (Summer) Sunday, 1:00 - 5:00 p.m. (May and September)

- ❏ Admission: $5.00 Adult, $4.50 Senior (65+)
  $2.50 Youth (12-18)
- ❏ Miscellaneous: Gift Shop and concessions.

This 19th Century Ohio Village includes the Wright Mansion, Annie Brown's log home that she owned for 82 years (early Ohio settler exhibits inside), a blacksmith shop, schoolhouse, Grandpa's barn, and the Cooper-Fries general store. All original buildings were moved to this location. Of special interest is the National Museum of Postmark Collector's Club (with the world's largest single collection of postmarks) in a restored post office.

HAYES PRESIDENTIAL CENTER
1337 Hayes Avenue (Rt. 6), **Fremont**

- ❏ Area: **NC**
- ❏ Telephone Number: (419) 332-2081 or (800) 998-7737
- ❏ Hours: Monday - Saturday, 9:00 a.m. - 5:00 p.m.
  Sunday and Holidays, Noon - 5:00 p.m.
- ❏ Admission: $7.50 Adult, $6.50 Senior (60+)
  $2.00 Youth (6-12)
  Covers museum and residence ($4.00 Adult, $1.00 Youth separately)
- ❏ Miscellaneous: Museum Store

The iron gates that greet you at the entrance were the same gates that once stood at the White House during the Hayes administration. The 33-room mansion estate was the home of President and Mrs. Rutherford B. Hayes and is full of family momentos, private papers and books. They give you the sense he dedicated himself to his country. The museum displays the President's daughter's ornate dollhouses and the White House carriage that the family used.

THOMAS EDISON'S BIRTHPLACE MUSEUM
North Edison Street (off State Route 250) Downtown, **Milan**

- Area: **NC**
- Telephone Number: (419) 499-2135
- Hours: Tuesday – Saturday, 10:00 a.m. – 5:00 p.m.
  Sunday, 1:00 – 5:00 p.m. (Summer)
  Tuesday – Sunday, 1:00 – 5:00 p.m. (February – May and September – November)
- Admission: $5.00 Adult, $4.00 Senior (59+) $2.00 Children (6-12)

Edison was born here in 1847 and raised in this home until age 7. The original family momentos give you a feeling of being taken back in time. The room full of his inventions (he had 1,093 American patents) gives you a sense of his brilliance. Most famous for his invention of the light bulb and phonograph (1st words recorded were "Mary had a little lamb"), you may not know he was kicked out of school for being a non-attentive/slow learner. So, his mother home-schooled him. Part of the Edison family belongings include slippers, Derby hat, cane, Mother Edison's disciplinary switch (still hanging in the original spot in the kitchen), butter molds and "Pop Goes the Weasel" yarner. Two practical inventions you'll want to see are the pole ladder (a long pole that pulls out to a full size ladder) and the slipper seat (a cushioned little seat, low to the ground, so it is easier to put your slippers or shoes on).

MILAN HISTORICAL MUSEUM
10 Edison Drive (Across the street from Edison's birthplace), **Milan**

- Area: **NC**
- Telephone Number: (419) 499-2968

- ❑ Hours: Tuesday - Saturday, 10:00 a.m. - 5:00 p.m., Sunday, 1:00 - 5:00 p.m. (Summer) Tuesday - Sunday, 1:00 - 5:00 p.m. (April, May, September, October)
- ❑ Admission: Donations. Small fee for guided group tours.
- ❑ Miscellaneous: Gift Shop with video and slide presentations.

Tour includes several buildings in a complex featuring different themes like the Galpin Home of local history, dolls, toys and a collection of mechanical banks. There are several other homes along with a blacksmith and carriage shop and everything you might want to buy from the 1800's is sold in the general store.

PERRY'S VICTORY AND INTERNATIONAL PEACE MEMORIAL

South Bass Island on the Lake, **Put-In-Bay**

- ❑ Area: **NC**
- ❑ Telephone Number: (419) 285-2184
- ❑ Hours: Daily, 10:00 a.m. - 7:00 p.m. (Mid-June - Labor Day) Daily, 10:00 a.m. - 5:00 p.m. (Late April - Mid-June and September and October)
- ❑ Admission: Observation Deck by elevator, $2.00 per person

Built of pink granite, 352 feet high and 45 feet in diameter, this memorial commemorates the Battle of Lake Erie and then the years of peace. Commodore Perry commanded the American fleet in the War of 1812. In September of 1813 he defeated the British and Perry then sent his famous message to General William Henry Harrison "We have met the enemy and they are ours".

AREA "NE"

HUBBARD HOUSE AND UNDERGROUND RAILROAD MUSEUM

Walnut Boulevard and Lake Avenue, **Ashtabula Harbor**

- Area: **NE**
- Telephone Number: (440) 964-8168
- Hours: Friday - Sunday and Holidays, Noon - 6:00 p.m. (Summer), 1:00 - 5:00 p.m. (September and October)

A northern terminal that was part of the pathway from slavery to freedom in the pre Civil War era.

HALE FARM AND VILLAGE

2686 Oak Hill Road (I-77 exit 143, follow signs), **Bath**

- Area: **NE**
- Telephone Number: (800) 589-9703
- Hours: Tuesday - Saturday, 10:00 a.m. - 5:00 p.m. Sunday and Holidays, Noon - 5:00 p.m. Memorial Day - October (Regular Season)
- Admission: $9.00 Adult, $7.50 Senior (59+) $5.50 Youth (6-12)
- Miscellaneous: Museum Shop and Snack Bar. Map and sample questions to ask towns people provided.

Tour a living museum with original buildings moved to the area to form a village. Jonathan Hale moved to the Western Reserve from Connecticut and prospered during the canal era building a brick home and farm typical of New England. The gate house prepares guests with an orientation movie, then begin your adventure around the homestead area with an old-fashioned sawmill and wood shop (where lumber is produced). Period tools and machines provide wood- working demonstrations. Other barns serve as shops for a blacksmith and basket maker (post-1850 transitional cut baskets). The Hall House (made of bricks made on site by Hale family and are still made today) has candle, broom making and pioneer cooking (and sampling!) demonstrations. You will feel like you're part of mid 1800' s life as crops are planted and harvested, glass items blown, textiles spun, barters made, and church and school attended. Kids are asked to help with chores and schoolwork.

CENTURY VILLAGE MUSEUM AND COUNTRY STORE

14653 E. Park Street (State Route 87 and State Route 700), **Burton**

- Area: **NE**
- Telephone Number: (440) 834-4012
- Hours: Tuesday – Sunday, 1:00 – 5:00 p.m. (June – October)
  Saturday and Sunday, 1:00 – 5:00 p.m. (November – March)
- Tours: 1:00 and 3:00 p.m. (June – October Only)
- Admission: $5.00 Adult, $3.00 Children (6-12)

A restored community with 12 buildings containing 19th Century historical antiques and a working farm. Best to attend during Apple Syrup Festivals, Civil War Festival, or Pioneer School Camp.

THE WESTERN RESERVE HISTORICAL SOCIETY

10825 East Boulevard, University Circle, **Cleveland**

- Area: **NE**
- Telephone Number: (216) 721-5722
- Hours: Tuesday – Saturday, 10:00 a.m. – 5:00 p.m. Sunday, Noon – 5:00 p.m.
- Admission: $6.00 Adult, $5.00 Senior $4.00 Youth (6-12) FREE Tuesday, 3:00 – 5:00 p.m.
- Miscellaneous: Crawford Auto-Aviation Museum. Library to discover your family tree.

Cleveland's oldest cultural institution boasts a tour of a grand mansion recreating the Western Reserve from pre-Revolution War to the 20th Century. The look (but mostly don't touch) displays include: baseballs, roller coasters, farming tools, clothing and costumes and over 150 classic automobiles (Cleveland built cars, oldest car, and heaviest car) and airplanes.

BOULEVARD OF FLAGS
35150 Lake Shore Boulevard, City Hall, **Eastlake**

- Area: **NE**
- Telephone Number: (440) 951-1416

Believe it or not, 500 American flags lining the entrances to City Hall. It's the largest display in The United States!

LAWNFIELD MUSEUM
8095 Mentor Avenue (2 miles East on US 20), **Mentor**

- Area: **NE**
- Telephone Number: (440) 255-8722
  Hours: Tuesday - Saturday, 10:00 a.m. - 5:00 p.m. Sunday, Noon - 5:00 p.m.
- Admission: $4.00 Adult, $2.50 Youth (6-12)

- Miscellaneous: Gift Shop

The Victorian mansion was the home of President James A. Garfield. Shortly after his election, an opponent at a railroad station in Washington D.C. assassinated him. Catch the funeral wreath sent by Queen Victoria when Garfield was killed. See the video showing Garfield's campaign on the front porch of his home in 1880. Journalists standing on the lawn covering the campaign nicknamed the property "Lawnfield".

NATIONAL McKINLEY BIRTHPLACE MEMORIAL AND MUSEUM
40 North Main Street, Niles

- Area: **NE**
- Telephone Number: (330) 652-1704
- Hours: Monday - Thursday, 8:30 a.m. - 8:00 p.m. Friday and Saturday, 8:30 a.m. - 5:30 p.m. Sunday, 1:00 - 5:00 p.m. (September - May Only)
- Admission: FREE
- Miscellaneous: Auditorium and Library

The classic Greek structure with Georgian marble which houses a museum of McKinley memorabilia. Also see artifacts from the Civil War and Spanish-American War.

AREA "NW"

SAUDER FARM AND CRAFT VILLAGE
2 miles Northeast on State Route 2, Archbold

- Area: **NW**

- Telephone Number: (800) 590-9755
- Hours: Monday – Saturday, 10:00 a.m. – 5:00 p.m. Sunday, 1:00 – 5:00 p.m. (Mid-April – October)
- Admission: $9.00 Adult, $8.50 Senior
  $4.50 Youth (6-16)
  $1.00 Carriage, Train or Wagon rides
  Group Rates available for 25+
- Miscellaneous: Barn Restaurant. Gift Shop. Bakery. Country Inn.

The farm consists of a barnyard house with a summer kitchen full of antique tools and hardware. Walk along the craft village where you can meet a weaver, glassblower, broom maker, tinsmith, blacksmith and potter all dressed in early 20th Century clothing.

AUGLAISE VILLAGE FARM MUSEUM

Off US 24 (3 miles SW of **Defiance** - follow signs)

- Area: **NW**
- Telephone Number: (419) 784-0107
- Hours: Weekends, 11:00 a.m. - 4:00 p.m. (June - Labor Day)
- Admission: $2.00 Adult, $1.00 Youth (6-16)

A recreated late 19th Century village - 17 new, restored or reconstructed buildings that serve as museums. The Red Barn with the Street of Shops and Hall of Appliances is probably the most interesting - especially the old-fashioned appliances and authentic period food they serve. Best to visit during festivals or special events when there is an abundance of costumed guides.

GHOST TOWN MUSEUM PARK
US 68 to County Road 40 West, **Findlay**

- Area: **NW**
- Telephone Number: (419) 326-5874
- Hours: Tuesday - Sunday, 9:30 a.m. - 6:00 p.m.
  Memorial Day Weekend - Mid-September
- Admission: $4.00 Adult, $2.00 Children (under 12)

A ghost town recreation with 28 buildings from the 1880's including a general store and barbershop.

FORT MEIGS
State Route 65 (1 mile Southwest of State Route 25), **Perrysburg**

- Area: **NW**
- Telephone Number: (419) 874-4121
- Hours: Wednesday - Saturday, 9:30 a.m. - 5:00 p.m.
  Sunday, Noon - 5:00 p.m.
  Memorial Day Weekend - Labor Day
  Weekends Only (September and October)
- Admission: $4.00 Adult, $3.20 Senior (59+)
  $1.00 Youth (6-12)
- Miscellaneous: Visitor's Center with Gift Shop at the stone shutterhouse.

A War of 1812 era authentic castle-like log and earth fort with seven blockhouses that played an important role in guarding the Western frontier against the British. The walls of the blockhouses are 2 feet thick with 4-inch deep windows and cannon hole ports on the second floor. See actual cannons fired as the air fills with smoke.

AREA "SC"

ADENA STATE MEMORIAL
West of State Route 104 off Adena Road, **Chillicothe**

- Area: **SC**
- Telephone Number: (740) 772-1500
- Hours: Wednesday - Saturday, 9:30 a.m. - 5:00 p.m. (Summer)
  Sundays and Holidays, Noon - 5:00 p.m. (Summer)
  Weekends Only (September and October)
- Admission: $4.00 Adult, $3.20 Senior
  $1.00 Youth (6-12)

View the overlook of the hillside that was used to paint the picture for the Ohio State Seal. See the 1807 stone mansion built by the 6th Ohio governor Thomas Worthington. Also visit a tenant house, smoke house, wash house, barn and spring house.

AREA "SE"

CAMPUS MARTIUS: MUSEUM OF NORTHWEST TERRITORY
2nd and Washington Street (Downtown), **Marietta**

- Area: **SE**
- Telephone Number: (740) 373-3750
- Hours: Monday - Saturday, 9:30 a.m. - 5:00 p.m. (May - September)
  Sundays and Holidays, Noon - 5:00 p.m. (May – September)
  Wednesday - Saturday, 9:30 a.m. - 5:00 p.m. (October –

November)
Sunday, Noon - 5:00 p.m. (October - November)
- ❑ Admission: $4.00 Adult, $3.20 Senior (65+) $1.00 Children (6-12)

Campus recreates early development of Marietta as the 1st settlement in the Northwest Territory. The Putnam House is the oldest residence in Ohio. The home and land office display replicas of the hardships of early pioneer life including old surgical and musical instruments. A new exhibit titled "Paradise Found and Lost: Migration in the Ohio Valley", highlights migration from farms to cities and from Appalachia to industry. See the stage jacket worn by Appalachian born Country Singer, Dwight Yoakum. Videos and interactive computer games on migration. You can actually create a feeling of being taken back in time by walking through the train passenger car and listening to actual stories of passengers taking a trip to the "big city" for business or jobs (Stories are told on telephone handsets). See actual huge photographs of downtown Columbus and Marietta in the early 1900's that take up an entire wall - you'll feel as if you're walking into them!

Area "SW"

HARRIET BEECHER STOWE HOUSE

2950 Gilbert Avenue, **Cincinnati**

- ❑ Area: **SW**
- ❑ Telephone Number: (513) 632-5120
- ❑ Hours: Tuesday - Thursday, 10:00 a.m. - 4:00 p.m.
- ❑ Admission: Donations

The home of the author of "Uncle Tom's Cabin" novel that brought attention to the evils of slavery. Displays describe the Beecher family, the abolitionist movement and the history of African-Americans. Request the video about the story of the book. Mrs. Stowe's journal is available for viewing.

THE WILLIAM HOWARD TAFT NATIONAL HISTORIC SITE
2038 Auburn Avenue, **Cincinnati**

- Area: **SW**
- Telephone Number: (513) 684-3262
- Hours: Daily, 10:00 a.m. – 4:00 p.m.
- Admission: Donations

Visit the birthplace and boyhood home of a US President and Chief Justice. Four of the rooms are furnished to reflect Taft's family life 1857-77. Other exhibits depict his public service career. See actual family portraits. We were told children's group tours give kids the opportunity to dress up from a truck of period hats and over-garments and play with old fashioned toys. This really helps the children understand life for a young person in the mid-1800's.

GOVERNOR BEBB PRESERVE
1979 Bebb Park Lane (Rt. 126), **Morgan Township**

- Area: **SW**
- Telephone Number: (513) 738-8119
- Hours: Saturday and Sunday, 1:00 - 5:00 p.m.
  May - September

Visit the small 1812 village with the restored log cabin (birthplace of William Bebb - born in 1802). He was the governor of Ohio from 1846 - 48 and a trial lawyer noted for his emotional zeal.

FORT ANCIENT STATE MEMORIAL

6123 State Route 350 and Middleboro Road (I-71 to Rt. 123 to State Route 350), **Oregonia**

- Area: **SW**
- Telephone Number: (513) 932-4421
- Hours: Wednesday - Sunday, 10:00 - 8:00 p.m.
  Memorial Weekend - Labor Day
  Museum closes at 5:00 p.m.
  Weekends Only (Spring and Fall)
- Admission: Yes

The newly renovated Ohio Historical Society museum has Ohio's entire Indian heritage displayed from prehistoric to modern times. The 100 acre field is where graves and artifacts were found and is also home to the second largest earthwork in the nation (constructed by Hopewell Indians between 300 BC - 600 AD).

ULYSSES S. GRANT HOMESTEAD MUSEUM

219 East Grant Avenue, **Point Pleasant**

- Area: **SW**
- Telephone Number: (513) 378-4222
- Tours: Tuesday – Saturday, 9:00 a.m. – 5:00 p.m.
  By Appointment
  5th grade and above

Civil War General and 18th Presidents birthplace cottage with period furniture. The small white home has no heat and is sparsely lit – daytime in comfortable weather is best.

RANKIN HOUSE STATE MEMORIAL
Rankin Hill (North off US 52), **Ripley**

- Area: **SW**
- Telephone Number: (937) 392-1627
- Hours: Wednesday – Sunday, Noon – 5:00 p.m. (Summer)
  Weekends Only (September and October)
- Admission: $2.00 Adult, $0.50 Children (5-12)

This restored home of Reverend John Rankin (early Ohio abolitionist) was part of the Underground Railroad and home to Eliza, a character in "Uncle Tom's Cabin", who found refuge off the Ohio River. Winding roads lead to the remote cabin hidden in a clearing in the woods.

SHARON WOODS VILLAGE
11450 Lebanon Pike (US 42, 1 mile south of I-275 exit 46), **Sharonville**

- Area: **SW**
- Telephone Number: (513) 563-9484
- Hours: Wednesday – Friday, 10:00 a.m. – 4:00 p.m.
  Saturday and Sunday, 1:00 – 5:00 p.m.
  May – October
- Admission: $5.00 Adult, $3.00 Senior (62+)
  $2.00 Youth (6-12)

See 18th Century Ohio. Nine actual buildings of Southwest Ohio including a farmhouse, train station, homes, icehouse, smokehouse, and medical office (see Civil War medical and pharmaceutical equipment). Dressed interpreters.

CITY HALLS
Your local area or:

COLUMBUS CITY HALL
Corner of Broad and Front Streets, **Columbus**

- Area: **C**
- Telephone Number: (614) 645-6404
- Tours: Weekdays, Allow 1 hour for the tour
  30 people or less
  Appointment Necessary
- Admission: FREE

The tour begins with a walk through the Columbus Hall of Fame. The Hall contains pictures of outstanding Columbus natives such as James Thurber, former Miss Americas, OSU Coach Woody Hayes, OSU Heismann Trophy Winner Archie Griffin, and professional golfing legend, Jack Nicklaus. Next, the group goes inside City Council chambers where City Council meetings are held every Monday night. After that, you will visit the Mayor's office and conference room. If the Mayor is in and not too busy, he will probably peek out to say "hello". Lastly, the tour walks outside to see the bronze statue of Christopher Columbus. This statue was a gift given many years ago to the city from Genoa, Italy. Did you know that there was a secret box hidden inside the statue but it was not discovered until 1988. Guess what was inside the box?

CINCINNATI CITY HALL
801 Plum Street, **Cincinnati**

- Area: **SW**
- Telephone Number: (513) 352-3636
- Tours: 2nd Grade and Older

See a beautiful depiction of the history of the Queen City with stained glass windows.

COMMUNITY MUSEUMS

BALTIMORE COMMUNITY MUSEUM

C – 209 East Market Street, **Baltimore**. Sunday, 1:00 – 5:00 p.m. (Mother's Day – Labor Day)

PICKAWAY COUNTY HISTORICAL SOCIETY –CLARKE MAY MUSEUM

C – 162 West Union Street, **Circleville**. (740) 474-1495. Tuesday – Friday, 1:00 – 4:00 p.m. (April – October). Ohio bird's eggs and nests, Indian artifacts, and early dental office.

DELAWARE COUNTY HISTORICAL MUSEUM

C – 157 East William Street, **Delaware**. (740) 369-3831. Wednesday and Sunday, 2:00 – 4:30 p.m. (Mid-March – Mid November). Famous people. "Little Brown Jug" history.

GRANVILLE HISTORICAL MUSEUM

C – 115 East Broadway, **Granville**. (740) 587-3951. Friday, Saturday, Sunday, 1:00 – 4:00 p.m. (Mid-April – Mid-October). Oldest building in the area. Early hand tools and furniture plus a history of the 1st settlers from Granville, Massachusetts.

GRANVILLE LIFE STYLE MUSEUM

C –121 South Main Street, **Granville**. (740) 587-0373. Sunday, 1:00 – 4:30 p.m. (Mid-April – Mid-October). Robinson family possessions dating from the 1st wagon train in Granville (1805) to the 1980's. See it as the family life it – Civil War period chairs next to 1960's TV.

KILLBUCK VALLEY MUSEUM

C – US 62 and State Route 60, **Killbuck**. (330) 377-4572. Friday – Sunday, 1:00 – 5:00 p.m. Small Admission. History from Ice Age to railroads with an emphasis on American Indians.

THE GEORGIAN / THE SHERMAN HOUSE MUSEUM

C – 105 East Wheeling and Broad Street and 137 East Main Street, **Lancaster**. (740) 654-9923. Tuesday – Sunday. 19th Century homes with period furnishings and war momentos of Civil War General Sherman. Admission.

RICHLAND COUNTY MUSEUM

C – 51 West Church Street (east of State Route 42 South), **Lexington**. Weekends only, 1:30 – 4:30 p.m. (May – October). An 1850 schoolhouse with tools, clothing, children's toys and furniture.

MEDINA COUNTY HISTORICAL SOCIETY – JOHN SMART HOUSE MUSEUM

C – 206 North Elmwood Street and Friendship Street, **Medina**. (330) 722-1341. Tuesday and Thursday, 9:00 a.m. – 5:00 p.m., 1st Sunday of Month, 1:00 – 4:00 p.m., East Lake style home. Victorian, Civil War, pioneer and Indian artifacts. Life-size photographs of real "giants", Anna Julian and Martin Bates (also boots and helmet).

LICKING COUNTY HISTORICAL SOCIETY

C – North 6th and West Main, **Newark**. Tuesday – Sunday, 1:00 – 4:00 p.m. (April – December). Early 1800's home with furnishings. Small admission.

GREEN'S HERITAGE MUSEUM

C – 10530 Thrailkill Road (State Route 762), **Orient**. (740) 877-4254. Historical village with Blacksmith Shop, Antique Farm, 1929 Gas Station, Ice House, Depot, Sawmill, 1871 Church, Country Store with original counters and benches, and original

White Castle Gift Shop. Carriage House with 50 antique horse drawn carriages.

PICKERINGTON-VIOLET TOWNSHIP COMMUNITY MUSEUM

C - 105 East Columbus Street, **Pickerington**. (614) 834-4137. Saturday, 10:00 a.m. - 3:00 p.m. (February - December)

WYANDOT COUNTY HISTORICAL SOCIETY

C - 130 South 7th Street, **Upper Sandusky**. (419) 294-3857. Thursday - Sunday, 1:00 - 4:30 p.m. (May - October). An 1853 mansion with displays including American Indian and pioneer days, antique toys and clothing. Also school house. Admission.

HISTORIC PUTNAM TOUR

C - **Zanesville**. (800) 743-2303. "Doorway to the Past" - a driving tour of buildings from early settlements and rich architecture of late Federal Greek Revival and Victorian period residential, religious, and commercial structures. Area started in 1801with the purchase of land for $4.25 per acre by local businessmen.

BELMONT COUNTY VICTORIAN MANSION MUSEUM

CE - 532 North Chestnut Street, **Barnesville**. (740) 425-2926. Thursday - Sunday, 1:00 - 4:30 p.m. (May - October). 26 rooms furnished in Gay 90's style home. Admission.

BYESVILLE MUSEUM

CE - 236 East Main Street, **Byesville.** Monday - Friday, 12:00 - 4:00 p.m. Historic Bank building and Byesville history.

CAMBRIDGE GLASS MUSEUM

CE - 812 Jefferson Street (I-70 to exit 178), **Cambridge**. (740) 432-3045. Monday - Saturday, 1:00 - 4:00 p.m. (June - October). Admission.

GUERNSEY COUNTY HISTORICAL MUSEUM

CE – 218 North 8th Street, **Cambridge**. (740) 432-3145. Sunday, 1:00 – 5:00 p.m. (Memorial Day – Labor Day). Famous people and local products. Small admission.

MUSEUM OF CAMBRIDGE GLASS

CE – 9931 East Pike (US 40 off I-77 exit 46), **Cambridge**. (740) 432-4245. Wednesday – Saturday, 9:00 a.m. – 4:00 p.m., Sunday, Noon – 4:00 p.m. (April – October) Weekends in March. Admission.

GREATER CANTON AMATEUR SPORTS HALL OF FAME

CE – 1414 North Market Street, **Canton**. (330) 453-1552. Tuesday – Sunday, Noon – 4:00 p.m., Exhibits highlight local area amateur athletes (some are known internationally).

MCCOOK HOUSE

CE – Downtown Square, **Carrollton**. (330) 627-3345. Friday and Saturday, 9:00 a.m. – Noon and 1:00 – 5:00 p.m., Sunday, 1:00 – 5:00 p.m. (June – Mid-October). Admission.

DELPHOS CANAL COMMISSION MUSEUM CENTER

CE – 111 West Third Street, **Delphos**. (419) 695-7737. Monday, Wednesday, Friday, 1:00 – 3:30 p.m. Canals and canal boats. Stained glass artist. Quilt club work in progress.

CARRIAGE HOUSE MUSEUM

CE – 325 East Iron Avenue, **Dover**. (330) 343-7040. Tuesday – Sunday, 10:00 a.m. – 4:00 p.m. (Summer), Tuesday – Friday, 10:00 a.m. – 4:00 p.m. (September and October), Daily, 12:00 – 8:00 p.m. (December), Admission.

MUSEUM OF CERAMICS

CE – 400 East 5th Street, **East Liverpool**. (330) 386-6001. Wednesday – Saturday, 9:30 a.m. – 5:00 p.m., Sunday and Holidays, Noon – 5:00 p.m. Good and bad times of the ceramic industry in town and the effects on its people. Life sized dioramas of kiln, jigger and decorating shops with a collection of old and new ceramics. Slide presentation. Admission.

SEDGWICK HOUSE MUSEUM

CE – 627 Hanover Street (off State Route 7), **Martin's Ferry**. (740) 633-3430. (May – September). See the beginnings from 1787 by the Martin family of surveyors, planners, and ferry boat operators.

MASSILLON MUSEUM

CE – 121 Lincoln Way East, **Massillon**. (330) 833-4061. Tuesday – Saturday, 9:30 a.m. – 5:00 p.m., Sunday, 2:00 – 5:00 p.m. History, Sports, Circus (100 Sq. Ft. Miniature), P.T. Barnum's cane, Tom Thumb's clothing.

VICTORIAN HOUSE

CE – Holmes County (State Route 83), **Millersburg**. (330) 674-3975. Tuesday – Sunday, 1:30 – 4:00 p.m. (May – October). A 28 room, Queen Anne Style house built in 1900. Hand painted ceilings, ballroom, 1920's steam bath. Admission.

VILLAGE OF MT. PLEASANT

CE – Historical Society, State Route 150, **Mt. Pleasant**. (740) 769-2893. By appointment, (April – December). $6.00 Adult, $4.00 Student. Store, Tin Shop, Mansion Museum.

PORT WASHINGTON UNION HALL

CE – 109 Main Street (State Route 36), **Port Washington**. (740) 498-8597. Wednesday, 1:00 – 4:00 p.m. (June – August)

JEFFERSON COUNTY HISTORICAL MUSEUM

CE – 426 Franklin Avenue, Downtown **Steubenville**. (740) 283-1133. Victorian mansion. Steamboat and river history.

ALPINE HILLS MUSEUM

CE – 106 West Main Street, **Sugarcreek**. (330) 852-4113. Daily, 10:00 a.m. – 4:30 p.m. (April – November). Donation. 3 floors of

Swiss, German and Amish heritage (includes kitchen, cheese house and woodworking displays).

WAYNE COUNTY HISTORICAL SOCIETY MUSEUM

CE – Wooster. (330) 264-8856. Tuesday – Sunday, 2:00 – 4:30 p.m. Log Cabin. Schoolhouse. Indians. Women's Vintage Dress Shop. Carpenter Shop. Admission.

LOGAN COUNTY HISTORICAL MUSEUM

CW – 521 East Columbus Avenue, **Bellefontaine**. (937) 593-9557. Wednesday, Friday – Sunday, 1:00 – 5:00 p.m. (May – October). Schoolroom, Physician's office, Indians, Battles.

MERCER COUNTY HISTORICAL SOCIETY MUSEUM

CW – 130 East Market Street, **Celina**. Wednesday – Friday, 8:30 a.m. – 4:00 p.m. and Sunday, 1:00 – 4:00 (October – April). Chronicles the past 200 years. Riley House.

CENTERVILLE HISTORICAL SOCIETY WALTON HOUSE

CW – 89 West Franklin Street, **Centerville**. (937) 433-0123. Thursday and Saturday. 1838 stone house with period tools, clothing, and furnishings.

OLD COURTHOUSE AND MONTGOMERY COUNTY HISTORICAL MUSEUM

CW – 7 North Main Street, Downtown **Dayton**. (937) 228-6271. Tuesday – Friday, 10:00 a.m. – 4:30 p.m., Saturday, Noon – 4:00 p.m. Wright Brothers and Pattersons.

PATTERSON HOMESTEAD AND GARDENS

CW – 1815 Brown Street, **Dayton**. (937) 222-9724. Tuesday – Friday, 10:00 a.m. – 4:00 p.m., Sunday, 1:00 – 4:00 p.m. The 1816 farmhouse of Col. Robert Patterson whose sons, John and Frank founded NCR.

PREBLE COUNTY HISTORICAL FARM

CW – Gratis. An 1860's farm house. 1813 log cabin and barns full of relics.

GARST MUSEUM, DARKE COUNTY HISTORICAL SOCIETY

CW – 205 North Broadway, **Greenville**. (937) 548-5250. Tuesday – Saturday, 11:00 a.m. – 5:00 p.m., Sunday, 1:00 – 5:00 p.m., Annie Oakley memorabilia. Lowell Thomas (world famous radio broadcaster), Anthony Wayne, Native American artifacts. Village of shops.

THE SULLIVAN-JOHNSON MUSEUM OF HARDIN COUNTY

CW – 223 North Main Street, **Kenton**. (419) 673-7147. Thursday – Sunday, 1:00 – 4:00 p.m. (April – December), Saturday and Sunday Only (Rest of Year). Victorian mansion with Indian relics, Alaskan Art, Wilson footballs (manufactured in Ada, OH), iron toys, children's hands-on Discovery Room of history.

ALLEN COUNTY MUSEUM

CW – 620 West Market Street, **Lima**. (419) 222-9426. Tuesday – Sunday, 1:30 – 5:00 p.m., Indian and pioneer artifacts. Railroad Items. Antique automobiles and bicycles. Barber Shop, Doctor's office, country store. Locomotive and log house on grounds. Next door is MacDonell House (wall of purses).

KETTERING-MORAINE MUSEUM

CW – 35 Moraine Circle, **Moraine**. (937) 299-2722. Seven building complex showcases aviation, automobiles, appliances, and Shaker histories. The barn is where the automobile self-starter was invented. Wright Brothers furniture.

NEW BREMEN HISTORIC MUSEUM

CW – 120-122 North Main Street, Luelleman House, **New Bremen**. (419) 629-3321. Sunday, 2:00 – 4:00 p.m. (Summer)

PIQUA HISTORICAL MUSEUM

CW – 509 North Main Street, **Piqua**. (937) 773-2307. Tuesday, Thursday, Saturday and Sunday, 12:30 – 4:30 p.m. (April – November)

MUSEUM OF TROY HISTORY

CW – 124 East Water Street, **Troy**. (937) 339-6206. Saturday and Sunday, 2:00 – 5:00 p.m. (March – November). Household items from 1850 – 1950.

GREEN COUNTY HISTORICAL SOCIETY MUSEUM

CW – **Xenia**. (937) 372-4606. Tuesday – Friday, 1:00 – 3:30 p.m., Saturday and Sunday, 2:00 – 4:00 p.m. (Summer). Weekends Only, (Rest of Year). Restored Victorian home and 1799 James Galloway cabin where Tecumseh tried to "woo" Rebecca Galloway. Admission.

ASHLAND COUNTY HISTORICAL MUSEUM

NC – 414 Center Street, **Ashland**. (419) 289-3111. Friday and Sunday, 1:00 – 4:00 p.m. 1859 house, carriage house, and barn with collections of 19th and 20th Century establishments.

HICKORIES MUSEUM

NC – Lorain County, 509 Washington Avenue (North of Broad Street), **Elyria**. Tuesday – Friday, 1:00 p.m. – 4:00 p.m., Sunday, Noon – 4:00 p.m. (March – December). 1894 Tudor home built by inventor Arthur Garford, (padded bicycle seat). Large amount of hickory trees. Admission.

FIRELANDS MUSEUM

NC – 4 Case Avenue (State Route 250 and State Route 20), **Norwalk**. (419) 668-6038. Tuesday – Sunday, Noon – 5:00 p.m. (Summer). Saturday and Sunday, Noon – 4:00 p.m. (Spring and Fall). Area that was given as compensation for Revolutionary War fire destruction. 1836 home with firearms, costumes, and toys. Grandpa's newspaper shop upstairs until the 13th grandchild was born. Admission.

OBERLIN HISTORIC SITES TOUR

NC – 73 South Professor Street (State Route 38 and State Route 511), **Oberlin**. (440) 774-1700. Tuesday – Thursday, 10:30 a.m. and 1:30 p.m., 1st Sunday of month, 1:00 and 2:30 p.m., 3rd

Saturday of month, 1:00 and 2:30 p.m. $4.00 Adult. Underground Railroad, former politicians and professor home, little red school house with collection of lunch pails and McGuffey Readers.

OTTAWA COUNTY HISTORICAL MUSEUM

NC – **Port Clinton.** (419) 732-2237. Fossils, Indian artifacts, and Military history.

LAKE ERIE ISLANDS MUSEUM

NC – 441 Catawba Avenue, **Put-in-Bay**. (419) 285-2804. Daily, 11:00 a.m. – 5:00 p.m. (May, June and September). Daily, 10:00 a.m. – 6:00 p.m. (July and August)

FOLLETT HOUSE MUSEUM

NC – US 6 and 404 Wayne Street, **Sandusky**. (419) 627-9608. Tuesday – Sunday, 1:00 – 4:00 p.m. (Summer), Tuesday, Thursday, Sunday, 1:00 – 4:00 p.m. (Spring and Fall). An 1827 stone mansion built by Oren Follett who fought against slavery and helped to establish the Republican Party. Lake Erie history.

SENECA COUNTY MUSEUM

NC – 28 Clay Street, **Tiffin.** (419) 447-5955. Wednesday and Sunday afternoons. Mid-1800's home. Tiffin Glass.

HOWER HOUSE

NE – University of **Akron** Campus, (Fir Hill at East Market Street). (330) 972-6909. Wednesday – Saturday, Noon – 3:30 p.m., Sunday, 1:00 – 4:00 p.m. A 28 room Victorian mansion owned by one of Ohio's leading Industrialists, John Henry Hower (Quaker Oats). Beautiful wood and family treasures. Admission.

PERKINS MANSION

NE – Copley and South Portage Path, **Akron.** (330)-535-1120. Tuesday – Sunday, 1:00 – 4:00 p.m. (February – December). $9.00 Adult, $4.00 Senior (60+), $4.00 Children (5-16). Built by the son of Akron's founder.

WORDEN HERITAGE HOMESTEAD

NE – Hinckley Historical Society, 895 Lodge Road, **Hinckley.** (440) 278-2154. 1860 home with famous carvings and Hinckley history.

INDIAN MUSEUM OF LAKE COUNTY

NE – 391 West Washington Street (Lake Erie College), **Painesville.** (440) 352-1911. Monday – Friday, 10:00 a.m. – 4:00 p.m., Saturday and Sunday, 1:00 – 4:00 p.m. Interactive matching game of Indian tribes. Dig for arrow heads in sand. Grinding corn to flour. Small admission.

SHAKER HISTORICAL MUSEUM

NE – 16740 South Park Boulevard (off I-271), **Shaker Heights.** (440) 921-1201. Tuesday – Friday and Sunday, 2:00 – 5:00 p.m. Shaker Community remnants. Furniture and inventions (apple peeler, flat broom, tilter chair, clothes pins).

SHANDY HALL

NE – State Route 84, **Unionville.** (440) 466-3680. Tuesday – Saturday, 10:00 a.m. – 5:00 p.m., Sunday, 1:00 – 5:00 p.m. (May – October). Admission.

TRUMBULL COUNTY HISTORICAL SOCIETY MUSEUM

NE – 303 Monroe Street, **Warren.** (330) 394-4653. Saturday and Sunday, 1:00 – 4:00 p.m. John Stark Edwards/Thomas Denny Webb House.

MAHONING VALLEY HISTORICAL SOCIETY MUSEUM

NE – 648 Wick Avenue, **Youngstown.** (330) 743-2589. Tuesday – Friday, 1:00 – 4:00 p.m., Saturday – Sunday, 1:30 – 5:00 p.m. Small Admission. "The Valley Experience".

EHRHART MUSEUM

NW – 118 North Main Street, **Antwerp.** (419) 258-8161. Monday – Thursday, Noon – 5:00 p.m. See Otto Ehrhart's (a local naturalist) collection of mounted birds and animals caught and preserved. Indian artifacts.

WOLCOTT HOUSE MUSEUM

NW – 1031 River Road, **Toledo** area. (419) 893-9602. Wednesday – Sunday, 1:00 – 4:00 p.m., (April – December). Life in the mid-1800's in the Maumee Valley. Log home, depot, church and gift shop. Admission.

LAWRENCE COUNTY MUSEUM

SC – 506 S 6th Street (6th and Adams Street),. (740) 532-1222. Friday – Sunday, 1:00 – 5:00 p.m. (Mid-April – Mid-December). $2.00 Adult, Children under 12 Free. 1870 Victorian home of Rev. Runkin and served as a station for the Underground Railroad. Iron industry.

ROSS COUNTY HISTORICAL MUSEUM

SC – 45 West 5th Street, **Chillicothe**. (740) 772-1936. Daily (except Monday), 1:00 – 5:00 p.m. (April – September), Weekends, (December – March). See the table upon which Ohio's Constitution was signed. Civil War. Franklin House women's museum.

OUR HOUSE MUSEUM

SC – 434 1st Avenue (off State Route 7), **Gallipolis.** (740) 446-0586. Tuesday – Saturday, 10:00 a.m. – 5:00 p.m., Sunday, 1:00 – 5:00 p.m. (Summer). Weekends, (May, September, October). A restored river inn with furnishings of early Americana. Admission.

ADAMS COUNTY HERITAGE CENTER

SC – State Route 247, **West Union**. Thursday and Saturday, 12:00 – 4:00 p.m. Sheriff's murder exhibit. Oldest band in Ohio.

THE CASTLE

SE – 418 Fourth Street, **Marietta**. (740) 373-4180. Monday - Sunday, (Summer), Thursday – Monday, (April, May, September, - December), Weekdays, 10:00 a.m. – 4:00 p.m., Weekends, 1:00 –

4:00 p.m., $3.50 Adult, $3.00 Senior, $2.00 Student (6+). Historic area furnishings. Impressive parlor and chandelier. Video.

BUTLER COUNTY HISTORICAL SOCIETY MUSEUM

SW – 327 North 2nd Street, **Hamilton**. (513) 893-7111. Tuesday – Sunday, 1:00 – 4:00 p.m., Benninghofen House, a 19th Century Victorian mansion. Period furnishings.

LANE-HOOVEN HOUSE

SW – 319 North Third Street, **Hamilton**. (513) 863-1389. Monday – Friday, 9:00 a.m. – 4:00 p.m. Octagonal home with spiral staircase. Donations.

WARREN COUNTY HISTORICAL SOCIETY MUSEUM

SW – 105 South Broadway, **Lebanon**. (513) 932-1817. Tuesday – Saturday, 9:00 a.m. – 4:00 p.m., Sunday, Noon – 4:00 p.m. Village Green with shops. Collection of Shaker furniture.

LOVELAND MUSEUM

SW – **Loveland**. (513) 683-5692. History of Little Miami River Valley with 1862 house, 1797 log cabin, and herb garden.

ALVERTA GREEN MUSEUM

SW – 207 Church Street, **Mason**. (513) 398-6750. Thursday and Friday.

MIAMI-ERIE CANAL MUSEUM

SW – **Middletown**. (513) 422-7161. Restored lock tender's home with local artifacts.

COURT WATCHING

(See Government Section or Community Services of the White Pages)

Call for agenda of trials (docket information) for the following:

- ❑ Common Pleas
- ❑ Small Claims

- Municipal
- Domestic/Juvenile

Did you know as citizens we have the right to enter a courtroom to observe except when a "Do Not Disturb" sign warns otherwise? Watching trials in session can be a wonderful exposure to our legal system, especially for children who have studied law and government at school. Be sure your children have self-control before planning a visit. Call ahead and discover which trials would be most interesting.

Chapter 6

OUTDOOR EXPLORING

AREA "C"

WAHKEENA NATURE RESERVE
US 33 to County Road 86 West, follow signs, **Lancaster**

- Area: **C**
- Telephone Number: (740) 746-8695
- Hours: Wednesday - Sunday, 8:00 a.m. - 4:30 p.m. April - October
- Admission: $2.00 per vehicle
- Miscellaneous: Museum and Nature Trails

Trees, ferns, mountain laurels, wildflowers and orchids. All that beauty plus 70 species of birds and 15 species of mammals including woodpeckers and white-tailed deer.

MYSTERIOUS REVOLVING BALL
Marion Cemetery, **Marion**

- Area: **C**
- Hours: Dawn - Dusk

Can you scientifically solve the "Marion Unsolved Mystery"? Here's the scoop! The ball is a grave monument for the Merchant family erected in 1896. The 5200-pound granite ball turns mysteriously with continuous movement. There has been no scientific explanation for this revolution and the phenomenon is featured in many newspapers including "Ripley's Believe It or Not"!

OUTDOOR EXPLORING

AREA "CE"

ALPINE - ALPA
US 62, **Wilmont**

- Area: **CE**
- Telephone Number: (440) 359-5454
- Hours: Daily, 9:00 a.m. - 4:00 p.m. (Spring - Thanksgiving)

This is home of the World's Largest Cuckoo Clock. The Guinness Book of World Records has it listed as 23 ½ feet high, 24 feet long and 13 ½ feet wide. Trudy, a life-size mannequin with a German accent, opens shutters to greet you. The Swiss Village Market has viewing windows (to watch cheese making), restaurants and shops. Look for the 40-foot diorama with waterfalls and a moving train.

AREA "CW"

MIAMISBURG MOUND
I-75 to State Route 725 exit, follow signs, **Miamisburg**

- Area: **CW**
- Telephone Number (937) 297-2300
- Hours: Daily, Dawn to Dusk
- Miscellaneous: Park, Picnic

Take the stairs up a 68-foot high and 1.5 acre wide mound built by American Indians. This is the largest conical burial mound in Ohio.

CEDAR BOG AND NATURE PRESERVE

980 Woodburn Road (off Route 68 North / I-70 to **Springfield** / off State Route 36)

- Area: **CW**
- Telephone Number: (937) 484-3744
- Hours: Wednesday - Sunday, 9:00 a.m. - 4:30 p.m. (April - September)
  By Appointment (October – March)
  Admission: Small fee

A bog is a remnant of the Ice Age (glaciers and mastodons) and public tours take you to the boardwalk over this bog. Below you'll see the black, wet, slimy muck and chilly dampness created by a constant water table and cool springs.

HOBART WELDED SCULPTURE PARK

400 Trade Square East (State Route 41 to Ridge), **Troy**

- Area: **CW**
- Telephone Number: (937) 332-5000
- Hours: Dawn to Dusk

An outdoor collection of a dozen welded sculptures from students at the Hobart Institute of Welding Technology (an esteemed welding school). Be sure to check out the "Checkmarks" or "Unity of Man" (one of the nation's largest bronze fountains). The column represents *family* while the water expresses *continuity of life*. The "Sound Chamber" actually allows visitors to "play" with the sculpture as its steel and aluminum structure gives an Island Pacific sound when thumped on, strung, or beat with sticks.

OUTDOOR EXPLORING

AREA "NE"

TOWER CITY CENTER OBSERVATION DECK
50 Public Square, 42nd Floor, Terminal Tower, Downtown
Cleveland

- Area: **NE**
- Telephone Number: (216) 621-7981
- Hours: Weekends, 11:00 a.m. - 4:30 p.m. (Summer)
  11:00 a.m. - 3:30 p.m. (Rest of Year)
- Admission: $2.00 Adult, $1.00 Youth (6-16)

The Tower deck offers a full view of the city (best if you choose a clear day) with a few displays of the history of the Terminal Tower and downtown.

THE MAILBOX FACTORY
7857 Chardon Road (US 6), **Kirtland**

- Area: **NE**
- Telephone Number: (440) 256-MAIL
- Hours: Monday - Friday, 10:00 a.m. - 6:00 p.m.
- Saturday, 9:00 a.m. - 5:00 p.m.

You can't miss this place! As you approach the workshop, finished decorative mailboxes are adorning the lawn and many boxes and totem poles (yes!) are works in progress. Owner Wayne Burrwell used to drive a snow plow and occasionally knocked down mailboxes during his work. When he replaced them, he did it with such a unique mailbox that others on the street became envious. Now his livelihood is making mailboxes shaped like cows (with a cowbell), pelicans, trucks, flamingoes, and our favorite (and the special of the week), a "pig box". A must see!

MILL CREEK PARK

South of Mahoning Avenue off Glenwood Avenue, **Youngstown**

- Area: **NE**
- Telephone Number: (330) 740-7115 (Lanterman's Mill) (330) 740-7107 (Ford Nature Center)
- Hours: Tuesday - Friday, 10:00 a.m. - 5:00 p.m. Saturday and Sunday, 11:00 a.m. - 6:00 p.m.
- Miscellaneous: Gift Shop. Lanterman's Mill (May - October). Admission.

This park has your basic scenic trails, lakes, falls, gardens and covered bridges but it also has more. The Ford Nature Center is a stone house with live reptiles and hands-on exhibits about nature. Lanterman's Mill is a restored 1845 water powered gristmill with a 14-foot oak wheel. As you travel through the park, be on the look out for the Silver Bridge (reminiscent of Old England and Mary Poppins).

Area "SC"

HOPEWELL CULTURE NATIONAL HISTORICAL PARK

16062 State Route 104, 3 miles north of **Chillicothe**

- Area: **SC**
- Telephone Number: (740) 774-1125
- Hours: Daily, 8:00 a.m. - 6:00 p.m. (Summer) Daily, 8:30 a.m. - 5:00 p.m. (Rest of year)
- Admission: $2.00 per person. Maximum charge per vehicle is $4.00

OUTDOOR EXPLORING

- ❑ Miscellaneous: Visitor Center with a 15 minute "Legacy of the Moundbuilders" orientation film. Junior Ranger free booklet guide and badge.

The 120-acre park with 13-acre earthwall enclosure is home to 23 prehistoric burial and ceremonial mounds of the Hopewell Indians.

SERPENT MOUND STATE MEMORIAL
3850 State Route 73, **Locust Grove**

- ❑ Area: SC
- ❑ Telephone Number: (937) 587-2796
- ❑ Hours: Daily, 10:00 a.m. - 5:00 p.m. (Summer) Weekends, 10:00 a.m. - 5:00 p.m. (September, October, April, May)
- ❑ Admission: $4.00 per vehicle
- ❑ Miscellaneous: Profile of the "cyptoexplosion" doughnut shape can be seen off State Route 770 - East of Serpent Mound.

The largest earthwork in the United States, it measures 1335 feet from head to tail and is about 15 feet high. The mound appears as a giant serpent uncoiling in seven deep curves. The oval doughnut at one end probably represents the open mouth of the snake as it strikes.

AREA "SE"

CAPTAIN HOOK'S TOMB
State Route 376, Old Brick Cemetery (along river), **Stockport**

- ❑ Area: SE

Legend says that Captain Isaiah Hook designed his grave monument to be sharp on top so that it would be impossible for his wife to dance on his grave!

AREA "SW"

CAREW TOWER

441 Vine Street (5th and Vine). Downtown, **Cincinnati**

- Area: **SW**
- Telephone Number: (513) 241-3888 or (513) 579-9735
- Hours: Monday - Friday, 9:30 a.m. - 5:30 p.m.
  Saturday, 10:00 a.m. - 9:00 p.m.
  Sunday, 11:00 a.m. - 4:45 p.m.
- Admission: $2.00 Adult, $1.00 Children (under 12)
- Miscellaneous: A 1930's Art Deco building that is the tallest building downtown. Observation deck.

PYRAMID HILL SCULPTURE PARK

1763 Hamilton-Cleves Road, **Hamilton**

- Area: **SW**
- Telephone Number: (937) 868-8336

This park currently has 10 titled sculptures. Especially noticeable is "Abracadabra" by internationally famous sculptor, Alexander Liberman. Many passengers flying into Cincinnati can see the 2 1/2 story high, bright red contemporary walk through sculpture from above.

(The following listings are sorted by area/city within each category)

OUTDOOR EXPLORING

ARBORETUMS & GARDENS

FRANKLIN PARK CONSERVATORY AND BOTANICAL GARDENS
1777 East Broad Street (off I-71), **Columbus**
- Area: **C**
- Telephone Number: (614) 645-TREE.
- Hours: Tuesday – Sunday, 10 a.m.-5:00 p.m.
  Monday, Wednesday & Holidays, 5:00-8:00 p.m.

A place where you can learn where coffee comes from or watch the careful pruning of Bonsai trees. The large 1895 glass structure resembles the style of London's Crystal Palace. Walk through a simulated tropical rain forest, a desert, a tree fern forest, a Pacific Island water garden and then on to the Himalayan Mountains. Outside is a sculpture garden. Admission.

TOPIARY GARDEN

C – Deaf School Park, 408 East Town Street, **Columbus**. (614) 645-3300. The topiary (greenery shaped like people, boats, animals, etc.) garden depicts the theme "A Sunday Afternoon on the Island of La Grande Jaffe". Free.

DECKER ARBORETUM

C – Ohio Wesleyan campus, downtown **Delaware**. (740) 368-3020. Includes a sulfur spring and Ginkgo tree. Maps and tour info at Slocum Hall.

KINGWOOD CENTER

C – I-71 exit State Route 30, **Mansfield**. (419) 522-0211. Forty-seven acres of gardens, woods and ponds. Greenhouses with a specialty of tulips and perennials. Daily, 8:00 a.m. – 5:00 p.m.

DAWES ARBORETUM

State Route 13, **Newark**

- ❑ Area: **C**
- ❑ Telephone Number: (800) 443-2937
- ❑ Hours: Monday – Saturday, 8:00 a.m. – 5:00 p.m. Sunday & Holidays, 1:00 – 5:00 p.m.

Meadows, woods, gardens, cypress swamp, holly and a special Japanese Bonsai garden. If you were flying over the gardens you could see a 2100-foot long series of hedges that spell out "Dawes Arboretum". Free.

SECREST ARBORETUM

CE – 1680 Madison Avenue, **Wooster.** (330) 263-3761. Over 2000 species of native and exotic plants and trees, especially Old World roses.

COX ARBORETUM

CW – 6733 Springboro Pike, **Dayton.** (937) 434-9005. 160 acres including the nationally recognized Edible Landscape Garden. Daily 8:00 a.m. to dusk.

CLEVELAND BOTANICAL GARDEN

NE – 11030 East Blvd. (University Circle), **Cleveland.** (216) 721-1600. Display gardens as well as a great resource for advise on horticulture, landscape design and floral design.

HOLDEN ARBORETUM

NE – 9500 Sperry Road, **Kirtland.** (330) 946-4400. 3000 acres of gardens and walking trails. Admission over age six. Tuesday – Sunday, 10:00 a.m. – 5:00 p.m.

SCHOEPFLE ARBORETUM

NC – State Route 113 & State Route 60, just east of **Milan.** Harem of Holly, topiary garden. Free.

TOLEDO BOTANICAL GARDENS

NW – 5403 Elmer Drive (off North Reynolds Road), **Toledo**. (419) 936-2986. Fifty-seven acres of meadows and gardens. Gallery and gift store. Open dawn to dusk.

KROHN CONSERVATORY

SW – Eden Park Drive, **Cincinnati**. (513) 421-4086. A rainforest full of 5000 varieties of exotic desert and tropical plants. Small admission.

CAMPING

OHIO DEPARTMENT OF NATURAL RESOURCES

- (614) 764-0279 (Ohio Campground Owner's Association)
- (614) 265-7000 (State Parks Information - Calendar of Events)
- (800) 376-4847 (Ohio Camping)

The State Parks offer camping, horseback riding, boating, fishing, golfing, hiking, winter sports, and vacation planning assistance. The camping facilities can be lodges, cabins, or tents. The ODNR offers Rent-A-Camp. It is a unique program for beginning or infrequent campers to enjoy the experience of camping without purchasing the equipment. The cost is $11 to $17 per night. You will arrive at your campsite to find a 10 x 12-foot sleeping tent already set up complete with a dining canopy. Inside are two cots, sleeping pads, cooler, propane stove, lantern, broom, dustpan and welcome mat. Outside, you will find a fire ring and picnic table. This way of camping allows you to pick up and go without packing up a lot of gear. The campsites are limited, so make your plans early and call to make your reservation.

CAVERNS

OLENTANGY INDIAN CAVERNS

1779 Home Road (US 23 North to Home Road, follow signs), **Delaware**

- Area: **C**
- Telephone Number (740) 548-7917
- Hours: Daily, 9:30 a.m. - 5:00 p.m.
  April - October
- Admission: $7.50 Adult, $6.75 Senior
  $4.00 Children (7-12)
- Miscellaneous: Reservations needed for camping. Large picnic facilities.

Wyandotte Indians used these underground caves until 1810 for protection from the weather and their enemies. The caves were formed by an underground river that flows to the Olentangy River hundreds of feet below the surface. The caves were originally discovered during a search for oxen that broke loose from a wagon train. Their owner, J. M. Adam's name and date can be seen on the entrance wall. The tour lasts 30 minutes and takes you through winding passages and spacious underground rooms. Then you visit the museum where Indian artifacts found in the caves are displayed. Gift Shop, playground, sports activities, campsites, picnic grounds and shelter houses are available.

ZANE CAVERNS

7092 State Route 540, **Bellefontaine**

- Area: **CW**
- Telephone Number: (937) 592-9592
- Hours: Daily, 10:00 a.m. - 5:00 p.m. (May - September)
  Weekends Only (April and October)
- Admission: $7.00 Adult, $4.00 Children (under age 12)

The tour and slide show lasts about 45 minutes. See crystals in objects formed like straws, draperies, and popcorn. Kids will be in awe! There are a lot of extras like hayrides, gift shop, snack bar, and camping. Remember to dress appropriately because the temperature in the caverns is a constant 48-50 degrees F.

SENECA CAVERNS

State Route 269, South of **Bellevue**

- Area: **NC**
- Telephone Number: (419) 483-6711
- Hours: Daily, 9:00 a.m. - 7:00 p.m. (Summer)
  Weekends, 10:00 a.m. - 5:00 p.m. (May, September, October)
- Admission: Yes
- Miscellaneous: Light jacket is suggested as the cave is a constant 54 degrees F.

Take a one hour tour of the 110 foot deep limestone cave with many small rooms, seven levels and the "Ole Mist'ry River". The cave is actually an earth crack discovered by two boys out hunting in 1872. To make the tour really fun, stop by Sandy Creek Gem Mining and let your little explorers pan for gems.

PERRY'S CAVE

979 Catawba Avenue, **Put-in-Bay**

- Area: **NC**
- Telephone Number: (419) 285-2405
- Tours: Daily, 11:00 a.m. - 6:00 p.m. (20 minutes) (Summer)
- Admission: $4.00, Adult, $2.00 Youth

Inside the cave you'll see walls covered with calcium carbonate (the same ingredient in antacids) that has settled from years of dripping water. Rumor says Perry kept prisoners and stored supplies in the cave during the Battle of Lake Erie. At the Gem Mining Company buy a bag of sand at the gift shop. Take the bag outside to the mining station and dig through it to find gems. Compare your stones to a display in the survey stations.

SEVEN CAVES

7660 Cave Road (US 50, 4 miles Northwest, follow signs), **Bainbridge**

- Area: SC
- Telephone Number: (937) 365-1283
- Hours: Daily, 8:00 - Dusk
- Admission: $8.00 Adult, $4.00 Youth (5-11)
- Miscellaneous: Many stairs

Three trails lead to caves with cemented walkways, handrails, and lighting showing specific formations. See cliffs, canyons, and waterfalls.

HOCKING HILLS STATE PARK

20160 State Route 664 (Route 33 south to Route 664, follow signs), **Logan**

- Area: SC
- Telephone Number: (800) HOCKING
- Hours: 6:00 a.m. - Sunset (Summer), 8:00a.m.(Winter)

Overnight accommodations, bed and breakfasts, camping, recreation, picnic grounds, and hiking. Nature trails are found throughout the park, many of them lead to obscure, out-of-the-way natural creations. The park includes: Ash Cave (an 80 acre cave and stream), Cantwell Cliffs, Cedar Falls, Conkle's Hollow, Rock House, and the most popular, Old Man's Cave (a wooded, winding ravine of waterfalls and caves). Your children's sense of adventure will soar. Concessions available at Old Man's Cave or dining in the Lodge. We recommend close supervision on the hiking trails for your child's safety.

OUTDOOR EXPLORING

OHIO CAVERNS

2212 East State Route 245, **West Liberty**
- Area: **C**
- Telephone Number: (513) 465-4017
- Hours: Daily, 9:00 a.m. – 5:00 p.m. (April – October)
  9:00 a.m. – 4:00 p.m. (November – March)
- Admission: $7.50 Adult, $4.00 Children (5-12)

This tour is a one hour guided tour of the largest caves in Ohio. The temperature here is 54 degrees F. constantly so dress appropriately. On the premises is a park and gift shop.

HOBBIES

BIRDWATCHING

The Audubon Society meets every month, (September - May) at various parks. Bird watching is exciting but your child would need to have a full understanding of the importance of s-i-l-e-n-c-e! There are two 24-hour recording services to report bird sightings: (614) 221-WREN and Dial-A-Bird.

KITE FLYING

Contact your local organization (or kite shop) or the Central Ohio Kite Flyers Association. They fly kites every 2nd Saturday and the last Sunday of each month at the Ohio State School for the Deaf (550 Morse Road), Columbus, from 1:00 - 5:00 p.m. (614) 431-5483.

STAMP COLLECTING

Main Post Office in your area. Collect your favorite nature scenes!

RECREATION AREAS

Ohio Department of Natural Resources: (614) 265-6565

LEGEND OF SYMBOLS		
C = Camping	**P** = Picnicking	**BR** = Boat Rental
W = Winter Sports	**F** = Fishing	**H** = Hiking Trails
S = Swimming	**V** = Visitor Center	**PL** = Pets on Leash
L = Lodge or Cabins	**B** = Boating	**BT** = Bicycle Trails
FS = Food Service	**RP** = Boat Ramp	

A.W. MARION

C – (5 miles East of *Circleville* of US 22). 454 acres. (740) 869-3124. **FS, W, B, PL, F, BR, RP, H, P, C**

ALUM CREEK

C – (7 miles Southeast of *Delaware* off State Route 36/37, 1 mile West of I-71). 8,600 acres. (740) 548-4631. **FS, W, PL, S, F, BR, RP, B, H, P, C**

DELAWARE

C – (6 miles North of *Delaware* on US 23). 3,145 acres. (740) 369-2761. **FS, W, PL, S, F, BR, RP, B, H, P, C**

BURR OAK

C – (6 miles Northeast of *Glouster* off State Route 13). Nature programs. Bridle trails. (740) 767-3570. **FS, L, W, S, F, BR, RP, B, H, P, C**

MADISON LAKE

C – (3 miles East of *London* off State Route 665). 186 acres. (740) 869-3124. **W, S, F, RP, B, P**

MOHICAN

C – *Loudonville.* Nature programs, scenic, bike rentals, bridle trails. 1,294 acres. (419) 994-4290. **FS, L, W, F, BR, B, H, P, C**

CHARLES MILL LAKE

C – (9 miles East of *Mansfield* on State Route 430). Nature programs. **FS, PL, S, F, BR, RP, B, H, P, C**

MALABAR FARM

C – *Mansfield.* Nature programs. Bridle trails. 917 acres. (419) 892-2784. **FS, W, PL, F, H, P, C**

MOUNT GILEAD

C – (1 mile East of *Mt. Gilead* on State Route 95). 172 acres. (419) 946-1961. **W, F, RP, B, H, P, C**

DEER CREEK

C – (7 miles South of *Mt. Sterling* on State Route 207). Nature Programs. Bike Rental. (740) 869-3124. **FS, L, W, PL, S, F, BR, RP, B, H, P, C**

BUCKEYE LAKE

C – (9 miles South of *Newark* off State Route 13). 3,557 acres. (740) 467-2690. **W, S, F, RP, B, P**

PLEASANT HILL LAKE

C – (3 miles Southwest of *Perrysville* on State Route 95). (419) 938-7884. Nature programs. 2,195 acres. **FS, L, V, PL, S, F, BR, RP, B, H, P, C**

DILLON

C – (5 miles Northwest of *Zanesville* off State Route 146). 7690 acres. (740) 453-4377. **FS, L, W, PL, S, F, BR, RP, B, H, P, C**

MUSKINGUM RIVER

CE – 120 acres along 80 miles of the Muskingum River extending from Devola to Ellis Locks. (740) 452-3820. **PL, F, RP, B, H, P, C**

BARKCAMP

CE – (1 mile East of *Belmont* off State Route 149). Nature Programs. 1,232 acres. (740) 484-4064. **W, PL,S,F, RP,B, H, P, C**

WOLF RUN

CE – (1 mile East of *Belle Valley* off I-77). 1,363 acres. (740) 732-5035. **W, PL, S, F, RP, B, H, P, C**

TAPPAN LAKE

CE – (12 miles Northwest of *Cadiz* off US 250). (740) 922-3649. Nature programs. 7,597 acres. **FS, L, V, PL, S, F, BR, RP, B, H, P, C**

SALT FORK

CE – (7 miles Northeast of *Cambridge* on US 22). Nature programs. Bicycle rental. 20,181 acres. (740) 439-3521. **FS, L, W, PL, S, F, BR, RP, B, H, P, C**

BEAVER CREEK

CE – (8 miles North of *East Liverpool* off State Route 7). 3,038 acres. (330) 385-3091. **W, PL, F, H, P, C**

CLENDENING LAKE

CE – (3 miles North of *Freeport* off State Route 800). 6,550 acres. **FS, L, S, F, BR, RP, B, P, C**

GUILFORD LAKE

CE – (6 miles Northwest of *Lisbon* off State Route 172) 488 acres. (330) 222-1712. **W, S, F, RP, B, P, C**

SENECAVILLE LAKE

CE – (3 miles Southeast of *Senecaville* on State Route 547). (740) 685-6013. Nature programs. 7,613 acres. **FS, L, V, PL, S, F, BR, RP, B, H, P, C**

LEESVILLE LAKE

CE – (4 miles South of *Sherrodsville* off State Route 212). 3,625 acres. **FS, L, PL, F, BR, RP, B, H, P, C**

PIEDMONT LAKE

CE – (2 miles Southeast of *Smyrna* off State Route 800). 6,642 acres. **FS, L, PL, F, BR, RP, B, P, C**

JEFFERSON LAKE

CE – (16 miles Northwest of *Steubenville* of State Route 43). 933 acres. (740) 765-4459. **W, PL, S, F, RP, B, H, P, C**

ATWOOD LAKE

CE – (2 miles Southeast of *New Cumberland* off State Route 212). (330) 343-6647. Nature programs. 4,536 acres. **FS, L, V, W, PL, S, F, BR, RP, B, H, P, C**

PIATT

CE – (4 miles East of *Woodsfield* on State Route 78). Bridle trails. 119 acres. **H, P, C**

BLUE ROCK

CE – (12 miles Southeast of *Zanesville* off State Route 60 and County Road 45). 350 acres. (740) 674-4794. **FS, W, PL, S, F, RP, B, H, P, C**

CARRIAGE HILL RESERVE

CW – (Northeast of *Dayton* at junction of I-70 and State Route 201). 868 acres. **PL, S, F, H, P, C**

POSSUM CREEK RESERVE

CW – (West of *Dayton* at junction of Gettysburg Avenue and State Route 4). 518 acres. **W, F, H, P, C**

SUGARCREEK RESERVE

CW – (Southeast of *Dayton* on Wilmington Pike). Horse rental. 596 acres. **W, H, P**

INDIAN LAKE

CW – (2 miles North of *Lakeview* on State Route 235). 6448 acres. (937) 843-2717. **W, PL, S, F, RP, B, H, P, C**

HUESTON WOODS

CW – (5 miles North of *Oxford* off State Route 732). Nature Programs. Bike rental. 3596 acres. (513) 523-6347. **FS, L, V, W, PL, S, F, BR, RP, B, H, P, C**

BUCK CREEK

CW – (4 miles East of *Springfield* on State Route 4). 4030 acres. (937) 322-5284. **FS, L, W, PL, S, F, BR, RP, B, H, P, C**

GRAND LAKE ST. MARY'S

CW – (2 miles West of *St. Mary's* on State Route 703). Nature programs. 14,000 acres. (419) 394-3611. **FS, W, S, F, BR, RP, B, P, C**

LAKE LORAMIE

CW – (3 miles Southeast of *Minster* off State Route 66). 2,055 acres. (937) 295-2011. **W, S, F, RP, B, H, P, C**

SYCAMORE

CW – (1 mile North of *Trotwood* on State Route 49). Snowmobiling. Bridle trails. 2,300 acres. (937) 854-4452. **W, F, H, C**

KISER LAKE

CW – (17 miles Northwest of *Urbana* on State Route 235). 870 acres. (937) 362-3822. **W, S, F, BR, RP, B, H, P, C**

JOHN BRYAN

CW – (2 miles Southeast of *Yellow Springs* on State Route 370). 750 acres. (937) 767-1274. **W, F, H, P, C**

HUNTINGTON BEACH

NC – Cleveland MetroParks, *Bay Village*. (440) 871-2900. Lake Erie Nature and Science Center. **FS, V, BT, S, F, RP, B, H, P**

CATAWBA ISLAND

NC – (off State Route 53). (419) 797-4530. **W, F, RP, B, P**

KELLEY'S ISLAND

NC – *Kelley's Island.* Scenic. 661 acres. (419) 797-4530. **W, PL, S, F, H, P, C**

CRANE CREEK

NC – (Northwest of *Locust Point* off State Route 2). 79 acres. (419) 836-7758. **W, S, F, H, P**

LAKEVIEW PARK

NC – *Lorain.* (440) 244-9000. Swimming.

EAST HARBOR

NC – (8 miles East of *Port Clinton* off State Route 269). Nature programs. 1,152 acres. (419) 734-4424. **FS,W,S,F, RP, B, H, P, C**

SOUTH BASS ISLAND

NC –A summer ferry takes you to explore over 35 acres on *South Bass Island.* (419) 797-4530. **L, W, S, F, RP, B, P, C**

MAUMEE BAY

NC – (8 miles East of *Toledo*, then 3 miles North off State Route 2). 1,845 acres. (419) 836-7758. **FS, L, W, PL,S,F, RP, B, H,P, C**

FINDLEY

NC – (3 miles South of *Wellington* on State Route 58). Nature programs. Bike rental. 931 acres. (440) 647-4490. **FS, W, PL, S, F, BR, RP, B, H,P,C**

PORTAGE LAKES

NE – (State Route 93 in *Akron*). 4,963 acres. (330) 644-2220. **W, PL, S, F, RP, B, H, P, C**

PYMATUNING

NE – (6 miles Southeast of *Andover* off US 85). Nature programs. 17,500 acres. (440) 293-6329. **L, W, S, F, BR, RP, B, H, P, C**

CLEVELAND LAKEFRONT

NE – (off I-90, downtown), *Cleveland*. (216) 881-8141. 450 acres. **FS, W, BT, S, F, BR, RP, B, P**

FAIRPORT HARBOR

NE – (Huntington Beach Drive). (440) 639-9972. **S**

GEVEVA

NE – (Shore of Lake Erie, *Geneva-on-the-Lake*). 698 acres. (440) 466-8400. **L, W, PL, S, F, RP, B, H, P, C**

QUAIL HOLLOW

NE – (2 miles North of *Hartville* on Congress Lake Road). Nature programs. Bridle trails. 700 acres. (330) 877-6652. **V, W, H, P**

LAKE MILTON

NE – (1 mile South of I-76 off State Route 534, *Lake Milton*). 2,856 acres. (330) 654-4989. **W, S, F, RP, B, P**

PUNDERSON

NE – (2 miles East of *Newbury* off State Route 87). Nature programs. Tennis. 996 acres. (440) 564-2279. **FS, L, W, PL, S, F, BR, RP, B, H, P, C**

HEADLANDS BEACH

NE – (2 miles Northwest of *Painesville* at State Route 44). (440) 257-1300. 125 acres. (440) 881-8141. **W, S, F, H, P**

TINKER'S CREEK

NE – (2 miles West of State Route 43 on Aurora-Hudson Road near *Portage*). 760 acres. (330) 296-3239. **W, S, F, H, P**

WEST BRANCH

NE – (5 miles East of *Ravenna* off State Route 5). Nature programs. Bridle trails. 8,002 acres. (330) 296-3239. **FS, W, S, F, BR, RP, B, H, P, C**

MOSQUITO LAKE

NE – (10 miles North of *Warren* off State Route 305). Bridle trails. 11,811 acres. (330) 637-2856. **W, S, F, BR, RP, B, H, P, C**

INDEPENDENCE DAM

NW – (4 miles East of *Defiance* on State Route 424). 604 acres. (419) 784-3263. **W, PL, F, RP, B, H, P, C**

HARRISON LAKE

NW – (4 miles South of *Fayette* off State Route 66). 249 acres. (419) 237-2593. **W, PL, S,F, RP, B, H, P, C**

MARY JANE THURSTON

NW – (2 miles West of *Grand Rapids* on State Route 65). 555 acres. (419) 832-7662. **W, F, RP, B, H, P**

VAN BUREN LAKE

NW – (1 mile East of *Van Buren* on State Route 613). 296 acres. (419) 299-3461. **W, BT, PL, F, B, H, P, C**

TAR HOLLOW

SC – (10 miles South of *Adelphi* off State Route 540). 634 acres. (740) 887-4818. **PL, S, F, RP, B, H, P, C**

STROUD'S RUN

SC – (8 miles Northeast of *Athens* off US 50A on County Road 20). 2,767 acres. (740) 592-2302. **W, PL, S,F, BR, RP, B, H, P, C**

PIKE LAKE

SC – (6 miles Southeast of *Bainbridge*). Nature programs. 613 acres. (740) 493-2212. **FS, L, W, S, F, BR, B, H, P, C**

GREAT SEAL

SC – (3 miles Northeast of *Chillicothe* on Marietta Pike). Cross-country skiing, Bridle trails.1,864 acres. (740) 773-2726.**W,H,P, C**

SCIOTO TRAIL

SC – (10 miles South of *Chillicothe* off US 23). 248 acres. (740) 663-2125. **W, PL, F, B, H, P, C**

PAINT CREEK

SC – (17 miles East of *Hillsboro* on US 50). Nature programs. Pioneer farm. 10,200 acres. (937) 365-1401. **W, PL, S,F, BR, RP, B, H, P, C**

ROCKY FORK

SC – (6 miles Southeast of *Hillsboro* off State Route 124). 3,464 acres. (937) 393-4284. **FS, PL, S, F, BR, RP, B, H, P, C**

LAKE VESUVIUS

SC – (6 miles North of *Ironton* off State Route 93). Nature program. 200 acres. **V, PL, S, F, BR, RP, B, H, P, C**

HOCKING HILLS

SC – *Logan*. Nature Programs. 2,348 acres. (740) 385-6841. **FS, L, W, S, F, B, H, P, C**

LAKE LOGAN

SC – (4 miles West of *Logan* off State Route 664). 717 acres. (740) 385-3444. **FS, W, S, F, BR, RP, B, H, P**

LAKE HOPE

SC – (12 miles Northeast of *McArthur* on State Route 278). Nature programs. 3,223 acres. (740) 596-5253. **FS, L,PL, S,F, BR, RP, B, H, P,C**

JACKSON LAKE

SC – (2 miles West of *Oak Hill* on State Route 279). 335 acres. (740) 682-6197. **W, S, F, RP, B, P, C**

SHAWNEE

SC – (8 miles West of *Portsmouth* on State Route 125). Nature programs. 1,168 acres. (740) 858-6652. **FS, L, W, PL, S, F, BR, RP, B, H, P, C**

OUTDOOR EXPLORING

LAKE WHITE

SC – (4 miles Southwest of *Waverly* on State Route 104). 358 acres. (740) 947-4059. **W, S, F, RP, B, P, C**

LAKE ALMA

SC – (3 miles Northeast of *Wellston* on State Route 349). 279 acres. (740) 384-4474. **PL, S, F, RP, B, H, P, C**

FORKED RUN

SE – (3 miles Southwest of *Reedsville* off State Route 124). 817 acres. (740) 378-6206. **FS, W, PL, S, F, BR, RP, B, H, P, C**

EAST FORK

SW – (4 miles Southeast of *Amelia* off State Route 125). Bridle trails. 10,580 acres. (513) 734-4323. **W, PL, S, F, RP, B, H, P, C**

MIAMI WHITEWATER FOREST

SW – (Northwest of *Cincinnati* off I-74). Golf. Playground. **V, F, BR, B, H, P, C**

SHARON WOODS

SW – (Northeast of *Cincinnati* off Reading Road). Golf, bicycle rental, playground. **FS, V, BT, H, P**

SHAWNEE LOOKOUT

SW – (West of *Cincinnati* via US 50). Golf, playground. **V, F, RP, B, H, P**

WINTON WOODS

SW – (North of *Cincinnati* off Winton Road). Golf, bicycle rental, horse rental, playground. **V, BT, F, BR, B, H, P, C**

LITTLE MIAMI

SW – (North of *Corwin*). Bridle trails. 452 acres. (513) 897-3055. **W, BT, F, H**

STONELICK

SW – (1 mile South of *Edenton* off State Route 727). 1,258 acres. (513) 625-7544. **FS, W, PL,S,F, RP, B, H, P, C**

CAESAR CREEK

SW – (State Route 73, 6 miles West of I-71, near *Waynesville*). Bridle trails. 10,771 acres. (513) 897-3055. **W, PL, S, F, RP, B, H, P, C**

COWAN LAKE

SW – (5 miles South of *Wilmington* off US 68). Nature programs. Bike Rental. 1,775 acres. (937) 289-2105. **FS, L, W, PL, S, BR, RP, B, H, P, C**

Chapter 7

SEASONAL SPECIAL EVENTS

Tony Staff

Most listings occur on weekends unless noted otherwise
Free = Free Admisson

(Listings sorted by Area and City within each month)

JANUARY

MARTIN LUTHER KING MARCH & PROGRAM

C - City Hall & Vets Memorial, **Columbus**. (614) 645-3343. Free. Saturday only.

WINTERFEST / MARTIN LUTHER KING JR. CELEBRATION

C - Secrest Auditorium, **Zanesville**. (740) 455-0609. Chili cook-off, prayer breakfast, floral contest, ice carving competition and parade tribute to Dr. King.

MARTIN LUTHER KING FESTIVAL

NC - Holiday Inn, 1825 Lorain Road, **Elyria**. (440) 366-5656. Saturday only. Admission.

WINTERFEST

NE – Alpine Valley Skiing, 10620 Mayfield Rd., **Chesterland**. (440) 285-2211. Enjoy volleyball in the snow, snowshoe obstacle race course, bikini slalom and a children's obstacle slalom. Lift ticket fee. Saturday only.

FEBRUARY

CHOCOLATE FANTASY FAIR

C - Columbus Convention Center, **Columbus**, Valentine's Day Weekend. Sample chocolate desserts. Entertainment. Demos. Admission.

SEASONAL & SPECIAL EVENTS

ICE FESTIVAL

NC - Public Square, **Medina**. (800) 463-3462. Cash prizes and medals for an ice carving competition. Free.

TRADITIONAL POWWOW

NW - UAW Hall, 1440 Bellefontaine Avenue, **Lima**. (419) 228-1097. Native American dance, song, crafts and food. Admission.

MARCH

BUZZARD DAY

NE - Cleveland Metroparks, **Hinckley** Reservation, (440) 351-6300. Annual migration of the buzzard with breakfast watch. Admission.

MAPLE SYRUP FESTIVALS

Syrup making demos. Pancake dinners/breakfasts. Sugarbush tours by foot or by wagon.

- **C** - *Dawes Arboretum*. (740) 323-2355.
- **C** - *Malabar Farm*. (419) 892-2784
- **NC** - *Teddy Bear Park*, Lima, (419) 221-1232
- **NE** - *Holden Arboretum*, (440) 946-4400. Daily except Monday. Admission.
- **NE** - *Township Park*, Boardman, (330) 726-8105. Admission.

ST. PATRICK'S DAY PARADES & CELEBRATIONS

Cincinnati, Cleveland, Dublin (Columbus), and Toledo. Downtown

APRIL

EASTER EGG HUNTS

- **C** - Columbus Recreation & Parks, (614) 645-3300.
- **C** - *Columbus Zoo*, (614) 645-3550, ages 2-12. Admission.
- **C** - *Slate Run Farm*, Egg decorating & egg rolling contests. Admission.
- **CW** – *Young's Dairy*, Yellow Springs, Over 4000 colored Easter eggs. Free.
- **SW** - *Easter Eggstravaganza*, Hamilton County Park, (513) 521-PARK.
- **SW** - *Great Easter Egg Scramble*, Cincinnati Zoo, (513) 281-4700.

TROUT DERBY

NC - Shawnee State Park, St. Route 125, W. of **Portsmouth**. (740) 858-6652. Fishing contest, dawn to dusk, with awards ceremony at nightfall. Free. Valid Ohio fishing license required. Saturday only.

GEAUGA COUNTY MAPLE FESTIVAL

NE - **Chardon**. (440) 286-3007. Sap Run contest, midway, parades, bathtub races and maple syrup production and sales. First weekend after Easter.

WALLEYE DERBY

NW - Maumee River, West River Road, **Maumee**. (419) 893-5805. Collect a prize for the longest walleye. Dawn-1:00 p.m. Saturday only. Fee.

MAY

ASIAN FESTIVAL

C - Franklin Park, 1777 East Broad Street, **Columbus**. (614) 222-4944. A dozen or more Asian ethnic cultures share their heritage through entertainment, costumes, foods and kid's crafts such as origami, rangoli and kite making. Free.

MEDIEVAL & RENAISSANCE FESTIVAL

C - O.S.U. South Oval, **Columbus**. (614) 292-2324. The first Saturday of May watch traditional Medieval performers in a human chess game or mock battles, food and crafts (face painting).

RHYTHM & FOOD FESTIVAL : A TASTE OF COLUMBUS

C - Downtown Riverfront, **Columbus**. (614) 645-7995. Performances by national and local artists in blues, Cajun, zydeco and world music. Local restaurants serve traditional international favorites. Free. Memorial Day Weekend.

SPRING PLOWING DAYS

C - Malabar Farm State Park, State Route 603, SE of **Mansfield**. (419) 892-2784. Horse teams test their strength and skill during log skidding, plowing matches and load pulling contests. Free.

OLD-FASHIONED ICE CREAM FESTIVAL

C - Ye Olde Mill, **Utica**. (740) 892-3463. Velvet Ice Cream hosts a tribute to our national dessert, ice cream, with family entertainment and lots of food made from ice cream. Kids can feel like they're in the movie, Babe, as they watch sheep herding with border collies. You must catch the kiddie tractor pull. Memorial Day Weekend. Admission.

HOPALONG CASSIDY FESTIVAL

CE - Downtown **Cambridge**. (740) 439-6688. William Boyd, better known as "Hop-a-long Cassidy" was originally from Cambridge. This celebration includes western entertainment, a cowpoke dinner and visiting Hollywood stars.

RAILROAD FESTIVAL

CE - Dennison. (800) 527-3387. Enjoy the heritage and history of the famous World War II Dennison Depot with food, games, contests, rides and parade.

A WORLD A'FAIR

CW - Convention Center, 22 East Fifth Street, **Dayton**. (937) 293-5173. 35 countries present their dances, foods, customs and culture. Admission.

WILDLIFE FESTIVAL

CW - Aullwood Audubon Farm, 9101 Frederick Road, **Dayton**. (937) 890-7360. Wild animals, live music, zoo cats, foods, crafts, wagon rides and children's activities. Admission.

SPRING FOUR-WHEEL JAMBOREE NATIONALS

CW - Allen County Fairgrounds, State Route 309 East, **Lima**. (317) 236-6515. 1400 vehicles compete in a tough and monster trucks show-n-shine competitions. Admission. Long weekend.

STRAWBERRY FEST

NC - **Norwalk**. (419) 663-2219. A Strawberry theme street fair with crafts and foods. Free. Memorial Day Weekend.

WALLEYE FESTIVAL

NC - Water Works Park, **Port Clinton**. (419) 732-2864. Fresh walleye sandwiches, entertainment, crafts, rides and parade. Free

TROUT DERBY

NW - Buckeye Quarry, **Bluffton**. (419) 358-6911. Stocked quarry with prizes offered by local businesses for tagged fish. Saturday afternoon only. Fee.

GREAT BALLOON CHASE

NW - Fort Meigs State Memorial, **Perrysburg**. (419) 241-4258. Brightly colored hot-air balloons all aglow with competition flights, entertainment and tethered balloon rides. Admission.

SEASONAL & SPECIAL EVENTS

INTERNATIONAL STREET FAIR

SC - Court Street, **Athens**. (740) 593-4330. Dance, music, food, arts and cultural displays by 40 international student and community organizations. Mid-month. Saturday only. Free.

VINTON COUNTY WILD TURKEY FESTIVAL

SC - **McArthur**. (740) 596-5033. Turkey calling contests, street fair and parade during the wild turkey hunting season. Free.

KIDS FEST

SW - Sawyer Point, **Cincinnati**. (513) 352-6168. Three stages of entertainment, boat rides and 130+ activities.

KIDS DAY

SW - Courthouse Square, Downtown **Hamilton**. The first Saturday in May, Hamilton has a kids appreciation day with a parade, clowns, face painting, contests, demos, food and entertainment.

JUNE

CRANBERRY BOG ANNUAL OPEN HOUSE

C - Cranberry Bog State Nature Preserve, **Buckeye Lake**. (740) 265-6453. Take a tour of the island's rare and fascinating plants by pontoon boat. Held the last Saturday in June. Admission.

PRAIRIE PEDDLER

C - Bunker Hill Woods, State Route 97, 3 miles east of **Butler**. (419) 663-1818. Almost 200 costumed craftspeople offer their items made with frontier style tools, foods cooked over open fires and bluegrass music. Stop by the Medicine Show and buy a bottle of elixir. Fee. Also held in September and October.

FESTIVAL LATINO

C - **Columbus** Downtown Riverfront. (614) 645-7995. Celebrate Latin culture, food (contemporary and traditional) and music (Mambo, Salsa, Conjunto, Flamenco). Free.

ROSE FESTIVAL

C - Whetstone Park, 3923 North High Street, **Columbus**. (614) 645-3343. Thousands of roses during peak blooming season. Mazes, games and a reunion of people with the last name, Rose.

ITALIAN AMERICAN FESTIVAL

C - Downtown **Crestline**. (419) 683-4466. Dancing, Italian American foods, folk music, a spaghetti cook-off, cultural booths and a parade. Free.

STRAWBERRY FESTIVAL

CE - B & O Depot, 300 East Church Street, **Barnesville**. (740) 425-4300. A day beginning with strawberry shortcake and maybe ending with strawberry sundaes. Also crafts and entertainment. Saturday. Free.

ITALIAN AMERICAN FESTIVAL

CE - Stark County Fairgrounds, 305 Wertz Avenue, **Canton**. (330) 494-0886. Italy in Ohio with entertainment, foods, dancing, exhibits, rides and a bocci tournament. Thursday-Sunday. Admission.

HOT AIR BALLOON FESTIVAL

CE - Coshocton County Fairgrounds, 707 Kenilworth Avenue, **Coshocton**. (740) 622-5411. Balloon launches at dawn and dusk; nightglow (Saturday); entertainment and rides. Free.

STRAWBERRY FESTIVAL

CE - Historic Roscoe Village, State Route 16/83, **Coshocton**. (800) 877-1830.

FORT STEUBEN FESTIVAL

CE - Historic Fort Steuben Site, **Steubenville**. (740) 283-4935. This first American Regiment was built to protect government surveyors from hostile Indians. Next to the fort site is the first Federal Land Office built in the U.S. in 1801. Watch mountain men reenactment groups, storytellers and craftspeople. Admission.

SEASONAL & SPECIAL EVENTS

KIDS DAY

CE - Downtown **Wooster**. (330) 262-6222. An afternoon devoted to children's art, activities, games and entertainment. First Saturday in June. Free.

GARLIC FESTIVAL

CW - Cox Arboretum MetroPark, 6733 Springboro Pike, **Dayton**. (937) 434-9005. Pro chefs demo food made with garlic. Tastings. Reservations only.

NATIONAL FOLK FESTIVAL

CW - Downtown **Dayton**. (937) 223-3655. Hundreds of the country's best folk performers and artists entertain you with shows, activities, games, crafts and food.

STRAWBERRY FESTIVAL

CW - **Troy**, the Strawberry Capital of the Midwest. (937) 339-7714. The first full weekend in June the fountain on Town Square runs pink water! Loads of fresh-picked berries and strawberry foods are sold. Parade, entertainment and hot-air balloons. Free.

POULTRY DAYS

CW - Versailles High School, Center Street, **Versailles**. (937) 526-3539. Famous barbecued chicken, parade, entertainment and rides. Free.

INTERNATIONAL FESTIVAL

NC - Sheffield Centre, State Route 254 & Lake Road, **Lorain**. (440) 282-6304. Dance, music and authentically prepared foods from many different countries throughout the world. Free.

OHIO SCOTTISH GAMES

NC - **Oberlin**. (440) 442-2147. A weekend of Scottish traditions from the parade of tartans to the drumming and piping competition. Admission.

OHIO IRISH FESTIVAL

NC - West Side Irish-American Club, 8559 Jennings Road, **Olmsted Falls**. (440) 779-6065. Celebrating the best of Ireland with lively Irish dance reels and lots of Irish food like tasty scones. Admission.

FESTIVAL OF FISH

NC - Victory Park, **Vermilion**. (440) 967-4477. Walleye and perch sandwiches, "crazy" craft race, entertainment, crafts and a lighted boat parade. Free.

STRAWBERRY FESTIVAL

NE - Village Park, **Canal Fulton**. (800) 435-3623. Strawberry cake and ice cream, a vintage baseball game and canal boat rides. Admission. Saturday only.

GREAT LAKES MEDIEVAL FAIRE

NE - 3033 State Route 534, 15 miles south of **Geneva**. (888) 633-4382. The recreation of a 13th century English village with jugglers, jesters, musicians, crafts, full-armored knights and sumptuous foods. Admission.

NORTHEAST OHIO POLKA FEST

NE - Old Firehouse Winery, 5499 Lake Road, **Geneva-on-the-Lake**. (800) 862-6751. Lots of ethnic foods and live polka music and dancing (Polish, Chicago and Slovenian). Free.

AFRICAN - AMERICAN HOMECOMING FESTIVAL

NE – Courthouse Square, **Warren**. (330) 393-7223. Parade, rides, food and lots of good gospel and jazz music. Free.

TRAINS, PLANES & AUTOMOBILES FEST

NW - Bluffton Airport, 1080 Navajo Drive, **Bluffton**. (419) 358-5675. Airplane rides, tandem skydiving, antique cars and model trains. Free. Saturday only. Fees for air rides.

GARLIC LOVERS FESTIVAL

NW - Downtown **Toledo**. (419) 243-2404.

SEASONAL & SPECIAL EVENTS

NATIONAL THRESHERS ANNUAL REUNION

NW - Fulton County Fairgrounds, State Route 108, **Wauseon**. (419) 335-6006. Working gas tractors and over 30 operating steam engines on the sawmill, threshing wheat and plowing machines. Admission.

APPALACHIAN DOWN HOME DAYS

SW - Butler County Courthouse, **Hamilton**. (513) 868-2585. Clogging contest, gospel choir competition, square dancing, live bands, crafts, rides and games. Free.

PORK RIND HERITAGE FESTIVAL

SW - **Harrod**. (419) 648-2063. Fresh popped pork rinds, hog roast, parade, crafts and live entertainment. Free.

FIESTA LATINO-AMERICANA

SW - Fraze Pavilion, 695 Lincoln Park Blvd., **Kettering**. (937) 296-3300. Enjoy hot Latin music, exciting dance, authentic foods, crafts and children's activities. Saturday only. Fee for concerts.

KIDS FEST

SW - Civic Commons Park, 675 Lincoln Park Blvd., **Kettering**. (937) 296-2587. Designed for young children and their parents to participate in activities ranging from hands-on crafts to face painting. Saturday only. Free.

PAPER FESTIVAL

SW - Civic Center, 300 East Central Avenue, **West Carrollton**. (937) 859-5909. A celebration of the city's paper making industry heritage with a parade, crafts and entertainment. Free.

JULY

JULY 4TH CELEBRATIONS

All cities listed (by area, alphabetically) include parades, entertainment and fireworks.

C - *Ashville* (740) 983-4797

C - *Columbus* (614) 263-4444 Red, White & Boom! July 3rd. Largest fireworks display synchronized to music and lights in the Midwest.

C - *Columbus* (614) 297-2300 Independence Day at Ohio Village. Old fashioned activities in a re-created Civil War-era town.

C - *Delaware* (614) 965-2860

C - *Dublin* (614) 761-6500

C- *Mansfield* (419) 938-7884 Beach Party & Fireworks.

C - *Mansfield* (419) 756-6839 Freedom Festival. Airport air show.

C- *Marysville* (937) 246-5733

C - *Zanesville* (740) 452-7571 Stars & Stripes on the River.

CE - *Deersville*, Tappan Lake Park (740) 922-3649

CE - *Martins Ferry* (740) 633-2565 Sky show.

CE - *Massillon* (330) 833-2233 Picnic in the Park, Stadium Park.

CW *-Beavercreek* (937) 427-5514

CW - *Centerville* (937) 433-5898. Americana Festival

CW - *Dayton* (937) 225-4674 Jefferson Township Days. July 3-6.

CW - *Huber Heights* (937) 233-5700 Soar to New Heights. July 2-5.

CW - *Jeffersonville* (740) 426-6331 Community Days. July 4-6.

CW - *Lakeview*, Indian Lake (937) 843-5392 Decorated boat parade.

NC - *Port Clinton* (419) 734-5522

NC - *Put-in-Bay* (419) 285-2184 Perry's Victory Memorial

NE - *Austintown* (330) 792-1129

NE - *Brunswick* (330) 225-2720

NE - *Cleveland* (216) 881-8141 Festival of Freedom Fireworks

NE - *Eastlake* (440) 951-1416 Freedom Festival. July 3-6. Boat races.

NE - *Fairport Harbor* (440) 357-6209 Mardi Gras. July 2-6.

NE - *Garfield Heights* (440) 475-1100 Home Days Festival. July 2-6.

SEASONAL & SPECIAL EVENTS

NE - *Ravenna* (330) 296-3247 Balloon A-Fair Fourth of July Celebration.
NW - *Oak Harbor* (419) 898-0479
NW - *Perrysville* (419) 938-7884 Fourth of July Beach Party, Pleasant Hill.
SE -*Marietta* (740) 376-0055 Red, White & Blues Fest.
SW - *Cincinnati* (513) 352-6168 All American Birthday Party
SW - *Hillsboro* (937) 393-1111 Festival of the Bells. July 3-5.

GREAT MOHICAN INDIAN POW-WOW

C - Mohican State Park, State Route 3, 1 mile south of **Loudenville**. (419) 994-4008. Nine different tribes gather to a pow-wow featuring foods, music, crafts, hoop dancers and storytellers. Learn the proper throwing of a tomahawk or a new Native American custom. Admission.

PROFESSIONAL FOOTBALL HALL OF FAME FESTIVAL

CE -**Canton**. (800) 533-4302. Check out the nine days of celebrating football greats including a parade, enshrinement ceremony and a televised professional game. Some fees.

CORN FEST

CE - Strasburg-Franklin Park, **Strasburg**. (330) 878-7115. Plenty of roasted corn with lots of other foods and entertainment. Free.

BLACK CULTURAL FESTIVAL

CW - Montgomery County Fairgrounds, 1043 South Main Street, **Dayton**. (937) 224-7100. Feel the richness of African and African-American cultures with entertainment like jazz and African drumming. Vendors. Admission.

U. S. AIR & TRADE SHOW

CW – Dayton International Airport, **Dayton**. (937) 898-5901. This is the leading event of its kind highlighted by the outstanding civilian and military air show performances. The event includes ground flight simulators, aerobatics, barnstormers, air races, pyrotechnics and sky divers. Admission. 3rd weekend in July.

ZUCCHINI FESTIVAL

CW - Eldorado. (937) 273-3281. This festival has zucchini baked, carved and eaten all weekend. Free.

GERMAN-AMERICAN FESTIVAL

CW - German Club Edelweiss, 531 East Wenger Road, **Englewood.** (937) 898-3059. German music bands, crafts, and foods. Admission.

ANNIE OAKLEY DAYS

CW - Darke County Fairgrounds, 752 Sweitzer Road, **Greenville**. (800) 504-2995. Annie Oakley's hometown celebrates with a parade, live entertainment, a sharpshooter's contest and a contest to name Miss Annie Oakley.

ASHLAND BALLOONFEST

NC - Main Street, **Ashland**. (419) 281-4584. Hot air balloon races and twilight balloon glow. Ashland is a top balloon manufacturer – factory tours available.

CLEVELAND'S IRISH CULTURAL FESTIVAL

NE - Cuyahoga County Fairgrounds, 164 Eastland Blvd., **Berea**. (440) 251-1711. Irish culture at its best with dancing, music, arts & crafts, storytelling and workshops. Admission.

GREATER YOUNGSTOWN ITALIAN FEST

NE - Canfield Fairgrounds, **Canfield**. (330) 757-2779. Celebrate Italy with food, music, crafts, contests, rides and games. Admission.

GRAND PRIX OF CLEVELAND

NE - Burke Lakefront Airport, Downtown **Cleveland**. (216) 781-3500. The world's top Indy Car drivers compete on the 213 miles of racing. Also a Grand Prix Parade on Friday. Admission.

PEPSI COUNTRY MUSIC FESTIVAL

NE - I-X Center, 6200 Riverside Drive, **Cleveland** (Brookpark). (216) 247-4386. Hot new country stars and good local talent entertain plus a fiddlers contest and western dance lessons. Admission.

ZOO BLOOMS

NE - Cleveland Metroparks Zoo, 3900 Brookside Park Drive, **Cleveland**. (216) 661-6500. Tours of the zoo's specialty gardens, a children's garden activity area and a ladybug release (100,000 ladybugs). Admission. Saturday only.

ITALIAN-AMERICAN FESTIVAL OF SUMMIT COUNTY

NE - Riverfront Centre Mall, Front Street, **Cuyahoga Falls**. (330) 922-3170. A celebration of everything Italian including live bands, food, bocci, and morri tournaments and children's fun activities. Free.

CELTIC HERITAGE FAIR

NE - City Hall Grounds, **Warren**. (330) 856-3432. Experience the arts, dance, foods and music of the Celtic nations, along with the special 1st Century Iron Age Celtic Encampment. Free.

LAGRANGE STREET POLISH FESTIVAL

NW - Lagrange Street between Central & Mettler Sts., **Toledo**. (419) 255-8406. All kinds of Polish foods, polish bands, dancers, a polka contest, rides and craft area. Free.

AUGUST

OHIO'S AGRICULTURAL FAIRS

(614) 728-6200. Schedules available through the Ohio Department of Agriculture.

GREEK FESTIVAL

C – Greek Orthodox Cathedral, Short North Area, **Columbus**. (614) 224-9020. Gyros, baklava, music, dance, tours of the church, cooking demos and videos about Greece. Admission. Labor Day Weekend.

OHIO STATE FAIR

C – Ohio Expo Center, I-71 & 17th Avenue, **Columbus**. (614) 644-4000. Includes the largest junior fair in the nation, small circus, laser light shows, petting zoo, rodeo, tractor pulls, horse shows, exhibitors from agriculture to the arts, rides and big name entertainment. Admission. Family Value Days.

CANAL FESTIVAL

C - **Coshocton**. (800) 877-1830. Historic Roscoe Village canal boat rides highlight the celebration of the canal boat era. Parade and crafts show. Admission.

IRISH FESTIVAL

C – Coffman Park, 6665 Coffman Road, **Dublin**. (614) 761-6500. A weekend of all things Irish, from entertainment, dance competitions and sports demos to the very best in Irish foods. Admission. 1st weekend each August.

NATIVE AMERICAN POWWOW

C – Helmat Haus, 4555 Jackson Pike, **Grove City**. (614) 443-6120. Authentic Native American dancing, arts, crafts and singing.

MARIGOLD FESTIVAL

C – Madison County Fairgrounds, State Route 38, **London**. (740) 852-1582. The "friendship flower" is admired in craft, entertainment, a Miss Marigold contest and parade. Free. Weekend before Labor Day.

ALL OHIO BALLOON FESTIVAL

C – Union County Fairgrounds, **Marysville**. (800) 642-0087. Unique hot-air balloons from all over the country in colorful ascensions and a balloon glow. Balloon rides, entertainment and crafts. Admission.

SEASONAL & SPECIAL EVENTS 159

SWEET CORN FESTIVAL

C – Lions Park, Chautauqua Blvd., **Millersport**. (740) 467-3943. Hot buttered corn on the cob, entertainment, large midway, nightly square dancing, parade and the Nashville Show on Saturday. Fee for parking.

ZUCCHINI FESTIVAL

C – Lancaster Park, **Obetz**. (614) 491-4546. Try some yummy zucchini fudge or burgers while seeing a parade, riding amusement rides, listening to music or looking over crafts. Free.

VIOLET FESTIVAL

C – **Pickerington**. (614) 837-1958. Spend the weekend in the "Violet Capital of Ohio" and explore crafts, foods and horticultural events.

FOLKLIFE CELEBRATION

C - Village Green, **Worthington**. (614) 431-0329. A celebration of living traditions in crafts, performances and foods. Includes the cultures of Africa, Asia, Germany, India, Europe and Appalachia.

PIONEER DAYS

CE – Gnadenhutten Historical Park & Museum, 352 Cherry Street, **Gnadenhutten**. (330) 254-4143. An 1840s pioneer encampment, entertainment, parade, arts and crafts. Free.

TUSCARAWAS COUNTY ITALIAN-AMERICAN FESTIVAL

CE– Downtown, **New Philadelphia**. (330) 339-6405. Italian ' foods, pizza eating contests, bocci and morri tournaments, music and dance. Free.

GRECIAN FESTIVAL

CE – Civic Center, 1101 Market Avenue, **North Canton**. (330) 494-8770. Live music, crafts shows, Greek imports gifts and delicious Greek foods and pastries. Admission.

KITE FESTIVAL

CW – U.S. Air Force Museum, Wright-Patterson AFB, **Dayton**. (937) 255-4704. Kite making, safety and flying workshops. Labor Day Weekend. Free. Fee for workshops.

SWEET CORN FESTIVAL

CW – Community Park East, Dayton-Yellow Springs Road, **Fairborn**. (937) 878-2860. Steamed corn-on-the-cob, entertainment, crafts and a corn eating contest. Free.

MELON FESTIVAL

NC – **Milan**. (419) 499-2766. Melons in baskets, by the slice, muskmelon ice cream and watermelon sherbet. Parade, rides, crafts and a kiddie pedal tractor pull. Free. Labor Day Weekend.

CORN FESTIVAL

NC – **North Ridgeville**. (440) 327-5144. Sweet corn prepared Amish-style, parade, midway, crafts and live bands every night. Free.

GREAT LAKES WOODEN SAILBOAT REGATTA

NC – Battery Park Marina, **Sandusky**. (419) 625-6142. Wooden sailboats large and small are raced for special awards in many categories. Free.

ALL AMERICAN SOAP BOX DERBY

NE – Derby Downs, I-77 & State Route 244 East, **Akron**. (330) 733-8723. The annual gravity "grand prix" of soap box derby racing is still run the same way since 1934. Youths from over 100 local competitions participate and learn workmanship, completing a project and competing. Parade at 10a.m.. 2nd Saturday of August. Admission.

NATIVE AMERICAN POWWOW

NE – Century Village, 14563 East Park Street, **Burton**. (440) 834-4012. Authentic Native American crafts, dances and foods in the restored village setting of the 1798-1900 period. Admission.

SEASONAL & SPECIAL EVENTS

IRISH FEST

NE – Yellow Duck Park, State Route 46, **Canfield**. (330) 533-3773. Irish entertainment, traditional foods, border collies and more. Admission.

CLEVELAND NATIONAL AIR SHOW

NE – Burke Lakefront Airport, downtown **Cleveland**. (216) 781-0747. One of the nation's top air shows featuring the best in military jet demonstrations and civilian aerobatics performers. Thunderbirds and Blue Angels Flybys. Labor Day Weekend. Admission.

KIDSFEST

NE – Nautica Entertainment Complex, **Cleveland**. (216) 247-4386. Playground World Pavilion, Treasure Island, sand castle building, Edible Art, Thomas the Train and great kid's entertainment. Admission.

SLAVIC VILLAGE HARVEST FESTIVAL

NE- Fleet Avenue, **Cleveland**. (216) 271-5591. An ethnic street fair on ten blocks of a historic Polish neighborhood with continuous entertainment, crafts, a Kielbasa cookoff and lots of Slavic foods. Free.

TWINS DAYS FESTIVAL

NE – Chamberlin High School, Ravenna Road, **Twinsburg**. (440) 425-3652. The largest gathering of twins in the world (usually over 2500) includes twins contests, entertainment, fireworks and the nationally televised "Double Take" parade. Small fee for non-twins. Twinsburg was originally named by the Wilcox twins in the early 1800s.

ITALIAN AMERICAN HERITAGE FESTIVAL

NE – Courthouse Square, **Warren**. (330) 393-3444. Celebrate Italian heritage with cultural exhibits, entertainment, foods, parade, competitions, games and rides. Admission.

RED HAWK AMERICAN INDIAN POWWOW

NE – Willow Ranch, off U.S. 422 on South Hubbard Road, East of **Youngstown**. (330) 534-0424. Native American traditions shown through dance, song, art and food. Admission.

GERMAN-AMERICAN FESTIVAL

NW – Oak Shade Grove, 3524 Seaman Street, **Oregon**. (419) 691-4116. Continuous live German music, foods and entertainment. Admission.

FIESTA MEXICANA

NW – Broadway & Segur Avenue, **Toledo**. (419) 242-7071. Folkloric dancing, ethnic foods, mariachi bands, arts and crafts and gifts. Admission.

RIVERFEST

NW – Promenade Park, downtown **Toledo**. (419) 243-8024. Festival and parade. Labor Day Weekend. Free.

RIVER DAYS

SC – **Portsmouth**. (740) 354-6419. Parade, rides, crafts, entertainment and children's events. Free. Labor Day Weekend

ALL ABOUT KIDS SHOW

SW – Convention Center, 525 Elm Street, **Cincinnati**. (513) 684-0501. Event for kids ages 2 to 12 including interactive play and entertainment. Admission.

RIVERFEST U.S.A.

SW – Sawyer Point, **Cincinnati**. (513) 352-6168. A kids carnival, entertainment, a sand volleyball open and spectacular fireworks draw hundreds of thousands of parents and children. Labor Day Sunday only.

OHIO HONEY FESTIVAL

SW – Courthouse Square, **Hamilton**. (513) 868-5891. Celebrate the "Ohio Bee & Honey Week" by enjoying honey in jars, ice cream, candy and other desserts. Parades, entertainment and the world famous "Living Bee Beard". Free.

OHIO RENAISSANCE FESTIVAL

SW – 5 miles East of Waynesville on State Route 73 at **Harveysburg**. (513) 897-7000. The recreation of a 16th century English Village complete with costumed performers, strolling minstrels, may pole dances, full-armored jousting, sword play or feast on giant turkey legs and hearty bread bowl meals. This event is often named as one of the "Top 100 Events in North America" by the American Bus Association. Admission. Begins end of August through mid-October.

CARAMEL FESTIVAL

SW – **Winchester**. (513) 695-0236. Caramel foods, live Nashville entertainment, rides and crafts. Free.

SEPTEMBER

AMERICAN SOYA FESTIVAL

C – **Amanda**. (740) 969-4525. The only festival that features the soybean. Contests, foods, parades and entertainment. Free. Wednesday – Saturday. Mid-September.

GERMAN VILLAGE OKTOBERFEST

C – Brewery District & German Village, **Columbus**. (614) 224-4300. Polka bands from local and distant towns, German foods and artists, Kinderplatz area for kids. Admission.

KIDSPEAK KIDSFEST

C – Franklin Park, 1777 East Broad Street, **Columbus**. (614) 645-3343. Hayrides, roving performers, games & prizes, hands-on crafts, rides, youth agencies and lots of freebies to take home. Free. 3rd Sunday of the month.

LITTLE BROWN JUG

C – Delaware County Fairgrounds, 236 Pennsylvania Avenue, **Delaware**. (800) 335-3247. The most coveted horse race for three-year old pacers held on the fastest half-mile track in the world. Admission. Saturday only. Mid-September.

POPCORN FESTIVAL

C – Marion. (800) 371-6688. Highlights include a parade, tours of the Popcorn Museum, popcorn sculptures and nationally known entertainment nightly. Free. Weekend after Labor Day.

BUCKEYE FLINT FESTIVAL

C – Courthouse Square, **Newark**. (740) 345-1282. Ohio's gemstone is flint rock and you'll learn everything you could want to know about flint through displays, entertainment, crafts and food preparation. Free. Last weekend.

TOMATO FESTIVAL

C – Civic Park, 6800 Daugherty Drive, **Reynoldsburg**. (614) 866-2861. Ohio's tomato harvest is celebrated with things like free tomato juice, fried green tomatoes, tomato pies, tomato fudge, tomato cakes & cookies, Tiny Tim Tomatoland, crafts, parade and The Largest Tomato Contest ($100 per pound). Fee for parking. Wednesday through Sunday.

OHIO PUMPKIN FESTIVAL

CE – Barnesville. (740) 695-4359. All kinds of pumpkin contests (largest pumpkin, pumpkin rolling and pie eating), parade, foods, fiddle contest, rides, crafts and entertainment. Free. Last Weekend in the month. Thursday – Sunday.

INTERNATIONAL MINING AND MANUFACTURING FESTIVAL

CE – Cadiz. (740) 968-3015. Parades, labor force bands, a coal house, coal products and crafts, ethnic foods and a coal shoveling contest. Free. Thursday through Sunday.

SEASONAL & SPECIAL EVENTS

ETHNIC FESTIVAL

CE – Thompson Park, Park Blvd. & Park Way, **East Liverpool**. (330) 385-0845. Ethnic artists, crafts, foods and entertainment. Saturday only. Free.

INDIAN FESTIVAL

CE – **Powhatan Point**. (740) 795-4869. An authentic Native American event including crafts, dancing, an historic reenactment, storytelling, archery and more. Free.

OHIO SWISS FESTIVAL

CE – **Sugarcreek**. (330) 852-4113. Experience the best of Switzerland from Polka bands, dancing, tons of Swiss cheese, Steinstossen (stone throwing) and Schwingfest (Swiss wrestling). Free. Last Friday/Saturday of the month.

POPCORN FESTIVAL

CW – **Beavercreek**. (937) 427-5514. A balloon rally, live entertainment and most of all, "popcorn showers". Free.

PREBLE COUNTY PORK FESTIVAL

CW – Preble County Fairgrounds, 722 South Franklin Street, **Eaton**. (937) 456-7273. Start your day feasting on sausage & pancakes, and then later try some hot off the grill barbecued pork chops. Enjoy crafts, entertainment, a parade and contests. Free.

PRETZEL FESTIVAL

CW – Veteran's Memorial Park, **Germantown**. (937) 855-7255. Food, games, rides and live music/shows. Free.

CORN FESTIVAL

CW – **South Vienna**. (937) 568-4345. A corn eating contest, corn products, parade, crafts, rides and entertainment. Free.

OHIO WATERFOWLERS FESTIVAL

NC – Magee Marsh Wildlife Area/Crane Creek State Park, 13229 West State Route 2, **Oak Harbor**. (419) 898-0960. Retriever trials, decoy carving and judging, duck and goose calling contests. Last Sunday of the month. Free.

NORTHERN OHIO GARLIC FESTIVAL

NC – Lorain County Fairgrounds, **Wellington**. (419) 499-4604. Enjoy (while learning about) all aspects of garlic including health, cooking, growing and eating. Crafts, live entertainment. Admission.

CHICKENFEST!

NE – Lake Anna, Park & Sixth Streets, **Barberton**. (330) 753-8471. "Chick-o-lympics", great chicken dishes to eat and entertainment. Free.

GRAPE JAMBOREE

NE – **Geneva**. (440) 466-5262. The local grape harvest is celebrated with parades, fresh-picked grapes, grape stomping contests, grape products, rides and entertainment. Free.

POTATO FESTIVAL

NE – Buchert Park, **Mantua**. (330) 274-8093. Potato foods, potato cook-off, potato stomp race, mashed potato eating contest, entertainment, rides and a parade. Fee for parking.

BALLOON A-FAIR

NE – **Ravenna**. (330) 296-3247. Downtown street festival with a parade, hot air balloon flights, fireworks and more. Fee for some events at Sun Beau Valley Farm.

SCARECROW FESTIVAL

SC – **Washington Court House**. (800) 479-7797. A street fair, parade, live entertainment and a living scarecrow contest. Free.

EMANCIPATION DAY

SE – Gallia County Junior Fairgrounds, **Gallipolis**. (800) 765-6482. A celebration of African-American and local heritage with crafts, area history, music and ethnic food. Free.

SEASONAL & SPECIAL EVENTS

OHIO RIVER STERNWHEEL FESTIVAL

SE – Marietta. (740) 373-5178. Twenty plus sternwheelers dock for the weekend, some for commercial and some for residential use. Continuous musical entertainment, fireworks and grand finale sternwheel races. Free.

CELTIC MUSIC & CULTURAL FESTIVAL

SW – Ault Park, 3600 Observatory Avenue, **Cincinnati**. (513) 533-4822. Celebrate the Celtic countries heritage with music, dance, art, cuisine and performances. Admission.

OKTOBERFEST-ZINZINNATI

SW – Fifth Street, downtown **Cincinnati**. (513) 333-6888. The nation's largest authentic Oktoberfest featuring seven areas of live entertainment, food and a children's area. 3rd weekend in September.

THUNDER-IN-THE-HILLS HYDROPLANE RACE

SW – Rocky Fork Lake State Park, **Hillsboro**. (937) 393-4883. Hydroplane boat racing, the third largest race in the country. Free.

APPLE FESTIVALS

Apples & cider. Apple pie eating contests. Apple peeling contests. Apple butter. Candy apples. Wagon/hayrides. Apple Dumplings. Parades. Pioneer crafts.

- September / October
- *Participating Areas*: Jackson, Smithfield, Lebanon, Piqua Historical Area, Aullwood Audubon Farm, Delta, Gnadenhutten, Clinton, Groveport, Van Buren, Forest, Oak Harbor, Historic Century Village, Enon, Grand Rapids, Roscoe Village and Zoar Village.

HARVEST FESTIVALS

Press cider. Apple butter making. Veggie harvest. Living history demos. Lumberjacks. Butter churning. Grainthreshing.

- September / October
- Participating Areas: Lake Farmpark, Atwood Lake, Cincinnati Zoo, Bloomington, Hale Farm, Granville Strongsville, Carriage Hill Metropark Farm, Heritage Reserve Park, Wolcott Museum Complex.

OCTOBER

OKTOBERFEST

German music, dancing, food (potato salad, brats), crafts, games and rides.

- *Participating Areas*: Cambridge, Beaver, Conneaut, Cuyahoga Falls, Galion, Minster, Harmar Village, Boardman, Wooster, Zanesville, Urbana, Bremen, Vandalia and Portage Lakes.

PUMPKIN PATCHES/ HAYRIDES/ CORN MAZES/ FALL PLAYLANDS

- **C** – *Circle S Farms*. Grove City. (614) 878-7980.
- **CW** – *Fulton Farms*. Troy. (937) 339-2077.
- **CW** – *Young's Jersey Dairy*. Yellow Springs. (937) 325-0629.
- **NE** – *Hillside Orchard*. Hinckley. (330) 225-4748.
- **NE** – *Mapleside Farms*. Brunswick. (330) 225-5576.
- **NE** – *Richardson Farms*. Medina. (330) 722-4029.
- **SW** – *Minges Farm*. Harrison. (513) 367-2035.
- **SW** – *Shaw Farm*. Milford. (513) 575-2022.

SEASONAL & SPECIAL EVENTS

SW – *Windmill Farm Market*. Springboro. (513) 885-3965.

PUMPKIN FESTIVALS

Largest Pumpkin Contest. Old fashioned games. Rides. Pie eating contests.

- *Participating Areas*: Hudson, Huntsburg, Huber Heights, Wellsville

PUMPKIN FESTIVAL

C – **Circleville**. (740) 474-7000. Ohio's largest and oldest harvest celebration has seven parades, lots of pumpkin, squash and gourds, pumpkin foods (cotton candy, burgers, chips and ice cream), rides and entertainment. See some of the largest pumpkins and the world's largest pumpkin pie (approx. 350 lbs. and 5 feet in diameter). Contests galore like hog calling, egg toss, pie eating and carved pumpkins. Free. Thursday through Sunday.

ALL AMERICAN QUARTER HORSE CONGRESS

C – Ohio Expo Center, I-71 & 17th Avenue, **Columbus**. (614) 943-2346 before October, (614) 294-7469 (during show). The world's largest single breed horse show with seven acres of commercial exhibits and demos. Fee per vehicle. Two weeks long during mid-to-late October.

OHIO GOURD SHOW

C – Morrow County Fairgrounds, U.S. 42 & State Route 61 South, **Mount Gilead**. (419) 362-6446. Gourd crafts, fresh gourds, gourd cleaning and carving demos, and the gourd show parade. Admission.

ENCHANTED FOREST

CW – Aullwood Audubon Farm, 9101 Frederick Road, **Dayton**. (937) 890-7360. A non-scary family Halloween event including a guided walk in the woods to meet costumed animal characters and stories around a campfire. Admission. Weekend night.

GREAT OUTDOOR UNDERWEAR FESTIVAL

CW – Piqua. (937) 773-1625. A fun festival celebrating Piqua's history as the "Underwear Capital of the World" (they used to have ten underwear factories, now there are none). Have fun as you enjoy a Long John parade, the Undy 500, Drop Seat Trot, Boxer Ball, Bed Races and Celebrity Underwear Auction. Free. 2nd weekend.

WOOLLYBEAR FESTIVAL

NC – Vermilion. (440) 432-4246. An annual tribute to the weather "forecasting" woollybear caterpillar with a huge parade, caterpillar races, woollybear contests for kids, crafts and entertainment. 1st Sunday. Free.

ASHTABULA COUNTY COVERED BRIDGE FESTIVAL

NE – Ashtabula County Fairgrounds, **Jefferson**. (440) 576-3769. Ashtabula is known as the working covered bridge capital of the Western Reserve. Enjoy a tour of 15 covered bridges during the beautiful fall season, plus entertainment, crafts, draft horse contests and a scarecrow contest. Admission.

JOHNNY APPLESEED FESTIVAL

NW – AuGlaize Village, off U.S. 24, 3 miles West of **Defiance**. (419) 393-2662. The historic village is busy with crafts, apple butter, cider and molasses making, and harvest demonstrations. Admission.

PAUL BUNYAN SHOW

SC – Hocking College Campus, **Nelsonville**. (740) 753-3591. Ohio's largest forestry exposition features lumberjack competitions, forestry displays, guitar pickers championship and chainsaw sculpting. Admission.

FARM FESTIVAL

SC – Bob Evans Farm, State Route 588, **Rio Grande**. (800) 994-3276. Down on the farm feeling with over 100 craftspeople, country music, square dancers, homestyle foods and contests such

SEASONAL & SPECIAL EVENTS

as apple peeling, cornshelling, cow chip throwing and hog calling. Admission. Mid-October.

HOCKING FALL COLOR TOUR

SC – Hocking State Forest, **Rockbridge**. (740) 385-4402. Enjoy a guided tour at Cedar Falls and a hayride through the fall colors, along with a bean dinner. Free.

MIDDFEST INTERNATIONAL CELEBRATION

SW – One City Centre Plaza, **Middletown**. (937) 425-7707. Experience the dance, crafts, music, sports, foods and cultural displays of many countries. Each year a different country is focused on. Donations. 1st weekend.

INDIAN SUMMER CAMPOUT

SW – Caesar Creek State Park Campground, Center Road, off State Route 380, near **Waynesville**. (513) 488-4595. A weekend of hayrides, pioneer crafts, fireside cooking and woodland hikes. Admission. Early October.

OHIO SAUERKRAUT FESTIVAL

SW – **Waynesville**. (937) 897-8855. All kinds of sauerkraut foods like cabbage rolls, sauerkraut candy, pizza, and desserts, fair food, crafts and live entertainment. Fee for parking. 2nd weekend.

NOVEMBER

COLUMBUS INTERNATIONAL FESTIVAL

C – Veterans Memorial, 300 West Broad Street, **Columbus**. (614) 885-7862. More the an 60 nationalities and cultures will participate in a mix of dance, music, foods and crafts. Educational interactive activities for kids. Admission. 1st weekend.

FESTIVAL OF TREES

C – **Columbus**. (614) 722-2993. More than 100 decorated trees, each with different themes, Kwanza and Hanukkah displays, music, visits with Santa and children's hands-on activities. Admission. Late November week-long.

DAYTON HOLIDAY FESTIVAL

CW – Downtown **Dayton**. (937) 224-1518. Dayton kicks off the holiday season with live entertainment, a large children's parade, a street fair with rides and the tree lighting. Free. Weekend after Thanksgiving.

SUGARPLUM FESTIVAL OF TREES

CW – Convention Center, 22 East Fifth Street, **Dayton**. (937) 226-8405. Beautifully decorated trees on display along with lots of crafts of the season. Admission.

BETHLEHEM EXPERIENCE

CW – Preble County Fairgrounds, State Route 122, **Eaton**. (937) 456-9665. A walk-through drama of the experience of Old Bethlehem the night Christ was born. Free. Weekend after Thanksgiving.

THANKSGIVING DAY PARADES

Downtown Cleveland, downtown Columbus, downtown Cincinnati, downtown Hamilton and downtown Toledo.

DECEMBER

CHRISTMAS DECORATIONS/OPEN HOUSES

Wolcott Museum Complex, Orrville Depot Museum, Allen County Museum, Paulding Museum, Shawnee State Park, Milan Museum Complex, Stan Hywet Hall & Gardens, Aullwood Audubon Center, Hanby House, Mac-O-Cheek Castle, Logan County Historical, Zoar, Belmont County Museum, Glendower State Memorial, Malabar Farm, Quail Hollow State Park, Lyme Village, City of Tiffin and Jefferson Depot.

CHRISTMAS TREE FARMS

Travel by wagon to the tree patch where you pick and hand cut your family tree.

- *Participating Farms*: **C** - Chippewa Farms, 741 Chippewa Road. **Lodi**. (330) 948-1142. **C** – Holekamp Family Farm 8656 SR 13 NW, **Somerset**, (740) 743-1359; **CE** – Pine Tree Barn 4374 Shreve Road, **Wooster,** (330) 264-1914; **CE** – Ruetenik Christmas Trees, Lawrence Township Road 57, **Zoar** (330) 874-2688;**CW** – Fulton Farms (SR 202, Troy, (937) 339-2077.

FESTIVALS OF LIGHTS

All include hundreds of thousands of lights and holiday /storybook characters. Daily, evenings (unless noted). Admission.

- **C** – *Fantasy of Lights*. Alum Creek State Park. (614) 228-5523. Drive vehicle or carriage through park.
- **C** – *Griggs Reservoir*. Columbus. (614) 461-6285. Drive thru.
- **C** – *Wildlight Wonderland*. Columbus Zoo. (614) 645-3550. Ice skating, carolers, delicious treats and wagon/train rides. Begins Thanksgiving weekend.
- **CE** – *Christian Indian Christmas*. Gnadenhutten Historical Park. (740) 254-4143. Drive through display depicting Christian Indians celebrating Christmas. Open daily every evening in December.
- **CW** – *Bluffton Blaze of Lights*. (419) 358-5675. Begins Thanksgiving weekend.
- **CW** – *Clifton Mill Legendary Light Display*. (937) 767-5501. Miniature village, Santa's workshop and 1802 log cabin. Closed Tuesdays.
- **CW** – *The Lights at Ludlow Falls*. (513) 698-3318.

- ❑ **NE** – *Country Lights*. Lake Farmpark. (800) 366-3276. Wagon rides, holiday shopping & music or make wooden toys at Santa's workshop.
- ❑ **NE** – *Holiday Lights*. Cleveland Metroparks Zoo. (216) 661-6500. Caroling, entertainment, model train display, Santa visits and Wolf Wilderness cabin. Weekends only.
- ❑ **NE** – *Holiday Lights Celebration*. Akron Zoological Park. (330) 375-2550. Santa and delicious food.
- ❑ **NW** – *Lights Before Christmas*. Toledo Zoo. (419) 385-5721. Begins the third weekend of November.
- ❑ **SW** – *Cincinnati Zoo*. (513) 281-4700. Ice skating, decorated villages, and Santa. Begins Thanksgiving weekend.
- ❑ **SW** – *Holiday in Lights*. Sharon Woods. (513) 381-2397. Begins the third of November.

TRAIN RIDES WITH SANTA

Train trip in decorated coaches with Santa. Songs and treats along the way. Weekends only.

- ❑ **C** – *Buckeye Central Scenic Railroad*. (740) 366-2029. Dress warmly.
- ❑ **CE** – *Ohio Central Railroad*. Dennison Depot.. (740) 922-6776.
- ❑ **NC** – *Trolleyville USA*. (440) 235-4725. Heated.
- ❑ **SW** – *Turtle Creek Valley Railway*. (513) 398-8584.

KWANZAA FESTIVALS

A celebration of the African-American people, their culture and unity.

- ❑ **NC** – *Elyria*. (440) 366-5656. Free.
- ❑ **NE** – *Tri – C*. (216) 987-4151.

SEASONAL & SPECIAL EVENTS

CAPITAL HOLIDAY LIGHTS

C – Ohio Statehouse, downtown **Columbus**. (800) 345-4386. A traditional candlelighting ceremony, family activities inside and a nightly outdoor stage show with high-tech lighting effects. Free. All December weekends.

HOLIDAYS AT OHIO VILLAGE

C– Ohio Village & Ohio Historical Center, I-71 & 17th Avenue, **Columbus**. (800) 653-6446. Celebrate a traditional 19th century holiday complete with old-fashioned music, games, foods and shopping. Admission. Daily for two weeks in mid-December.

LIVING CHRISTMAS TREE CONCERTS

C – Grace Brethren Church, 8225 Worthington-Galena Road, **Columbus**. (614) 431-8223. 150 voice choir fills the branches of two large trees as they sing along with a themed story and live animals. Admission.

CHRISTMAS CANDLELIGHTINGS

CE – Historic Roscoe Village, State Route 16/83, **Coshocton**. (800) 877-1830. Shop all day for holiday gifts in a 19th century holiday setting and then stay for the candlelighting ceremony each night at 6 p.m.. Fee for parking. Saturdays only.

CHRISTMAS MUSIC SPECTACULAR

CW – Palace Theatre, 605 North Market Avenue, **Canton**. (330) 454-8172. 85,000 lights along with toy soldiers, Victorian costumes and sing-alongs. Admission. Thursday – Sunday, mid – December.

BLACK NATIVITY

NE – Karamu House, **Cleveland**. (216) 795-7070.

WINTERFEST

NE – I-X Center, 6200 Riverside Drive, **Cleveland** (Brookpark). (800) 897-3942. A holiday extravaganza including games, rides, entertainment and ice skating. Begins the day after Christmas through the following weekend. Admission.

TOBOGGAN RUN

NE – Cleveland Metroparks Chalet in Mill Stream Run Reservation, **Strongsville**. (440) 572-9990. Well maintained toboggan chutes 1000 feet long and over 42 inches tall. Admission. Thursday – Sunday.

CAROLFEST

SW – Music Hall, **Cincinnati**. (513) 621-1919. Holiday music and caroling sing alongs. Admission. First Sunday of the month.

KROHN CONSERVATORY

SW – **Cincinnati**. (513) 421-4086. Huge lit evergreens, live nativity and a poinsetta Christmas tree. Admission.

CHRISTMAS FESTIVAL

SW – **Lebanon**. (513) 932-1100. Holiday characters, musicians strolling the streets, a candlelit parade of sixty horse-drawn carriages, a train display and warm food. Free. 1st Sunday of December.

CHRISTMAS IN THE VILLAGE

SW – **Waynesville**. (513) 897-8855. Carriage rides, Victorian street strollers, carolers and a live nativity depict a traditional Dickens holiday. Free. Two weekends in early December.

NEW YEARS EVE CELEBRATIONS

A family oriented non-alcoholic event with indoor and outdoor activities such as kid's/parent's food, entertainment and crafts, and a countdown to midnight.

- ❑ **C** – _First Night Columbus_, Ohio Statehouse Square, downtown Columbus. (614) 481-0020. Admission.
- ❑ **CE** – _Community New Year's Eve Gospel Sing_, Civic Center, 7033 West Glenn Highway, Cambridge. (740) 432-3787. Free.

SEASONAL & SPECIAL EVENTS

- ❏ **NC** – *First Night*, State Routes 20 & 83, North Ridgeville. (440) 327-3737. Admission.
- ❏ **NE** – *Opening Night*, Courthouse Square, Warren. (330) 399-1212. Admission.
- ❏ **NW** – *First Night*, Downtown Toledo. (419) 534-3303.

A QUICK LOOK AT SPECIAL EVENTS BY SEASON

WINTER (December, January and February)

Christmas Candlelightings
Christmas Concerts
Christmas Decorations/Open Houses
Christmas Tree Farms
Festivals of Lights
Ice Festivals
Kwanzaa Festivals
Martin Luther King Jr. Celebrations
Native American Indian Powwows
New Years Eve Celebrations
Train Rides with Santa
Toboggan Run
Winter Festivals
Valentine's Day Fair

SPRING (March, April and May)

Balloon Festivals
Easter Egg Hunts
Fishing Derbies/ Festivals
Ice Cream Festival
International Festivals
Maple Syrup Festivals
Medieval & Renaissance Festival
Railroad Festival
Rhythm & Food Festival
Spring Plowing Days
Strawberry Festivals
St. Patrick's Day Celebrations
Truck Nationals

SUMMER (June, July and August)

African – American Agriculture Fairs
Balloon Festivals
Boat Regattas
Church Festivals
Cranberry Bog Annual Open House
Ethnic Festivals
Fish/Poultry Festivals
Flowers/Fruits/Vegetables Festivals
Folklife Celebrations
Garlic Festivals
Heritage Fairs
International Festivals
Kids Festivals
Kite Festivals
July 4th Celebrations
Medieval Fare

SUMMER (*continued*)

Native American Indian Powwows
Paper Festivals
Pioneer Days
Polka Fests
Professional Hall of Fame Festival
Trains, Planes & Automobiles Fests/Shows

FALL (September, October and November)

All American Quarter Horse Congress
Apple Festivals
Balloon Fairs
Twins Days Festivals
Zoo Special Day

Ethnic Festivals
Farm Festivals
Forestry Expositions
Harvest Festivals
Hayrides, Corn Mazes & Fall Playlands
International Festivals
International Mining & Manufacturing Festival
Ohio River Sternwheeler Festival
Oktoberfests
Popcorn/Pretzel/Candy Festivals
Pumpkin Festivals
Sauerkraut Festivals
Thanksgiving Day Celebrations

Chapter 8

SPORTS

SPECTATOR SPORTS

CENTRAL OHIO KITE FLYERS ASSOCIATION

C – **Columbus**. (614) 431-5483. Fly kites twice a month on weekends from 1:00 – 5:00 p.m.

COLUMBUS CHILL

C – **Columbus**. (614) 488-4455. Semi-professional hockey. (October – March)

COLUMBUS CLIPPERS

C – Cooper Stadium, **Columbus**. (614) 462-5250. Semi-professional farm team for the New York Yankees. Kids Club and Mascot "Captain Clipper". (April – Labor Day)

COLUMBUS CREW

C – Ohio Stadium at OSU, **Columbus**. (614) 221-CREW. Major League Soccer (Mid April – Late September).

COLUMBUS INVADERS

C – **Columbus** Convention Center. (614) 645-5000. Indoor Semi-professional soccer.

COLUMBUS POLO CLUB

C – **Columbus**. (Bryn Du Field, Granville). (614) 492-4000. Oldest team sport in the world. Divot Stomps- half-time stroll by guests on the field to "toe" divots (patches of grass) back into place. (Weekends Late May – Early October)

COLUMBUS QUEST

C – **Columbus**. (614) 645-5000. Women's Professional Basketball.

THE OHIO STATE UNIVERSITY BUCKEYES

C – **Columbus**. Ticket Office: (614) 292-2624. Sports Information: (614) 292-6861. Big 10 College Sports. Football,

Ohio Stadium. Basketball (Men's & Women's), Hockey, OSU Ice Rink, Golf & Swimming, Tennis, Volleyball – Larkins Hall

OHIO VILLAGE MUFFINS

C – **Columbus**. (614) 297-2606. 19th Century Style baseball team. Authentic uniforms and rules. Commentator assists visitors to understand the "old-fashioned" ball game. Summers.

MEMORIAL GOLF TOURNAMENT

C – Muirfield Village Golf Course, **Dublin**. (614) 889-6700. PGA Tour. Course designed by Jack Nicklaus. TV coverage. Monday – Wednesday, Practice rounds. Thursday – Sunday, Tournament. (Early June)

ZANESVILLE GREYS

C – Municipal Stadium, **Zanesville**. (740) 454-7397. Minor League Baseball. (June – September)

MOCH SERIES HYDROPLANE RACING

CE – **Steubenville** Regatta. (800) 510-8124. (August)

CLEVELAND CAVALIERS

NE – Gund Arena, **Cleveland**. (216) 420-2200. Professional Basketball. (September – April)

CLEVELAND INDIANS

NE - Jacobs Field, 2401 Ontario, **Cleveland**. (216) 420-4200. Professional Baseball. Kids Club. (April – October)

CLEVELAND LUMBERJACKS

NE – One Center Ice (Gund Area), **Cleveland**. (216) 420-0000. International League Hockey. Jack Park Youth Club. (October – May)

CLEVELAND POLO CLUB

NE – Chagrin River Road & State Route 87, **Cleveland**. (440) 441-1804.

NATIONAL TRACTOR PULL CHAMPIONSHIPS

NW – **Bowling Green.** (419) 354-1434. (August)

OHIO NATIONAL CHAMPIONSHIP AMA MOTORCYCLE RACES

NW – **Lima.** (419) 991-8124. (June)

TOLEDO MUD HENS BASEBALL

NW – Ned Skeldon Stadium, **Toledo**. (419) 893-9483. Maumee. Semi-professional baseball (farm team for the Detroit Tigers). See "Muddy" the mascot.

TOLEDO STORM

NW – **Toledo** Sports Arena. (419) 691-0200. Semi-Professional hockey part of East Coast Hockey League (affiliate for Detroit Red Wings). Season starts in October.

CINCINNATI BENGALS

SW – 200 Cinergy Field, **Cincinnati**. (513) 621-3550. Professional football at Riverfront Stadium. Average ticket price $30.00. (August – January).

CINCINNATI CYCLONES & CINCINNATI SILVERBACKS

SW – 2250 Seymour Avenue, **Cincinnati**. (513) 531-PUCK & (513) 458-KICK. Semi-Professional hockey and soccer teams. Home games at Cincinnati Gardens. ($6.00 - $12.00 range) (October – March)

CINCINNATI REDS

SW – 100 Cinergy Field, **Cincinnati**. (513) 421-REDS. Professional Major League baseball at Riverfront Stadium. 1st professional baseball team. Autographs during batting practice. Tours available by appointment (513) 352-5400. ($4.00 - $12.00) (April – September)

CINCINNATI POLO CLUB

SW – Mason (**Cincinnati**). (513) 398-0278. Summer Sundays at 2:00 p.m.

SPORTS

UNIVERSITY OF CINCINNATI – DEPARTMENT OF ATHLETICS

SW – Cincinnati. (513) 556-CATS. Intercollegiate competition in 17 sports. Fall, Winter, Spring

RODEOS

GENERAL - (319) 668-2674 Dodge Trucks World's Toughest Rodeo, or (800) 357-6336, Longhorn World Championship Rodeo.

AUTO SPORTS

MID OHIO SPORTS CAR COURSE

C – Steam Corners Road, **Lexington**. (800) MID-OHIO. Indy Car, Sport Car, AMA Motorcycles, Vintage Car Races. General, Weekend, Paddock (walk through garages and see drivers) passes available. Weekends, (June – Mid September)

MARION COUNTY INTERNATIONAL RACEWAY

C - 2454 Richwood – LaRue Road (Route 37), **Marion**. (740) 499-3666. Quarter mile drag racing includes 7UP Pro Am and Sunoco IHRA Finals. Adult admission average $8.00, Youth admission average $2.00. Concessions available. (Saturdays, April – October)

NATIONAL TRAIL RACEWAY

C – US 40, **Newark**. (740) 587-1002 (office) or (740) 928-5706 (Raceday). Drag racing. Super Gas Races and Night Under Fire (jet cars and trucks with fire exhaust, drag racing, fireworks, funny car acts). Weekends and Wednesdays. Afternoon and Evening. (Late April – October)

COLUMBUS MOTOR SPEEDWAY

C – 1845 Williams Road, Obetz (**Columbus**). (614) 491-1047. Stock car racing. Kids Day (September). Climb into a real race car! 7:00 p.m. race starts Saturdays.

HOT ROD SUPER NATIONALS

CE – **Canfield**. (Late May)

ELDORA SPEEDWAY

CW – 13929 State Route 118. **Ansonia**. (937) 338-3815

LIMALAND MOTOR SPEEDWAY

CW – 1500 Dutch Hollow Road (off State Route 81), **Lima**. (900) 448-7225 ext. 5515 (Raceline). Race Headquarters, (419) 692-2692 or Raceday, (419) 339-6249

PAINESVILLE SPEEDWAY

NE – 650 Fairport Nursery Road, Painesville. (440) 354-3505.

TOLEDO SPEEDWAY

NW – **Toledo**. (419) 729-1634. Stock car racing. (May – October)

DODGE SKATE PARK
667 Sullivant Avenue, **Columbus**

- Area: **C**
- Telephone Number: (614) 645-8151
- Hours: Saturday and Sunday, 10:00 a.m. – 8:00 p.m. Weekdays hours vary – call for schedule (March – November)
  Membership required through Columbus Parks and Recreation
- Admission: $10.00 membership, $5.00 Day Pass

Dodge Skateboard Park is unique. This particular design is the only one east of the Mississippi River. There are in-ground bowls at 3, 4, and 6 feet deep. Skateboarders must wear helmet, and suggested elbow and kneepads, wrist guards. Some equipment is available for rent. No in-line skating.

SPORTS

SKIING

Usually December – early March. Ski Conditions, (800) BUCKEYE. Or contact local MetroParks or Ohio Department of Natural Resources for cross-country skiing.

- *C - Clearfork* – (800) 237-5673, Butler
- *C - Snow Trails* – (419) 522-7393, Mansfield
- *CW - Mad River Mountain* – (937) 599-1015, Bellefontaine
- *NE - Alpine Valley* - (440) 285-2211
- *NE - Boston Mills* – (440) 467-2242
- *NE - Cleveland MetroParks* – Cross Country
- *NE - Meadowridge Farm* – (440) 636-5420
- *NE - Pine Lodge Ski Center* – (440) 256-2255, Kirkland (cross country)
- *SC - Echo Hills* – (740) 385-8760, Hocking Hills

Chapter 9

THE ARTS

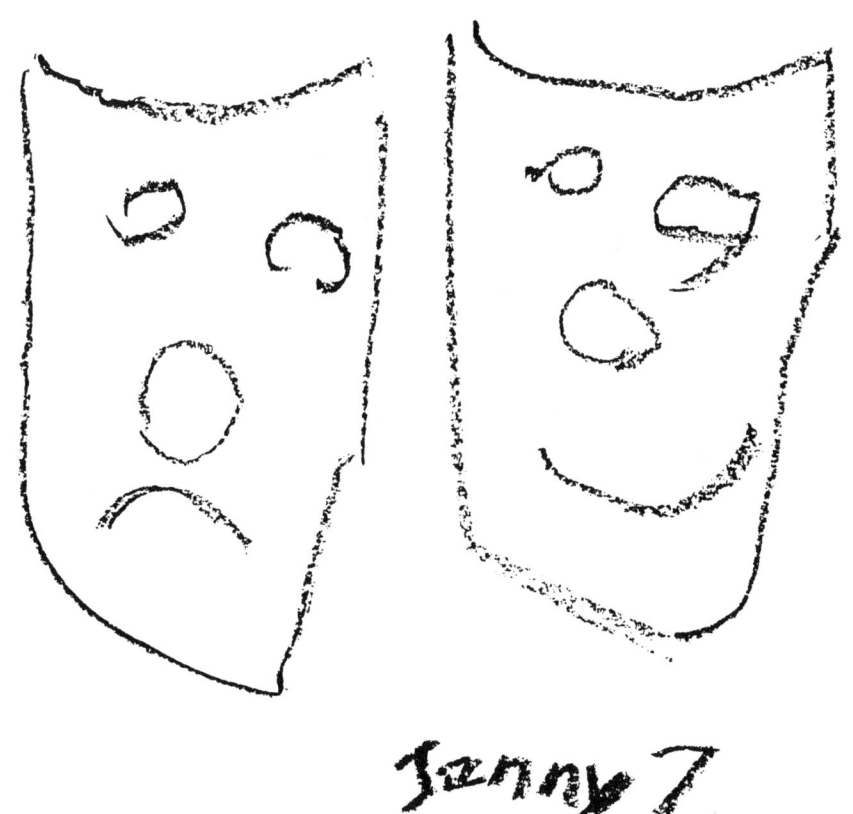

Jenny Z

GENERAL INFORMATION

(Areas are sorted alphabetically by city within each zone)

- Ohio Arts Council, Columbus, (614) 466-2613
- Most entries have admission fees.
- All entries have programming for children.

AREA "C"

ART FOR COMMUNITY EXPRESSIONS

C - 772 North High Street, **Columbus**. (614) 294-4200. ACE gallery with works of African American artists, interactive arts activities and educational programs.

BALLETMET

C – 322 Mt. Vernon Avenue, **Columbus**. (614) 229-4860. Classic to contemporary ballet. Kids Culture Corps - spend time with dancers.

COLUMBUS ASSOCIATION FOR THE PERFORMING ARTS

C - 55 East State Street, **Columbus**. (614) 469-0939. CAPA operates theatres and presents touring arts and entertainment including children's concerts.

COLUMBUS CULTURAL ARTS CENTER

C - 139 West Main Street, **Columbus**. (614) 645-7047. Family oriented workshops, demonstrations, performances, and exhibits.

COLUMBUS JUNIOR THEATRE

C - 504 North Park Street, **Columbus**. (614) 224-6672. Theatre activities for youth of all ages, backgrounds or cultures.

COLUMBUS MUSEUM OF ART

C - 480 East Broad Street, **Columbus**. (614) 221-4848. American and European art from 1850-1950. See the life-size horse of welded steel or the works of Columbus realist George Bellows and folk artist Elijah Pierce. Saturday parent/child workshops. Café and gift shop.

COLUMBUS SYMPHONY ORCHESTRA

C - 55 East State Street, **Columbus**. (614) 224-5281. Lollypop Concerts on Saturday mornings. Youth Orchestra. Popcorn Pops are outdoor theme concerts with games, crafts and food.

GALLERY PLAYERS

C - 1125 College Avenue, **Columbus**. (614) 231-2731. Oldest and largest community theatre company in Columbus performs at the Leo Yassenoff Jewish Center. Youth Theatre. (November-July)

GLASS AXIS

C - 280 Cozzins Street, **Columbus**. (614) 228-4011. Visit working glassblowing studio. (September –June)

GRANDPARENTS LIVING THEATRE

C - 51 Jefferson Avenue, **Columbus**. (614) 228-7458. Older actors perform theatre that is sensitive to issues of aging and speaks to audiences of all ages with a lasting impact.

HOPKINS HALL GALLERY

C - College of the Arts, Ohio State University, **Columbus**. (614) 292-5072. Exhibits by visiting artists, faculty and students.

KING ARTS COMPLEX

C - 867 Mount Vernon Avenue, **Columbus**. (614) 252-5464. Storytelling Festival. Activities to increase awareness of African American artists, develop talents and preserve culture.

MUSIC IN THE AIR

C - 549 Franklin Avenue, **Columbus**. (614) 645-7995. Free outdoor concerts and festivals of music, dance, poetry, theatre and Magical Musical Mornings children's programs. (May – September)

OPERA/COLUMBUS

C - 177 Naghten Street, **Columbus**. (614) 461-0022. Professional opera company produces three works each year with major guest artists in November, February and April. Dress Rehearsals the Tuesday before opening night are open for students to observe.

OSU DANCE

C - Ohio State University, **Columbus**. (614) 292-7977

OSU MUSIC

C -Ohio State University, **Columbus**. (614) 292-ARTS

OSU THEATRE

C - Ohio State University, **Columbus**. (614) 292- 2295

WEXNER CENTER FOR THE ARTS

C - North High Street & 15th Avenue, **Columbus**. (614) 292-3535. Features contemporary visual, performance and media arts in unique building and layout. Parental guidance suggested.

CENTRAL OHIO SYMPHONY ORCHESTRA

C - Ohio Wesleyan University Campus, **Delaware**. (740) 368-3724. Series of concerts with guest artists. (October-April)

ZIVILI

C – 1753 Loudon Street, **Granville**. (740) 855-7805. Performs music and dances of Southern Slavic nations.

LANCASTER CHORALE

C - **Lancaster**. (740) 569-4306. Choral music and other performances by ensemble of professional singers. (November-July)

LITHOPOLIS FINE ARTS ASSOCIATION

C – 150 East Columbus Street, **Lithopolis**. (740) 837-7003. Series of musical concerts and dramatic events in Wagnalls Memorial.

MANSFIELD ART CENTER

C - 700 Marion Avenue, **Mansfield**. (419) 756-1700. Displays invitational and juried exhibits. Offers lectures, movies, classes, special programs.

MANSFIELD PLAYHOUSE

C - 95 East Third Street, **Mansfield**. (419) 522-8140. Community and guest artists present adult and youth productions. (September – June)

MANSFIELD SYMPHONY SOCIETY

C - 142 Park Avenue West, **Mansfield**. (419) 524-5927. Performs classical works, opera, pops, ballet and special events in restored Renaissance Theatre. Summer musical and outdoor concerts.

RICHLAND ACADEMY OF THE ARTS

C - 75 North Walnut Street, **Mansfield**. (419) 522-8224. Performances in black box theatre, recitals, musicals, choral concerts, jazz, and children's plays.

PALACE CULTURAL ARTS ASSOCIATION

C - 276 West Center Street, **Marion**. (740) 383-2101. Presents theatre, music, dance, and film in restored historic theatre.

LICKING COUNTY ART ASSOCIATION

C - 391 Hudson Avenue, **Newark**. (740) 349-8031. Galleries, educational programs and art library.

WESTERVILLE CIVIC SYMPHONY

C - **Westerville**. (614) 895-1102. Community orchestra with concerts for children and a FREE Independence Day concert.

ZANESVILLE ART CENTER

C - 620 Military Road, **Zanesville**. (740) 452-0741. Visit a 300-year-old English panel room with classic works, glass, ceramics, ancient, Asian, African and contemporary art.

AREA "CE"

BEHALT

5798 County Road 77 (north of State Route 39), **Berlin**

- Area: **CE**
- Telephone Number: (740) 893-3192
- Hours: Monday – Saturday, 9:00 a.m. – 5:00 p.m.
- Tours: 30 minute guided or video (15 minute background to Amish area).

Behalt means "the remembering". This 10' x 265' cyclorama mural by artist Heinz Gaugel clearly explains the heritage of Amish and Mennonite people from beginnings of their faith to the present day. The circular mural took four years to paint using an old technique called "sgraffito" which means scratched. Mr. Gaugel applied five layers of plaster to the wall (green, dark red, dark yellow, white and black). This makes the mural almost 3D when viewing. The artist starts scratching through the layers to expose the colors he wants. The tour is narrated with stories so vivid that you feel a part of the scene. We were fortunate to meet Heinz Gaugel in the gift shop and it was amazing to meet such a humble man with such apparent and unique artistic talent.

THE LIVING WORD PASSION PLAY

College Hill Road (2 miles west of State Route 209), **Cambridge**

- Area: **CE**
- Telephone Number: (740) 439-2761
- Hours: Thursday – Saturday, 8:00 p.m. (Mid-June – Labor Day)
  Saturday Only, 7:00 p.m. (September)
- Admission: $10.00 Adult

$9.00 Senior (60+)
$6.00 Children (under 12)
Free Set Tours, 6:00 p.m.
- ❏ Miscellaneous: Concessions, Gift Shop, Rain Checks, Free Parking.

Experience an evening back in the Holy Land, in 30 AD with an authentic representation of Old Jerusalem. Watch as Jesus and his disciples travel into Jerusalem, he is then crucified, and raises from the dead. The play is full of biblical animals and costumes, even chariots!

CANTON BALLET

CE - Palace Theatre, 605 North Market Avenue, **Canton**. (330) 455-7220. Pre-professional training company performs with professional artists.

CANTON MUSEUM OF ART

CE - 1001 North Market Avenue, **Canton**. (330) 453-7666. Features traveling exhibitions and permanent collection of American watercolors, works on paper and ceramics.

CANTON SYMPHONY ORCHESTRA

CE - 2323 17th Street NW, **Canton**. (330) 452-2094. Presents classical, holiday, pops and youth concerts/symphony.

CULTURAL CENTER FOR THE ARTS

CE - 1001 North Market Avenue, **Canton**. (330) 452-4096. Presents FunFest, Family Arts Festival and educational programs.

PLAYERS GUILD CENTER FOR PUBLIC THEATRE

CE - 1001 North Market Avenue, **Canton**. (330) 453-7619. Family series presents plays based on award winning children's stories.

POMERENE CENTER FOR THE ARTS

CE - 317 Mulberry Street, **Coshocton**. (740) 622-0326. Art exhibits, music series, community celebration of the arts, art classes, workshops, school and community outreach programs.

POTTER PLAYERS THEATRE

CE - **East Liverpool**. (330) 385-9390. Youth theatre, mainstage and special productions.

MASSILLON MUSEUM

CE - 121 Lincoln Way East, **Massillon**. (330) 833-4061. Collection of art with photographs, Ohio quilts, pottery and folk art.

MUSKINGUM COLLEGE CULTURAL EVENTS SERIES

CE - Montgomery Hall, **New Concord**. (740) 826-8313. Presents lectures, music, dance, and theatre.

TRUMPET IN THE LAND

Shoenbrunn Amphitheatre (I-77 to Exit 81), **New Philadelphia**

- Area: **CE**
- Telephone Number: (330) 339-1132
- Hours: Daily, (except Sunday) 8:30 p.m. (Mid-June – August)
- Admission: $13.00 Adult, $6.00 Children under 12

In an Ohio Frontier setting meet historical characters like David Zeisgerber (missionary), Simon Girtz (renegade), Captain Pipe (young warrior chief who hated white men) and John Heikewelder (explorer). The Revolutionary War breaks out and Moravian Christians would not take sides. Sadly, in the end, American militia brutally massacre 96 Christian Indians at Gnadenhutten. 70 member cast.

THE ARTS

TUSCARAWAS PHILHARMONIC

CE - New Philadelphia. (330) 477-6153. Orchestra, chorus and children's chorus perform. (October – May)

STEUBENVILLE CITY OF MURALS
Tour Office. 100 North 4th Street. Downtown, **Steubenville**

- Area: **CE**
- Telephone Number: (740) 282-0938
- Tours: Guided tours include other tourist spots in the area. Admission.

Over twenty giant full color (almost 3D) murals with the theme "Preserving a Piece of America" on the sides of downtown buildings. Each has its own name with some of the most interesting being *Stanton Park, Ohio River Oil Company* and *Steam Laundry* – these all "jump" right off the wall and appear almost like a photograph.

OHIO LIGHT OPERA

CE - Freedlander Theatre, College of Wooster, **Wooster.** (330) 263-2345. Professional company presents 19th & 20th century operettas. (Summer)

WAYNE CENTER FOR THE ARTS

CE - 237 South Walnut Street, **Wooster.** (330) 264-2787. Presents chamber music series, dance programs, traditional arts festival, exhibits, classes and workshops.

AREA "CW"

DAYTON ART INSTITUTE

CW - 456 Belmonte Park North, **Dayton.** (937) 223-5277. Art collection spanning 5000 years. Experiencenter features 20 hands-on activities encourages interaction with art and experimentation with artistic elements of line, pattern, color, texture and shape.

DAYTON BALLET

CW - 140 North Main Street, **Dayton**. (937) 449-5060. Professional company performs new works by young American choreographers. (October – April)

DAYTON OPERA

CW - 125 East First Street, **Dayton**. (937) 228-0662. Presents opera, operetta and musical theatre featuring international and rising young American talent. (October – May)

DAYTON PHILHARMONIC ORCHESTRA

CW - 125 East First Street, **Dayton**. (937) 224-9000. Plays classical, pops, and chamber series. Summer outdoor concerts.

DAYTON VISUAL ARTS CENTER

CW - 40 West Fourth Street, **Dayton**. (937) 224-3822. Enjoy programs that showcase regional artists in Terra Cotta District.

HUMAN RACE

CW - 126 North Main Street, **Dayton**. (937) 461-3823. Resident, professional theatre company produces bold shows in intimate space. Best to attend a youth oriented presentation.

WRIGHT STATE UNIVERSITY ARTIST SERIES

CW - Student Union, 3640 Colonel Glenn Highway, **Dayton**. (937) 873-5544. Presents culturally diverse programs and artists.

FAIRBORN SUMMER PARK SERIES

CW - 44 West Hebble Avenue, **Fairborn**. (937) 754-3090. Free outdoor concerts from big band to jazz to jugglers. (Friday) (June – July)

THE ARTS

ARTSPACE/LIMA

CW - 65/67 Town Square, **Lima**. (419) 222-1721. Features exhibits of local/regional artists and classes. Art fair in September. Holiday festival in December.

LIMA SYMPHONY ORCHESTRA

CW - 67 Town Square, **Lima**. (419) 222-5701. Plays series of concerts plus holiday, family, children's and summer concerts. (October – May)

CLARK STATE PERFORMING ARTS CENTER

CW - 300 South Fountain Avenue, **Springfield**. (937) 328-3874. Hosts national and regional performers, recording artists, Broadway shows, and family programs. (September- June)

SPRINGFIELD MUSEUM OF ART

CW - 107 Cliff Park Road, **Springfield**. (937) 325-4673. Permanent collection of 19th & 20th century American/ European art.

SPRINGFIELD SUMMER ARTS FESTIVAL

CW - 150 Cliff Park Road, **Springfield**. (937) 324-2712. Five weeks of free music and theatre in Veterans Park. (June – July)

SPRINGFIELD SYMPHONY ORCHESTRA

CW - **Springfield**. (937) 325-8100. Community orchestra presents series with guest artists.

MAD RIVER THEATER WORKS

CW - **West Liberty**. (937) 465-6751. Professional company creates and presents plays that communicate regional ways of life and community concerns.

BLUE JACKET

Caesar's Ford Park Amphitheater. (US 35 to Jasper Road, south to Stringtown Road), **Xenia**

- Area: **CW**
- Telephone Number: (937) 376-4318
- Hours: Tuesday – Sunday at 8:00 p.m. (Mid–June – Labor Day)
  Dinner at the Pavillon, 5:30 – 7:30 p.m.
  Backstage guided tours at 4:00 and 5:00 p.m.
- Admission: $8.00 - $14.00 Adult, $ 6.00 Children (1-12)
  $3.50 Adult, $2.00 Children (Backstage tour)
  Reservations please.

Over two hour outdoor drama recounts the true story of a pure white man adopted by Indians. Blue Jacket became a Shawnee Indian Chief and fought to keep the land and heritage from frontiersmen like Daniel Boone. To add life to the drama, they use live horses, real muskets, cannons, flaming arrows and torches.

AREA "NC"

ASHLAND SYMPHONY ORCHESTRA

NC - Ashland University, **Ashland**. (419) 289-5115. Community orchestra performs at University. (September – May)

LAKESIDE ASSOCIATION

NC - 236 Walnut Avenue, **Lakeside**. (419) 798-4461. Chautaqua – like assembly with programs in historic enclave on Lake Erie. (June – September)

LORAIN PALACE CIVIC CENTER

NC - 617 Broadway, **Lorain**. (440) 245-2323. Presents arts and theatre events, educational programs.

THE ARTS

ALLEN MEMORIAL ART MUSEUM

NC - Oberlin College, 87 North Main Street, **Oberlin**. (440) 775-8665. See European art, 17th Century Dutch and Flemish painting, contemporary art, Japanese woodblock prints, Islamic carpets.

FIRELANDS ASSOCIATION FOR VISUAL ARTS

NC - New Union Center, 39 South Main Street, **Oberlin**. (440) 774-7158. Regional and national artists, art classes, photography and quilt shows.

FIRELANDS SYMPHONY ORCHESTRA

NC - **Sandusky**. (419) 621-4800. Professional and semi-professional musicians perform series concerts, children's concerts at State Theatre. Summer concerts at Put in Bay, Lakeside.

THE SPIRIT OF '76 MUSEUM

NC - 201 North Main Street, **Wellington**. (440) 647-4531. Gallery of paintings and murals done by Archibold Willard (famed painter of "Spirit of '76" painting of three Revolutionary War soldiers playing fife & drum through battle). See objects used as models for works.

AREA "NE"

AKRON ART MUSEUM

NE - 70 East Market Street, **Akron**. (330) 376-9185. An intimate setting for discovering beautiful, new art.

AKRON RECREATION BUREAU

NE - 220 South Balch Street, **Akron**. (330) 375-2804. Offers free symphony performances, ballet and summer concerts.

AKRON SYMPHONY ORCHESTRA

NE - 17 North Broadway, **Akron**. (330) 535-8131. Professional orchestra offers pops, classical and educational concerts. Youth Symphony. (September – July)

OHIO BALLET

NE - 354 East Market Street, **Akron**. (330) 972-7900. Professional company performs at E.J. Thomas Hall in Akron and Ohio Theatre in Cleveland. Produces free outdoor performances in summer.

SUMMIT CHORAL SOCIETY

NE - 715 East Buchtel Avenue, **Akron**. (330) 434-7464. Children's choir program.

UNIVERSITY OF AKRON THEATRE

NE - Guzzetta Hall, University of Akron, **Akron**. (330) 972-7890. Several shows each year in Kolbe/ Sandefur Theatres. (October-April)

WEATHERVANE PLAYHOUSE

NE - 1301 Weathervane Lane, **Akron**. (330) 836-2626. Offers mainstage and children's productions.

ASHTABULA ARTS CENTER

NE - 2928 West 13th Street, **Ashtabula**. (440) 964-3396. Home of Straw Hat Theatre, (June-August), GB Community Theatre, (September-April). Host of other drama, dance & musical performances.

BALDWIN-WALLACE COLLEGE ACES

NE - 275 Eastland Road, **Berea**. (440) 826-2157. Performing arts series with multi-cultural appeal and cross-cultural interaction features known artists performing with local talent.

BEREA SUMMER THEATRE

NE - **Berea**. (440) 826-2240. Community theatre with musicals and dramas during the summer.

AFRICAN AMERICAN MUSEUM

NE - 1765 Crawford Road, **Cleveland**. (216) 791-1700. Storytelling and artifacts tell the story of contributions to human progress made by people of African descent.

CENTRO CULTURAL HISPANO DE CLEVELAND

NE - 3200 Franklin Boulevard, **Cleveland.** (216) 961-9110. Preserves and promotes Latino culture through arts and crafts exhibits, music, dance, and drama presentations.

CLEVELAND BALLET

NE - One Playhouse Square, Suite 330, **Cleveland.** (216) 621-2260. Resident ballet company presents classical and contemporary dance. (September – March)

CLEVELAND CENTER FOR CONTEMPORARY ART

NE - 8501 Carnegie Avenue, **Cleveland.** (216) 421-8671. Displays of avant-garde paintings, sculpture, drawings, prints, and photographs by regional and national artists.

CLEVELAND CHAMBER ORCHESTRA

NE - 3659 Green Road, Suite 118, **Cleveland.** (216) 464-1755. Performs annual series in Waetjen Auditorium at CSU, neighborhood chamber series and free outdoor summer concerts.

CLEVELAND INSTITUTE OF MUSIC

NE - 11021 East Boulevard, **Cleveland.** (216) 791-5000. Concert series offers broad range of performances including family concerts. Most events free.

CLEVELAND MUSEUM OF ART

NE - 11150 East Boulevard, **Cleveland.** (216) 421-7340. See collection of objects from all cultures and periods including European and American paintings, medieval, Asian, Islamic, pre-Columbian, African masks, Egyptian mummies and Oceanic art. Free general admission; charge for parking.

CLEVELAND OPERA

NE - State Theatre, 1519 Euclid Avenue, **Cleveland.** (216) 241-6000. Internationally famous professional resident company. (October-March)

CLEVELAND ORCHESTRA

NE - 11001 Euclid Avenue, **Cleveland**. (800) 686-1141. Concerts in Severance Hall (September-May), at Blossom Music Center (Summer).

CLEVELAND PLAYHOUSE

NE - 8500 Euclid Avenue, **Cleveland**. (216) 795-7000. America's longest running regional theatre presents contemporary and classical plays; children's series and student festival.

CLEVELAND SIGNSTAGE THEATRE

NE - 8500 Euclid Avenue, **Cleveland**. (216) 229-2838. Performances combine the beauty of sign language, mime and the theatre to create cultural experiences shared by deaf and hearing people

CLEVELAND STATE UNIVERSITY DANCE PROGRAM

NE - Euclid Avenue & East 24th Street, **Cleveland**. (216) 687-4883. Presents activities and performances by dance artists. (September – June)

DANCE CLEVELAND

NE – 1148 Euclid Avenue, Suite 311, **Cleveland**. (800) 766-6048. The nation's oldest modern dance association presenting the best in contemporary dance.

EAST CLEVELAND THEATER

NE - 14108 Euclid Avenue, **Cleveland**. (216) 851-8721. Produces theatre programs for adults and children that further racial understanding and create a sense of community. (September – May)

GREAT LAKES THEATER FESTIVAL

NE -1501 Euclid Avenue, Suite 423, **Cleveland**. (216) 241-6000. Professional resident company produces Shakespeare, Shaw, Ibsen, Chekov, Moliere, Greek dramatists and modern classics. (October – May)

THE ARTS

KARAMU HOUSE

NE - 2355 East 89th Street, **Cleveland**. (216) 795-7070. Community based arts and education organization rooted in African American cultural heritage.

LYRIC OPERA CLEVELAND

NE - **Cleveland**. (216) 231-2484. Innovative productions of opera and musical theatre from standard and unusual repertoires. Summer festival and picnics.

CUYAHOGA VALLEY YOUTH BALLET

NE - Akron Civic Theatre, **Cuyahoga Falls**, (440) 258-8010. Pre-professional youth ballet presents ballet/modern dance. (September – May)

CROATIAN HERITAGE MUSEUM AND LIBRARY

NE - 34900 Lakeshore Boulevard, **Eastlake**. (440) 946-2044. Features collection of Croatian and Croatian American history/folk art.

KENT STATE UNIVERSITY MUSEUM

NE - Rockwell Hall, East Main & South Lincoln Streets, **Kent**. (330) 672-3450. Features work of the world's greatest artists and designers.

BECK CENTER FOR THE CULTURAL ARTS

NE - 17801 Detroit Avenue, **Lakewood**. (440) 521-2540. Visual and performing arts center offers community theatre, gallery, artists' collective, education, outreach programs, and children's theatre.

WESTERN RESERVE FINE ARTS ASSOCIATION

NE - 49 Park Street, **Madison**. (440) 428-5913. Presents performances, art shows and student recitals plus education in music, art, and dance.

LAKE ERIE COLLEGE FINE AND PERFORMING ARTS DEPARTMENT

NE - 391 West Washington Street, **Painesville**. (440) 352-3361. Offers theatre, dance, music and art programs. (September – April)

GREENBRIER THEATRE

NE - 6200 Pearl Road, **Parma Heights**. (440) 842-4600. Semi-professional community theatre offers mainstage and café-style productions, usually Broadway hits. (September – June)

DUFFY LITURGICAL DANCE ENSEMBLE

NE - 20310 Chagrin Boulevard, **Shaker Heights**. (440) 921-0734. Programs focus on heritage of African American song and dance.

HUDSON BANDSTAND CONCERT SOCIETY

NE - 4936-C Friar Road, **Stow**. (330) 673-5985. Sunday series includes band concerts, dance, bluegrass, jazz, choral and youth groups on Hudson Green or Barlow Community Center. (Summer)

BALLET THEATRE OHIO

NE - **Warren**. (330) 399-8106. Brings original, contemporary and classical works. (September – June)

WARREN CIVIC MUSIC ASSOCIATION

NE - **Warren**. (330) 369-5670. Presents yearly concert series of instrumental and vocal music, opera and dance. (September – May)

WILLOUGHBY FINE ARTS ASSOCIATION

NE - 38660 Mentor Avenue, **Willoughby**. (440) 951-7500. Cultural center gives opportunity to see, hear and participate in the arts.

BUTLER INSTITUTE OF AMERICAN ART

NE - 524 Wick Avenue, **Youngstown**. (330) 743-1711. Showcases American art from colonial times to the present. Children's Gallery (hands on) and American Sports Art Gallery.

MCDONOUGH MUSEUM OF ART

NE - Youngstown State University, **Youngstown**. (330) 742-1400. Presents visual art works of old and new artists. (September – July)

OAKLAND CENTER FOR THE ARTS

NE - Youngstown. (330) 545-3006. Presents comedies, musicals, children's plays.

YOUNGSTOWN PLAYHOUSE

NE - Youngstown. (330) 788-8739. Community theatre offers mainstage, summer musical and youth shows.

YOUNGSTOWN SYMPHONY

NE - 260 Federal Plaza West, **Youngstown**. (330) 744-4264. Performs Pops Concerts with guest artists in Powers Auditorium (tours).

AREA "NW"

FREED CENTER FOR PERFORMING ARTS

NW - Freed Center, Ohio Northern University, **Ada**. (419) 772-1900. Offers musicals/dramas, music and dance concerts, famous performers. (September – July)

BOWLING GREEN STATE UNIVERSITY FINE ARTS CENTER GALLERIES

NW - Fine Arts Building, **Bowling Green**. (419) 372-8525. Galleries and a Japanese ceremonial room exhibit national/student art.

DEFIANCE COLLEGE

NW - 701 North Clinton Street, **Defiance**. (419) 784-4010. Presents music and theatre, literary and artistic events. (September – May)

FINDLAY AREA ARTS COUNCIL

NW - 112 West Front Street, **Findlay**. (419) 422-4624. Annual arts festival (June). Presents performance series. (September – April)

FRANCISCAN CENTER

NW - 6832 Convent Boulevard, **Sylvania**. (419) 885-1547. Summer arts camp. Presents season of music and theatre. (September – May)

JEWISH COMMUNITY CENTER JUNIOR THEATRE GUILD

NW - 6465 Sylvania Avenue, **Sylvania**. (419) 885-4485. See professional touring artists from the US and Canada in productions ranging from classics to new works in theatre, puppetry, opera and dance.

RITZ THEATRE

NW - 30 South Washington, **Tiffin**. (419) 448-8544. A 1928 vaudeville/movie theatre presents performing arts events/films.

OHIO THEATRE

NW - 3114 LaGrange Street, **Toledo**. (419) 241-6785. Former vaudeville/movie house presents classical music, live stage, film and children's series.

TOLEDO MUSEUM OF ART

NW - 2445 Monroe at Scottwood, **Toledo**. (419) 255-8000. Discover treasures from the riches of the medieval, the splendors of a French chateau and the tombs of Egypt. Also glass, sculpture, paintings.

TOLEDO OPERA

NW - Masonic Auditorium, 4645 Heatherdowns Boulevard, **Toledo**. (419) 255-7464. Professional regional company presents three shows with guest artists.

THE ARTS

TOLEDO SYMPHONY ORCHESTRA

NW - 2 Maritime Plaza, **Toledo**. (800) 348-1253. Regional symphony performs orchestral masterpieces with guest artists, chamber, contemporary, pops, youth and summer concerts.

WASSENBERG ART CENTER

NW - 643 South Washington Street, **Van Wert**. (419) 238-6837. Displays works by traveling exhibits and local artists. Art, camera & wood carvers clubs.

AREA "SC"

DAIRY BARN CULTURAL ARTS CENTER

SC - 8000 Dairy Lane, **Athens**. (740) 592-4981. Festivals. Hayrides and storytellers for kids. Arts and crafts exhibits.

OHIO UNIVERSITY OFFICE OF PUBLIC OCCASIONS

SC - Templeton-Blackburn Memorial Auditorium, **Athens**. (740) 593-1761. Presents theatre, music, dance, ethnic and folk art programs. (October – May)

OHIO UNIVERSITY ART GALLERY

SC - OU Art Gallery, **Athens**. (740) 593-0796. Presents traditional and contemporary art by national/regional artists. (September – June)

TECUMSEH

Sugarloaf Mountain Amphitheater. Delano Road off State Route 159, **Chillicothe**

- Area: **SC**
- Telephone Number: (740) 775-0700
- Hours: Monday – Sunday, Show time, 8:00 p.m. Reservations please. (March – September)

❑ Admission: Monday – Thursday, $13.00 General
Friday – Saturday, $15.00 General
$6.00 Children (under 10)
Backstage Tours 2 –5 p.m. $3.50 Adult. $2.00 Children.
❑ Miscellaneous: Mountain Valley Gift Shop
Restaurant with buffet served a few hours before the show.
<u>Backstage Tour</u> - one hour long, demonstrations on weaponry, stunts & makeup.

This production has received national attention. More than 1.6 million people have already seen the outdoor re-enactment of Shawnee Leader, Tecumseh's life and death. Fast action horses, loud firearms and speeding arrows make the audience part of the action especially when costumed actors enter the scene from right, left and behind.

PUMP HOUSE ART GALLERY

SC - Enderlin Circle, Yoctangee Park, **Chillicothe**. (740) 772-5783. Visit art gallery and cultural center in restored water pumping station.

ARIEL THEATRE

SC - 426 Second Avenue, **Gallipolis**. (740) 446-2787. Restored opera house is home to Ohio Valley Symphony, Ariel Players.

PORTSMOUTH MURALS

SC - State Route 23 South, Washington Street to Ohio River (follow green mural signs), **Portsmouth**. Artist Robert Dafford (internationally known muralist) can be seen working on new murals in the months of May – September. Look for the paint dotted scaffold and the artist dressed in paint dotted white painter's pants and shirt. He plans to create 35-40 murals by 1998. Our two favorites were Chillicothe Street 1940's (a very colorful, tremendously detailed, cartoon-like mural) and Twilight (a modern day view of the bridge over the river, looks like a photograph).

SOUTHERN OHIO MUSEUM AND CULTURAL CENTER

SC- 825 Gallia Street, **Portsmouth**. (740) 354-5629. Changing exhibits in fine arts and history, performing arts events.

UNIVERSITY OF RIO GRANDE VALLEY ARTISTS SERIES

SC - Fine and Performing Arts Center, **Rio Grande**. (800) 282-7201. Series presents regional and national touring artists.

AREA "SE"

SHOWBOAT BECKY THATCHER

SE - 237 Front Street on the River, **Marietta**. (740) 373-6033/4130 (restaurant). Vintage early 1900's sternwheeler that has a theater that was once a boiler room. Talented performers create a "Mark Twain" mood with melodramas like "Little Mary Sunshine" and favorites of composer Stephen Foster ("Oh Susanna" and "Camptown Races"). Funny signs appear during the performance instructing you when to "boo" or "cheer". The restaurant on board serves basic American food and Riverboat Pie (secret recipe) for dessert! Hours: Daytime/Evening (Summer and Fall)

THE BARN

SE - State Route 78, **McConnelsville**. (740) 962-4284. 1904 stained glass studio used by nationally known artist, Chuck Borsari.

AREA "SW"

CINCINNATI ART MUSEUM

SW - Eden Park, **Cincinnati**. (513) 721-5204. Art collection presents 5000 years of visual arts. Favorites include medieval armor and arms, old musical instruments, Andy Warhol's Pete Rose and the futuristic robot. Family Fun Tours, Saturday, 1:00 – 3:00 p.m. – FREE.

CINCINNATI BALLET

SW - Cincinnati. (513) 621-5219. Classically based professional ballet company performs classic and contemporary works. Pirouette Club - meet with dancers backstage, Adopt-a-Dancer - have meals together, Sugar Plum Parties. (September – May)

CINCINNATI OPERA

SW - 1241 Elm Street, **Cincinnati**. (513) 621-1919. Second oldest opera group in the US produces grand opera in Music Hall.

CINCINNATI PLAYHOUSE IN THE PARK

SW - 962 Mount Adams Circle, **Cincinnati**. (513) 421-3888. Professional resident theatre offers dramas, comedies and musicals.

CINCINNATI SYMPHONY ORCHESTRA

SW - 1241 Elm Street, **Cincinnati**. (513) 621-1919. The CSO presents soloists, pops concerts and an artist series in Music Hall. CSO RiverBend Music Center hosts Symphony/Pops Orchestra, plus contemporary artists (May-September). Lollipop Concerts for kids.

CONTEMPORARY ARTS CENTER

SW - 115 East Fifth Street, **Cincinnati**. (513) 721-0390. Contemporary kids workshops and clubs.

ENSEMBLE THEATRE OF CINCINNATI

SW - 1127 Vine Street, **Cincinnati**. (513) 421-3555. Professional resident theatre develops and produces new works with an emphasis on Ohio and Cincinnati artists. (September – June)

IMAGES IMAGES IMAGES

SW - 1310 Pendleton Street, 6th floor, **Cincinnati**. (513) 241-8124. Center for the exhibition and advancement of art photography.

SHOWBOAT MAJESTIC

SW - Moored at Broadway Street Landing, **Cincinnati**. (513) 241-6550. Live riverfront shows like musicals, comedies and dramas.

The original owner, actor Thomas Jefferson Reynolds, raised eleven kids on board while moving from rivertown to town entertaining folks in the early 1900's. Open daily Summers, Weekends (April, May, September, October)

TAFT MUSEUM

SW - 316 Pike Street, **Cincinnati**. (513) 241-0343. See works of European and American painters, Chinese porcelains, Limoges enamels displayed in a federal period mansion.

SORG OPERA HOUSE

SW - **Middletown**. (513) 425-0180. Historic 1891 theatre presents opera productions. (October – April)

MIAMI UNIVERSITY ART MUSEUM

SW - Patterson Avenue, **Oxford**. (513) 529-2232. Collection of 16,000 plus art objects from ancient to contemporary.

MURPHY THEATRE FOR THE ARTS

SW - 50 West Main Street, **Wilmington**. (513) 382-3643. Historic theatre hosts performing arts groups. (September – April)

Chapter 10

THEME RESTAURANTS

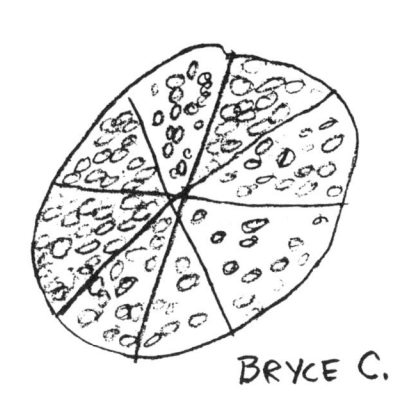

Allison Hoyt

Bryce C.

ASHLAND WOOSTER DRIVE-IN

C – 1134 East Main Street, **Ashland**. (419) 289-9808. Since 1957 they have been serving root beer, coneys, fries, chicken, onion chips, etc. with carhop service.

94TH AERO SQUADRON

C – 5030 Sawyer Road, **Columbus** Airport. (614) 237-8887. WWI French Countryside Inn décor with a view of the planes taking off and landing.

BUCKEYE HALL OF FAME CAFÉ

C – Olentangy River Road & West 5th Avenue, **Columbus**. (614) 291-2233. Fun casual dining. While waiting for your food order, walk down the hallway named the Ohio State Walk of Fame (memorabilia displayed from all sports at Ohio State University including Archie Griffin's 1975 Heismann Trophy) on your way to the Arena gameroom. Floor tiles throughout the restaurant are inscribed with the names of famous Ohio State University greats.

ENGINE HOUSE NO. 5

C – 121 Thurman Avenue, German Village, **Columbus**. (614) 443-4877. A real 100 year old firehouse converted into a fine dining restaurant (their specialty is seafood). When celebrating birthdays, the server slides down a shiny brass fire pole complete with cake and a lit sparkler.

KAHIKI RESTAURANT

C – 3583 East Broad Street, **Columbus**. (614) 237-5425. Inside or out it's Polynesian with lots of tropical plants and fish. Order fun juice drinks with umbrellas as you look over their extensive children's menu.

HAMBURGER INN

C – 16 North Sandusky Street, **Delaware**. (740) 369-3850. Chrome stools and soda fountains remain as they were in the 1950's. Great place for a burger and shake.

POPEYE'S RESTAURANT

C – 416 Main Street, **Dresden**. (740) 754-6330. A 50's décor with hostesses wearing poodle skirts and a jukebox at every booth. Soda fountain serving Wimpy Burgers and Spinach Salads plus many basic favorites. Kids' meals are served in a paper box 50's corvette. Try their 25-cent one bite ice cream sundae – almost too cute to eat!

THE STABLES

CE – 2317 13th Street NW (I-77 exit 106), **Canton**. (888) GO-STABLES. The circular brick building was once the Timken Family Stables. Festive football and sports atmosphere with many large screen televisions, tableside trivia games, fame room and a huge 10,000 pound carved redwood "football catch" sculpture. "Located a football field away from the Pro Football Hall of Fame."

THE DEPOT CANTEEN RESTAURANT

CE – 400 Center Street, **Dennison**. (740) 922-6776. Railroad canteen for WWII servicemen is now used as a museum of local history, a gift shop, an old fashioned candy counter and a theme restaurant.

356TH FIGHTER GROUP RESTAURANT

CE – 4919 Mount Pleasant Road, **North Canton**. (330) 494-3500. WWII theme with high windows that overlook runways of the Akron/Canton airport.

JAGGIN' AROUND

CE – 5th & Washington Street (off Route 7), downtown **Steubenville**. Modern art deco décor with kid's meals served in cardboard classic cars. Free admission (with food purchase) to attached Welsh Jaguar Classic Car Museum. The museum features displays of the "Glory Days of the Jaguar". Also, see a Mercedes Gull Wing and 60's Muscle cars.

DER DUTCHMAN / DUTCH VALLEY RESTAURANTS

CE – **Sugarcreek, Walnut Creek, Plain City and Bolivar**. Amish kitchen cooking with family style dinners, markets and gift shops. Amish crafts and buggies create an authentic atmosphere.

CLIFTON MILL RESTAURANT

CW – 75 Water Street (off State Route 72), **Clifton** (near Springfield). (937) 767-5501. An actual working gristmill with restaurant seating with a view of a waterwheel, river and covered bridge. Pancakes, mush, grits and bread are made from product produced at the mill. Best pork barbecue sandwich ever! Breakfast and lunch only.

JIM'S DRIVE IN RESTAURANT

CW – 100 Martz Street, **Greenville**. (937) 548-5078. Car hops, root beer, Spanish hot dogs. Lunch and dinner only. Late March through mid-August.

KEWPEE

CW – (three locations), **Lima**. (419) 228-1778. Burgers since 1928 with wrappers that say "Hamburger with pickle on top, makes your heart go flippity flop".

MAPLESIDE FARMS

NC – 294 Pearl Road, **Brunswick**. (330) 225-5576. 5000 apple tree orchard view at the restaurant. Apple house, gift house and ice cream parlor.

THE DEPOT RESTAURANT

NE – 120 East Mill Street, Quaker Square, **Akron**. (330) 253-5970. Sit inside coaches of a former Railway Express Train as the waiters/waitresses take your order dressed as conductors. A large model train display greets you in the lobby and once seated, you are surrounded by railroad cars and memorabilia.

100TH BOMB GROUP

NE – 2000 Brookpark Road, **Cleveland**. (440) 267-1010. A WWII English farmhouse décor with a view of Hopkins Airport runways.

HORNBLOWER'S

NE – **Cleveland** Lakefront. (216) 363-1151. Dine in an actual barge used on Lake Erie. Indoor/Outdoor dining with a view of the harbor from every seat.

PUFFERBELLY RESTAURANT

NE – **Kent & Berea**. (330) 673-1771 & (440) 234-1144. Sit down and dine in a restored historic train depot.

COVERED BRIDGE PIZZA

NE – State Route 193 & US 20, **North Kingsville** or 380 East Main Street, **Andover**. (440) 224-0497 or (440) 992-8155. Actual covered bridge with built in pizza parlor. Located in the heart of Ashtabula County that features 14 covered bridges that can be toured. Daily except Monday.

McDONALD'S

NE – 2891 Elm Road, **Warren**. (330) 372-6282. Ohio's largest McDonald's Play Place with five slides over two stories high, talking equipment (mirrors, trash cans), two ball pits and interactive computers. Open daily.

THE MOST MAGNIFICENT McDONALD'S IN AMERICA

NE – 162 North Road, **Warren**. (330) 856-3611. A three story building complete with brass and marble fixtures, a glass elevator, an indoor waterfall and a baby grand piano. Open daily.

MOM'S DINER

NW – State Route 2/20 to Route 66, downtown **Archbold**. (419) 445-5060. Milkshakes, burgers, 50's style décor, jukebox music and servers that wear poodle skirts. Open daily at 11:00 a.m.

JIGGS DRIVE IN

NW – 111 Holgate Avenue, **Defiance**. (419) 782-4393. A 50's carhop drive in with servers dressed in Jiggs shirts and jackets that come out to your car and hook trays to your car window. They serve food like chili dogs and rootbeer. Daily for lunch and dinner. (Mid – April through August)

TONY PACKO'S CAFÉ

NW – 1902 Front Street, **Toledo**. (419) 691-6054. Corporal Klinger (Jamie Farr) in the TV series M*A*S*H raved about it. See it for yourself and try some ethnic Hungarian style food such as cabbage rolls, chicken paprikash, chili dogs and Packo's famous chili. Be sure to look for the hot dog buns signed by TV stars that have visited the café.

SUMBURGER RESTAURANT

SC – 1487 North Bridge Street, **Chillicothe**. (740) 772-1055. Casual lunch or dinner menu items ordered from table telephones.

FOREST VIEW GARDENS

SW – 4508 North Bend Road (1 mile South off I-71 exit 14), **Cincinnati**. (513) 661-6434. Bavarian styled restaurant with singing servers. Thursday – Sunday.

ROOKWOOD POTTERY

SW – 1077 Celestial, **Cincinnati**. (513) 721-5456. An actual historic pottery shop where you dine in original pottery kilns. Casual food – voted best burgers, sundae bar.

SHADY – NOOK

SW – 879 Millville – Oxford Road (US 27), **Millville**. (513) 863-4343. Bring your grandparents who remember the famous Moon

River radio program. As you eat you're treated to a theater organ, tapes of 1930's and 1940's radio shows or a sing along.

SKY CREAM & DELI

SW – 4925 North State Route 42, **Waynesville** Airport. (513) 897-7717. May through October watch skydivers jump while you enjoy a snack. Fifteen-minute airplane rides available.

Chapter 11

TOURS

Basket Factory

Tony Starr

AREA "C"

COOPER'S MILL AND JELLY FACTORY

1414 North Sandusky Avenue, (U.S. Route 30 bypass and State Route 4) **Bucyrus**

- Area: **C**
- Telephone Number: (419) 562-4215
- Miscellaneous: Farm Market - taste test jellies and homemade fudge.

Jelly Factory tour lets you watch fruit spreads being made the old fashioned way.

AMERICAN WHISTLE CORPORATION

6540 Huntley Road (I-71 to Route 161), **Columbus**

- Area: **C**
- Telephone Number: (614) 846-2918
- Tours: (March – September)
  Monday – Friday (1 Hour Long)
  15-40 people
  Appointment Necessary
- Admission: $3.00 per person

Do you know what a lanyard is? Do you know what makes a whistle louder? See and hear the only small metal whistle manufactured in the United States (used by police, referees, coaches, etc.) Each person gets to take home a whistle they just watched being made.

BIG BEAR WAREHOUSE
770 West Goodale Blvd (Route 315 to Goodale Exit), **Columbus**

- Area: **C**
- Telephone Number: (614) 464-6750
- Tours: Tuesday or Wednesday (Appointment Necessary)
  10:00 a.m. (1 hour long)
  35 people maximum
  3rd grade and up
- Admission: Free

Tours include both the grocery and refrigerated areas. Some highlights for children include going into the large freezer, watching the fork lifts, seeing the train cars come in and out of the railroad room, and walking through the banana ripening room. Wear comfortable shoes.

COLUMBUS SOUTHERN POWER PLANT
Picway Plant (U.S. Route 23 South), **Columbus**

- Area: **C**
- Telephone Number: (740) 464-7779
- Tours: 1 hour, Any Weekday (By Appointment Only)
  10 years and up, 10 person minimum
- Admission: FREE

On June 15, 1752 Ben Franklin flew his kite in an experiment that proved that lightning contained electricity. Modern science has created many ways to generate electricity today, but what goes on with the flip of a switch? Visit a generation plant where coal is processed and within a few seconds converted to energize generators. Because coal can be dirty, wear old, comfortable clothes.

OHIO STATE HIGHWAY PATROL TRAINING FACILITY
740 East 17th Avenue, (West of I-71 and 17th Avenue Exit), **Columbus**

- Area: **C**
- Telephone Number: (614) 466-4896
- Tours: Tuesday and Wednesday, 10:00 a.m. or 2:00 p.m.
  Approximately 45 minutes
  Minimum 15 people, Maximum 40 people
- Admission: FREE

A State Trooper guide will escort you through the life of a highway patrol trainee. Your children learn the history of the patrol and how Ohio has developed its programs. You will probably bump into a few trainees as you pass through the weight room, swimming pool and gymnasium. Most favorite stop on the tour is the practice firing range. Gun safety and legal use will be discussed.

THE POPCORN OUTLET
1500 Bethel Road, **Columbus**

- Area: **C**
- Telephone Number: (614) 451-7677
- Tours: By Appointment
  Approximately 20-30 minutes
  No minimum or maximum number of people

What a treat to meet Al, The Popcorn Man! This wonderfully enthusiastic owner will answer every question you've ever had about popcorn. Kids love the large poppers and closely watch the popped corn flow out. They have a tremendous assortment of spices and sweet flavors to coat the popcorn. We tasted bubble gum when we were there! You won't leave without trying your favorite flavor.

LONGABERGER MUSEUM AND FACTORY TOUR
5563 Raiders Road (on State Route 16), **Dresden**

- Area: **C**
- Telephone Number: (740) 754-6330
- Hours: Monday – Saturday, 8:00 a.m. – 5:00 p.m. Sunday, Noon - 5:00 p.m.
- Admission: FREE
- Miscellaneous: World's Largest Basket! Fifth and Main Street. (Off State Route 60). Arrive before 1:00 p.m. Monday – Friday to see actual production. No production on Saturday or Sunday. Weaving demonstrations daily in the Gallery with same setup as one of the factory stations. *Just For Fun Shop* - Tour baskets, souvenirs. *Corporate Headquarters*. (State Route 16) Newark. Seven story Market Basket design with towering heated handles (to melt the winter ice) on top and painted/stenciled to look like wood. *Make a Basket Shop*. 417 Main Street. (740) 754-6327. Actually create your own hardwood maple Longaberger basket with the help of a Master Artisan. Takes 1 hour.

Fascinating tours and lots to see in this tiny little town. Longaberger manufacturers high quality, handmade hard maple baskets. The one-quarter mile long factory is home to 1000 weavers who make 100,000 baskets per week (each initialed and dated). It's best to watch a 13 minute video of the company's history and the manufacturing process that takes sugar maple logs (poached and debarked) that are cut into long thin strips. You'll be mesmerized when you go upstairs to the mezzanine to view 400 crafters, each with their own station, weaving damp wood strips around "forms", Each basket takes about 20-30 minutes to make. Can you guess what a weaving horse is? Before you leave the area you must view the new corporate headquarters and the large basket – they are difficult to visualize except in person. The village shops are quaint and the restaurants are cute and fun!

JAPAN MINI-TOUR AND EDUCATIONAL CENTER

99 South State Street, (270 North to Westerville Road exit), **Westerville**

- Area: **C**
- Telephone Number: (614) 882-2964
- Tours: Appointment Necessary
  Seasonal, (1 to 1 1/2 hours long)
- Admission: Age 4 and under free

George Henderson and his wife brought a traditional Kyoto Tea House and Shinto Shrine back to Westerville after their travels to Japan. The Tea House has authentic furniture, bathrooms, and food displayed. The garden is traditional style with large bamboo trees. The Shinto Shrine is now a classroom used to demonstrate Japanese ceremonies, schoolrooms, musical instruments and games. As a custom, be sure to remove your shoes before entering the Tea House!

AREA "CE"

SCHROCK'S AMISH FARM AND HOME

State Route 39 (1 mile East of Downtown) **Berlin**

- Area: **CE**

- Telephone Number: (330) 893-3232
- Hours: Monday – Friday, 10:00 a.m. - 5:00 p.m.
  Saturday, 10:00 a.m.- 6:00 p.m.
  Memorial Day - October
- Tours and Admission:
  Buggy Ride - $3.00 Adult, $2.00 Children (3-12)
  Home Tour and Slides - $3.00 Adult, $2.00 Children (3-12)
  Farm Only - $1.50 Adult, 1.50 Children (3-12)
  All Three - $6.00 Adult, $4.00 Children (3-12)
- Miscellaneous: Gifts shops (many)

We started with a buggy ride driven by an Amish man and his horse named "Leroy". After our ride, we were given a sticker to wear that says, "I rode my first Amish buggy ride with Leroy". We then stopped at the farm to pet animals and then watched a slide show about Amish lifestyles. The guide then shows you through the home. Kids, even adults, were surprised to see that all appliances were gas fueled including the lamps (the gas generated light source was hidden in the table under the lamp). We learned why there are no faces on Amish dolls and why only pins and occasional buttons are used in clothing.

WENDALL AUGUST FORGED GIFT TOUR
State Route 62 (3 miles West of **Berlin**)

- Area: **CE**
- Telephone Number: (800) 923-4438 or (216) 893-3713
- Tours: Monday – Friday, 9:00 a.m. – 6:00 p.m.
  Saturday, (Showroom open and workshop viewing only)

Free tour of the production workshop as metal giftware is taken through a fascinating eleven step process. The gift metal is hammered over a pre-designed template with random hand, or machine operated hammer motions. It was interesting to think someone close to the craft had to design the machine operated hammer for this specific purpose – probably a craftsman who's hands got tired! The impression is now set in one side and the signature hammer marks will stay on the other side. The artist stamps his seal and then the item is forged (put in a log fire) to get smoke marks that bring out the detail of the design. After the item cools, it is cleaned to remove most of the dark smoke color and the metal object is then thinned by hand hammering. For $5.00 you can have a crack at hammering a design into metal. It's well worth the fee to actually try it for yourself and have a personally crafted souvenir. The facility also features a video highlighting the company's history and the showroom has the World's Largest Amish Buggy – over 1200 pounds, and each wheel is over 5 feet tall!

BOYD'S CRYSTAL ART GLASS COMPANY

1203 Morton Avenue (off State Route 209 North)
Cambridge

- Area: **CE**
- Telephone Number: (740) 439-2077
- Tours: Monday – Friday, 7:00 a.m. – 11:00 a.m. and Noon – 3:30 p.m. Tours are 15 minutes long, (September – May)

The Cambridge area became popular for glass manufacturing because of good sand and abundant wells of natural gas. Boyd's specialty is antique glass reproductions and collectibles. Typical shapes made are trains, airplanes, cars, small animals and Teddy the Tugboat. Watch molten glass being poured into one of 300 molds and put in a furnace. When they cool, they are hand-painted.

HOOVER HISTORICAL CENTER
2225 Easton Street, (I-77 Portage Street/North Canton Exit), **Canton**

- Area: **CE**
- Telephone Number: (330) 499-0287
- Hours: Tuesday – Sunday, 1:00 -5:00 p.m.
- Admission: FREE
- Miscellaneous: Only known vacuum cleaner museum in the world.

See the Hoover Industry beginnings as a leather tannery. When automobiles came on the scene, W. H. Hoover searched for a new product. He bought the rights to inventor Murray Spangler's upright vacuum player and introduced it in 1908 - The Hoover Suction Sweeper Model O (On display). A short video details the history of the company. Guided tours of the farmhouse with a display of antique vacuums. A favorite is the Kotten Suction Cleaner (1910) that requires a person to rock bellows with feet to create suction. An early 1900's electric vacuum weighed 100 pounds (and they advertised it as a portable!).

WARTHER CARVINGS TOUR
331 Karl Avenue (I-77 to exit 83 to State Route 211), **Dover**

- Area: **CE**
- Telephone Number: (330) 343-7513
- Hours: Daily, 9:00 a.m. – 5:00 p.m. (March – November) Daily, 10:00 a.m. – 4:00 p.m. (December – March)
- Miscellaneous: Tree of Pliers – 500 interconnecting pairs of working pliers carved out of 1 piece of walnut wood! Mrs. Warther's Button Collection – Over 70,000 in museum! Gift Shop.

A must see tour of the visions of a master craftsman! Mr. Warther started carving at age 5 with a pocketknife while milking cows and during breaks working at a mill. A favorite carving of ours was the steel mill (3 x 5 feet) with moving parts depicting the foreman raising a sandwich to eat, and another worker sleeping on the job. The Abraham Lincoln Funeral Train has thousands of mechanized movements powered by a sewing machine motor. See models of steam locomotives and trains using mostly walnut, ivory, and arguto (oily wood) for moving parts which still run without repairs for over 60 years! He was dissatisfied with the knives that were available, so he developed his own line of cutlery, which is still sold today. The late Mr. Warther loved entertaining children with his carvings (we actually met him in the 1970's) and he would carve a pair of working pliers with just a few cuts in a piece of wood in only a few seconds!

YODER'S AMISH HOME

6050 State Route 515 (between Trail and Walnut Creek), **Millersburg**

- Area: **CE**
- Telephone Number: (330) 893-2541
- Hours: Monday – Saturday, 10:00 a.m. – 5:00 p.m. (April – October – Including Holidays)
- Admission: Tours $3.50 Adult, $1.50 Children (under 12) Buggy Rides $2.00 Adult, $1.00 Children (under 12)

One home was built in 1866 and shows authentic furnishings from that period. Learn what a "hoodle stup" is. Then step into an 1885 barn with animals to pet. Most popular tends to be the turkeys – (Yes, you can try to pet turkeys!). Buggy rides are given by retired real Amish farmers who are personable and tell stories during the ride.

CREEGAN COMPANY ANIMATION FACTORY
510 Washington Street. (I-70 to State Route 7 North)
Steubenville

- Area: **CE**
- Telephone Number: (740) 283-3708
  Tours: Reservations Preferred. (45 minute tour)
  Monday – Friday, 10:00 a.m. - 4:00 p.m.
  Saturday, 10:00 a.m. - 2:00 p.m.
- Miscellaneous: Christmas Shop (year round). Retail store sells Creegan's most recent animated figures and scenery. Fancy Food Department (Cake and candy – Free Samples)

Start with the Craft Area where ribbon, yarn, and puppet props abound. Then, to the Art Department where workers paint faces on molded plastic heads and make costumes. (To make the plastic heads they use a machine press that uses molds to form faces out of sheets of plain white plastic.) In the sculpting area, shelves of hundreds of character head, feet, and hand molds line the walls and a woman sculpts new molds. Finally, peek inside some of the bodies of automated figures to view the electronics that produce body movements. A costumed mascot (Beary Bear) greets and guides your tour. Their theme is "We Make Things Move" and they're the nation's largest manufacturer of animated and costumed characters. (Some customers are Sea World and Walt Disney)

THE BUGGY HAUS
County Road 160 off Route 62, **Winesburg**

- Area: **CE**
- Telephone Number: None (Amish)
- Hours: Monday – Saturday, 8:00 a.m. – 5:00 p.m.

See the world's largest buggy or take a one hour guided tour of a working Amish buggy shop and three floors of warehouse and displays. You'll see over 500 units of buggies, carts, sleighs, and wooden riding horses for sale. Climb aboard them to test them out. Their tour includes the history and cultural differences of buggies around the country.

OHIO AGRICULTURAL RESEARCH AND DEVELOPMENT CENTER
1680 Madison Avenue (State Route 83 and US 250), **Wooster**

- Area: **CE**
- Telephone Number: (330) 263-3700
- Hours: Monday – Friday, 7:30 a.m. - 4:30 p.m. (Summer) Monday – Friday, 8:00 a.m. - 5:00 p.m. (September – June)
- Tours: Guided tours by appointment. Self guided maps at visitor center.

This center is the foremost, nationally known agricultural research Ohio State University facility with inventions to their credit such as crop dusting and adding vitamin D to milk. See the famous cow with the window in it's stomach (actually neuroscopic implant line that allows researchers to study nutrition and digestions) or the electronic sensor detectors that record milk production. Many experiments on insects, greenhouses, honeybees and composting are going on. One project is to turn cornstarch (89 cents/lb.) into xanthum gum ($7. 00/lb). This might spark the future scientist within your child.

AREA "CW"

THE POPCORN GALLERY
927 North Cable Road, Suite H-1, **Lima**

- Area: **CW**
- Telephone Number: (419) 227-2676
- Tours: Monday – Friday, Mornings.
  Reservations Required
  45 minute tour and store browsing
- Admission: FREE

See how 40 flavors of popcorn are made. Begin with an explanation of why corn pops. Then see industrial poppers spill out oodles of popped corn that is then flavored using a slurry that is cooked onto corn. The American Indians had over 700 varieties of popcorn and brought some to the first Thanksgiving.

UNITED STATES PLASTIC CORPORATION
1390 Neubrecht Road (off I-75, exit 127 to State Route 81), **Lima**

- Area: **CW**
- Telephone Number: (419) 228-2711
- Monday – Friday, 8:00 a.m. – 5:00 p.m.
  Minimum 10 persons for viewing film of owner's personal inspirational story
- Miscellaneous: Factory outlet with 18,000 square feet of plastics displayed

This factory makes large industrial plastics for commercial applications. Their first product (1950) was a bucket. Now they have the largest assortment of plastics (13,000 items) in the world!

GENERAL MOTORS CORPORATION ASSEMBLY PLANT

2601 Stroop Road. I-7 south to Springboro Pike South, **Moraine**

- Area: **CW**
- Telephone Number: (937) 455 - 2776
- Tours: Thursdays, 9:30 a.m. and 1:00 p.m.
  Reservations Required
  1 1/2 hour long. Lots of walking. Wear closed-toe shoes.
  Ages 8 and above

This plant makes GMC Blazers, Chevy Jimmys and Oldsmobile Bravadas. Watch how they take 1500 - 1800 parts and 2 ½ days to make the finished vehicle roll off the assembly line. Lots of larger parts float above you on conveyors. The highlight is the "body drop" where painted frames meet their chassis by robots. Any child into trucks will enjoy this visit!

THE TIN MAN

537 North Elm Street (State Route 25 North off State Route 41), **Troy**

- Area: **CW**
- Telephone Number: (513) 339-2315
- Tours: Monday - Saturday, 9:00 a.m. - 5:00 p.m.
  Some evenings by appointment

Jim Hastings is the "Tin Man" and he makes lamps and wall decor in Colonial fashion out of brass, copper and tin. Watch him in the workshop form (with only hand tools) each piece so no two are alike (each piece has its own personality). During the tour, you can choose (from the wall of templates) a design and actually make some simple objects learning fundamental techniques. On your way out, search for the life-size TINMAN (*like the one from* the *Wizard of Oz*) in the retail store. This is one of our favorite tours.

MAC-O-CHEE AND MAC-O-CHEEK CASTLES (PIATT CASTLES)
2 miles East of **West Liberty** (Route 33 West to State Route 245 East)

- Area: **CW**
- Telephone Number: (937) 465-2821
- Each Castle: Daily, Noon – 4 p.m. (April – October), 11:00 a.m. – 5:00 p.m. (Summer)
- Admission: $6.00 Adult
  $5.00 Senior (60+) and Students (13-21)
  $3.00 Children (5-12), Under 5 Free

Castles in Ohio? Catch the eerie, yet magnificent old castles furnished with collections ranging from 150-800 years old. Both castles were built in the mid-1800's and give a good sense of what the lifestyle of the upper-class Piatt brothers family was like. This tour is very manageable for children and includes lots of land to explore outside. Telling friends they were in a real castle is fun too. Because the furniture is original, the homes have an old smell and the rooms look frozen in time. Ceiling paintings and the kitchen/dining area were most interesting.

AREA "NC"

DIXON TICONDEROGA CRAYON FACTORY
1706 Hayes Avenue, **Sandusky**

- Area: **NC**

- Telephone Number: (419) 625-9545
- Tours: 10:00 a.m., Tuesday, Wednesday, Thursday (September – June)
  Tours booked a couple of years in advance.
  Minimum 8 people/maximum 30 people
  Reservations Required-1 hour tour
- Admission: FREE
- Miscellaneous: Part of American Crayon Company.

What fun! See how crayons are mixed (colors), poured in molds, cooled, labeled and then boxed. This is a very popular factory tour with free samples at the end of your tour.

BALLREICH'S POTATO CHIPS

186 Ohio Avenue, (East on Market then left on Dwight St, then right on Ohio), **Tiffin**

- Area: **NC**
- Telephone Number: (419) 447 – 1814
- Tours: Monday, Tuesday, Thursday, Friday, 8:00 – 9:30 a.m. (every ½ hour).
  By Appointment (May – December)
  30 minute tour (try one fresh off the production line)

Started by Fred and Ethel Ballreich in the 1920's when they peeled fried chips by hand and then packaged them in brown paper sacks that were stapled shut. Today it takes only 18 minutes from raw potato to bagged chips! They produce 2000 lbs. of potato chips a day (takes 8000 lbs. of potatoes) or 40 millions lbs. per year with 100% soybean shortening.

TRIVIA ABOUT POTATOES - Which chips are naturally sweet? – The burnt ones because they release sugar. How were potato chips invented? – In New York as a joke!

AREA "NE"

GOODYEAR WORLD OF RUBBER
1201 East Market Street, (Downtown, Goodyear Hall, 4th floor of headquarters), **Akron**

- Area: **NE**
- Telephone Number: (330) 796-7117
- Hours: Monday – Friday, 8:30 a.m. – 4:30 p.m.
  Admission: FREE
- Tour: Introductory film (by request) of tire production. 1 hour. Guided Tours by reservation only (minimum 20 people)
- Miscellaneous: Gift Center

Discover how Charles Goodyear vulcanized rubber in his kitchen in a replica of his workshop. Other attractions include a simulated rubber plantation (hands on), Indy race cars, an artificial heart, a moon buggy, history of blimps, history of the trucking industry, and of course an array of Goodyear products. Everyone leaves knowing about at least one unusual new product made from rubber to tell his or her friends about.

CARNATION BASKET COMPANY
104-112 Prospect Street (US 62 to State Street to Park Street-north) **Alliance**

- Area: **NE**
- Telephone Number: (330) 823-7231
- Hours: Weekdays, 9:00 a.m. – 3:00 p.m.
- Tours: Reservations Suggested
  30 minutes (includes Factory Outlet Store)
- Admission: FREE

❏ Miscellaneous: Factory Outlet Store (Weekdays, 9:00 a.m. – 4:30 p.m.) Saturday 10:00 a.m. – 2 p.m. Private Label basket for clubs, church or organization available with pre-order. Lasting souvenir that you can use.

See a handmade basket made from start to finish. Includes watching the maple wood clipped and cut to form veneers in different widths and lengths. Watch weavers begin at the bottom of a basket (over a form) and buildup sides. Seamstresses make cloth liners and basket shirts in the sewing department. These finish off the baskets and give them decorating appeal.

GLAMORGAN CASTLE
200 Glamorgan Street, Alliance

❏ Area: **NE**
❏ Telephone Number: (330) 821-2100
❏ Tours: By Appointment

Home of the City School Districts Administration office and once the early 1900's home of the late Col. William Henry Morgan (inventory/businessman). The building measures 185 feet high and truly looks like a giant castle.

AREA "NW"

MURPHY'S LIGHTHOUSES, INC.
Erie Street Market, Toledo

❏ Area: **NW**
❏ Telephone Number: (419) 244-6444
❏ Tours: Daily, 8:00 a.m. - 5:00 p.m.

- Miscellaneous: Retail store selling lighthouses and nautical novelties

Tour the workshop where pieces of wood are turned into lighthouses shapes. Also, see a museum of collected lighthouses.

U.S. GLASS SPECIALTY OUTLET
1367 Miami Street (I-75 exit 199), **Toledo**

- Area: **NW**
- Telephone Number: (419) 698-8046
- Hours: Retail - Monday – Friday, 9:00 a.m. – 5:30 p.m. Saturday – Sunday, 11:00 a.m. – 4:00 p.m.
  Viewing – Tuesday – Sunday, 11:00 a.m. – 4:00 p.m.
  Watch glass blowers at work
- Miscellaneous: Gift Shop sells decorated glass and ceramics

AREA "SC"

MITCHELLACE SHOESTRING FACTORY
830 Murray Street (Corner of Gallia Street off US 52), **Portsmouth**

- Area: **SC**
- Telephone Number: (740) 354-2813
- Tours: Groups of 10 (no more than 50)
  One hour tour
  Age 8 and up
- Miscellaneous: Company store (laces for 25 cents) at the end of tour

The former shoe factory works 2-3 shifts per day to make more than 4,000,000 pairs of shoelaces per week. They are the world's biggest shoelace manufacturers for shoes and skates (especially RollerBlades). Family descendants still run the company started in 1902. Start the tour by watching weaving and braiding machines (over 1300) producing strands of fabric. This process takes up an entire floor and when you step onto the floor, all you see are flashes of color. The tipping department takes long strands and cuts them into different lengths and then they are tipped with aglets of nylon or metal. Automatic machines band, fold, label and seal. Other laces are blister packed (plastic pouch over laces is melted onto backing card). The shortest lace is 10 inches. The longest made is 120 inches (for ice skates).

AREA "SE"

LEE MIDDLETON ORIGINAL DOLL FACTORY

1301 Washington Boulevard (State Route 618 West), **Belpre**

- ❑ Area: **SE**
- ❑ Telephone Number: (740) 423-1717 or (800) 233-7479
- ❑ Tours: Monday – Friday, 9:00 a.m. – 2:00 p.m. (Hourly) March – December.
  Approximately 20 minutes.
  Reservations Suggested. FREE
- ❑ Miscellaneous: Factory Store with bargain buys and Nursery where you can adopt a life-sized Middleton infant baby doll complete with papers, promises and pictures.

Hopefully during your visit you'll get to experience a little girl adopting her first Middleton baby. It's so real, you'll swell with emotion as you see the new "Mom" promise the nursery worker to care for her baby properly. Lee Middleton started making dolls at her kitchen table in 1978 and modeled them after her children and children she knew. On tour a guide (dressed like a Middleton doll) shows you techniques critical to the distinctiveness of these expensive collectable dolls that look and feel almost real. One machine makes feet, hands and heads out of liquid vinyl cured in molds. Watch them put eyes in by blowing up the mold head like a balloon (with an air compressor) and popping in the eyes. Then they release the air and the eye is set in place. See the artists hand paint each doll's face using stencils and paint makeup. What a fun "girl's place" to visit. Prepare to fall in love with a doll and want one for your own!

ROSSI PASTA
114 Greene Street, Downtown **Marietta**

- Area: **SE**
- Telephone Number: (740) 376-2065
- Hours: Monday - Saturday, 9:00 a.m. - 7:00 p.m.
  Sunday, Noon - 5:00 p.m.
  Pasta making times vary, best weekdays before 3:00 p.m.
- Miscellaneous: Upscale gourmet pasta with unusual twists of flavors like Artichoke, Wild Mushroom, Calamari, Linguini. Free sample bag of pasta to first time visitors.

They hand roll dough adding fresh flavor ingredients as they "turn" the dough. Their secret is using spring wheat flour instead of highly manufactured semoline flour. A machine cuts the pasta into very long and wide strips (linguini) or thin soup noodles. Teardrop shapes are stamped out. Next, the cut pasta go into one of two large drying chambers which are precisely regulated to insure even temperatures. Finally, the pasta is packaged in clear Rossi-labeled bags. Be sure you invite your favorite gourmet cook along for this tour - it's a new level of pasta to experience!

AREA "SW"

FRISCH'S COMMISSARY
3011 Stanton Avenue. (I-71 to Taft Road West Exit)
Cincinnati

- Area: **SW**
- Telephone Number: (513) 559-5288
- Tours: Wednesday and Thursday, 9:00 a.m.
  Ages 8 and above
  Maximum 15 people
  One hour. Reservations required

This commissary supplies 85 Big Boy Restaurants in Ohio, Indiana, and Kentucky (and they're still family owned). They prepare cooked soups, salad dressings, raw meats, vegetables, and baked goods. Children will marvel at large-scale production, especially when the tour guide describes the quantities of ingredients used for each product. For example, two men peel 600 pounds of carrots by hand each day. The bakery ovens can hold 24 pies at one time. They save the restaurants time by pre-slicing or shredding vegetables and bagging them. We understand they use an air compressor to blow the skins off onions.

UNITED DAIRY FARMERS
3955 Montgomery Road, **Cincinnati**

- Area: **SW**
- Telephone Number: (513) 396-8700 - Ask for Consumer Relations
- Tours: Mondays and Fridays, 9:30 a.m.
  1 ½ hours, Ages 6 and up
  Maximum 25 persons
- Admission: FREE

See milk being filled in containers (and the large vats where they store raw and treated milk). The plastic bottles are also made on the premises from blown pellets of plastics. Best of all, watch ice cream packed and get a free ice cream cone as a souvenir.

CHATEAU LaROCHE "*Loveland Castle*"
12025 Shore Drive, (2 miles South of Kings Island),
Loveland

- Area: **SW**
- Telephone Number: (513) 683-4686
- Hours: Daily, 11:00 a.m. – 5:00 p.m. (April – September) Weekends, 11:00 a.m. – 5:00 p.m. (October – March)
- Admission: $1.00 per person. Self-guided tour.
- Miscellaneous: Only medieval castle in the US. Took 50-years to build using limestone from the river and "milk carton" hand-made bricks.

This is a real hidden castle! Chateau LaRoche was the vision of Harry D. Andrews and construction spanned some 50 years beginning in 1929. He actually did 99% of the work himself! The castle is authentic in its rugged structure with battlement towers, a princess chamber, a dungeon, narrow passageways, tower staircases, a "kings" dining room, and tower bedrooms. Over 32,000 hand-made (cast in milk cartons donated by neighbors) bricks were used to build the structure. Learn a lot about castle building and why the front door has over 2500 nails in it. Don't miss this real adventure that your children and you will love!

ELECTRIC COMPANY

1781 US 52. Cincinnati Gas and Electric Zimmer Station, **Moscow**

- Area: **SW**
- Telephone Number: (513) 287-2767
- Tours: 60-90 minutes
  Long pants and ear plugs required
  Children over 12
  Starts with 10-minute video

Coal arrives by river barge from the Ohio River. When the coal is fired to 2500 degrees F, it heats water, which produces steam that propels turbines (high insulated cylinders), that drive generators, that make electricity. The control room has dials, monitors, colored lights, pressure and temperature gauges, and graphing equipment on all four walls. Two operators watch and problem solve - always ready to jump into action (like firemen)!

MISCELLANEOUS BUSINESSES

Listed alphabetically by business type (and area/city within type)

AIRPORTS

PORT COLUMBUS INTERNATIONAL AIRPORT

C - 4600 East 17th Avenue (or International Gateway), **Columbus.** (614) 239-4038 (Airport Ambassadors). Tours: Monday – Friday, Late Morning, 1 hour, School age (K-up). Appointment necessary. FREE admission.

DAYTON INTERNATIONAL AIRPORT

CW - (937) 454-8225. **Dayton.**

TOURS

CLEVELAND-HOPKINS INTERNATIONAL AIRPORT

NE - (216) 265-6030. **Cleveland.**

BURKE LAKEFRONT AIRPORT

NE - (216) 781-6411. **Cleveland.**

CINCINNATI / NORTHERN KENTUCKY INTERNATIONAL AIRPORT

SW – (606) 767-3144. Can add a tour of the National Weather Service for 6th grade and up. (*actually in northern Kentucky*)

BLUE ASH AIRPORT

SW - 4273 Glendale Milford Airport, **Cincinnati.** (513) 791-8500.

All children love to visit the airport! Why not take a tour and understand all the jobs it takes to run an airport. The group will tour the terminal, baggage claims, ticket and gate areas and the security office (where there is even a small jail). Your guide also explains how foreign currency is exchanged and describes different types of airplanes used by certain airlines. If you are lucky, you may get a chance to board an airplane.

BANKS

Any local bank office

- ❑ Tours: Call to arrange
- ❑ Admission: Free

Take a "behind the scenes" look at automated teller machines, bank vaults, safe deposit boxes and the drive-through window chutes. You may want to take this tour and then open a savings account for your child.

CANDY FACTORIES

ANTHONY THOMAS CANDY COMPANY

1777 Arlingate Lane, (I-270W to Roberts Road Exit), **Columbus**

- Area: **C**
- Telephone Number: (614) 272-9221
- Hours: Weekdays, 9:00 a.m. – 3:00 p.m.
- Tours: Reservations Required
  Minimum 10 people, 30 minutes
  Free sample at end of tour
  Factory Candy Shop
- Admission: FREE

Have you seen "Willy Wonka's Chocolate Factory?" This tour will remind you of that movie, especially when you first see the clean bright white equipment, near spotless flours and dozens of silver insulated pipes running to several production lines. Walk along a glass enclosed mezzanine as you view chocolate and fillings being prepared and molded in rooms remaining at a constant 90 degrees F. with 0% humidity (so workers and chocolate don't sweat!) A couple of wrapping machines are exclusively for fundraisers and airline chocolates, but most of the production line packers can be seen hand packing chocolates for stores. All employees are taste testers – they can pop a morsel anytime to be sure it meets high standards – What a job!

SAVANNAH SWEETS CHOCOLATE FACTORY

West Main Street, **Berlin**

- Area: **CE**
- Telephone Number: (330) 893-3737
- Tours: Monday – Friday, 10:00 a.m. – 5:00 p.m.
  Saturday, 10:00 a.m. – 6:00 p.m.

Watch chocolate being made. One of the largest selections of homemade and hand dipped chocolates, especially truffles, bon-bons and molded chocolates.

HARRY LONDON CHOCOLATE FACTORY

5353 Lauby Road, (I-77 Exit 113 Airport), **North Canton**

- Area: **CE**
- Telephone Number: (800) 321-0444
- Hours: Monday – Saturday, 9:00 a.m. – 4:00 p.m.
  Sunday, NOON – 3:30 p.m.
  (Actual production only on weekdays)
- Tour: 45 minutes – 1 hour
  Reservations suggested (if group tour)
  Every half hour
- Admission: $2.00 Adult and Senior
  $1.00 Youth (6-18)
- Miscellaneous: Chocolate Hall of Fame, Candy Store

Learn about cocoa beans and the history of chocolate (we didn't know the beans grow in pods on trunks of trees near the equator). Live the fantasy of making, molding, wrapping, and boxing chocolate candy, fudge, and butterscotch. Be sure to try a London Mint (money wrapped candy) or a London Buckeye.

COBLENTZ CHOCOLATE COMPANY

4917 State Route 515 and State Route 39, **Walnut Creek**

- Area: **CE**
- Telephone Number: (800) 338-9341
- Monday – Saturday, 9:00 a.m. – 6:00 p.m. (June – October)
  9:00 a.m. – 5:00 p.m. (November – May)

Watch though the kitchen windows as chocolate is stirred in large vats with automatic paddle stirs. Caramels, fruits, and nuts are hand dipped and layered on large trays to cool and dry. Also, see molds for chocolate forms used to create bars of barks and holiday shapes. Savor the sweet smell of fresh milk and dark chocolate as you decide which treats to buy. Our favorite was the chocolate covered Dutch pretzels with sprinkles or nuts on top.

MALLEY'S CHOCOLATES

13400 Brookpark Road. (I-480 and West 130th street) **Cleveland**

- Area: **NE**
- Telephone Number: (800) 835-5684
- Tours: Monday-Friday, 9:00 a.m. –3:00 p.m. (By Appointment)
  Strollers allowed, No cameras
  30-45 minute tour, 15-45 person limits
- Admission: $2.00 Adult, $1.00 children (4-11)

See and hear about the story of chocolate from a professional at Malley's family business (since 1935). We learned it takes 400 cocoa beans to make one pound of chocolate. You'll watch them roast nuts, dip chocolates, and wrap goodies along with samples at the beginning and end of the tour (plus a candy bar to take home). They sell one half million pounds per year with the most sales at Easter, then Christmas, then Valentine's Day. Allow time to shop in their factory store.

OLYMPIA GOURMET CHOCOLATES & CARAMEL CORN

15155 Pearl Road (off I-71 near Cleveland Hopkins Airport), **Strongsville**

- Area: **NE**
- Telephone Number: (800)0574-7747
- Hours: After 3:00 p.m. or Weekends
  October, January, February, early March, late April, early May

- Tours: $100.00 group
  Maximum 16 people
  Minimum age 6 years old
- Miscellaneous: Includes chocolates and caramel corn goodies to take home. Factory Candy Store.

This is truly an "I Love Lucy" –Chocolate Factory Episode, reenacted! During the off hours at a real candy factory, you can arrange to have your group be actual candymakers. An experienced guide will first request you to put on an apron, gloves and hair net. Then you are escorted to the manufacturing line where chocolate is poured and filled under your direction. The most fun has to be waiting at the end of the process as a fast conveyor line speeds by. Your job is to inspect (of course, taste-tasting is allowed) and package boxes of gourmet chocolates! This is the most hands-on tour of any factory you'll ever want to take – YUM!

GORANT CANDIES

8301 Market Street (State Route 7, Boardman) **Youngstown**
- Area: **NE**
- Telephone Number: (800) 572-4139 Ext. 236
- Tours: Weekdays until 1:30 p.m.
  Maximum 50 people
  1st grade and above
- Miscellaneous: Candy store. Displays of chocolate history.

Put on your paper hat and watch up to 375,000 pieces of chocolate candy being made each day. See the 2000-pound chocolate melting vats and color-coded rooms. The brown walls are the molding room where chocolate is poured and shook on vibrating tables (takes out the air bubbles). The yellow room is the coating room. A personalized hand dipper (only one) dips 3600 candies a day. Receive a free candy bar at the end of the tour.

DIETSCH BROTHERS

400 W. Main Cross Street (State Route 12). **Findlay**

- ❏ Area: **NW**
- ❏ Telephone: (419) 422-4474
- ❏ Tours: Tuesday – Sunday (Daytime)
  ½ hour long, 20 people maximum
  Reservations required

Three brothers (2nd generation) run an original 1937's candy and ice cream shop. In the summer, see ice cream made with real cream. They make 1500 gallons per week. Fall, heading into the holidays, is the best time to see 500 pounds of chocolate treats made daily.

CHEESEHOUSES

BROAD RUN CHEESEHOUSE

6011 County Road 139 NW (4 miles west of I-77), **Dover**

- ❏ Area: **CE**
- ❏ Telephone Number: (800) 332-3358
- ❏ Tours: Monday – Saturday (Mornings)
- ❏ Admission: $1.50 per person
- ❏ Miscellaneous: Gift Shop with novelties, cheese and sausage.

Not just a window view but an actual tour of Swiss, Baby Swiss, Brick, and Muenster productions. They make 640,000 pounds of cheese from 8,000,000 pounds (yes, pounds!) of milk each year. After your factory tour you can sample cheese and as a souvenir, get an official cheesemaker paper cap (the one you wore for sanitary reasons during the tour).

MIDDLEFIELD CHEESE HOUSE

State Route 608, **Middlefield**

- Area: **CE**
- Telephone Number: (216) 632-5228
- Hours: Monday – Saturday 7:00 a.m. – 5:30 p.m.
- Admission: Free

Over 20 million pounds of Swiss cheese are produced here each year. Your tours begins with the film "Faith and Teamwork" describing the cheese-making process. Then wander through the Cheese House Museum with Swiss cheese carvings, antique cheese-making equipment, and Amish memorabilia. Lastly, sample some cheese before you buy homemade cheese, sausage and bread.

GUGGISBERG CHEESE FACTORY

5060 State Route 557 (Off State Route 39) **Millersburg**

- Area: **CE**
- Telephone Number: (330) 893-2500
- Hours: Daily, 8:00 a.m. – 6:00 p.m. (Except Sunday, 11:00 a.m. – 4:00 p.m.) (April – November)
  Daily, 8:00 a.m. – 5:00 p.m. (December – March)

Home of the original Baby Swiss – you can watch through a window as cheese is being made (best time to view is 8:00 a.m. – 2:00 p.m. weekdays). We learned milk is brought in the early mornings from neighboring Amish farms. Cultures and enzymes are added to form curd. Curd is pressed into molds and brine salted. Each cheese is aged at least a month for flavor. A short video is always playing that details this process if you can't view it personally.

COLLEGE TOURS

THE OHIO STATE UNIVERSITY MAIN CAMPUS

C - Mershon Auditorium (West 15th and North High St.), **Columbus**. (614) 292-8027. Geological Museum (dinosaur skeletons, meteorites, fossils, rocks) Orton Hall Bell Tower, Ohio Stadium - GO BUCKS!, Sports Center, Main Library, and the Oval (kids run and play). Ohio buckeye (nut) and Ohio State University souvenirs.

UNIVERSITY OF TOLEDO

NW - 2801 West Bancroft Street, **Toledo**. (800) 586-5336. Includes Ritter Planetarium.

OHIO UNIVERSITY

SC - **Athens**. (740) 593-2097. College Green tour starts at Visitor Center. Self-guided tour includes walk to oldest part of Campus buildings. Also tree tour shows 50 of the 115 different species of trees on campus (some are from Japan, China, and Siberia).

MIAMI UNIVERSITY

SW - **Oxford**. (513) 529-1809. Points of interest include formal gardens, Anthropology Museum, Zoology Museum, Geology Museum, Art Museum, Library and Chapel.

FIRE STATIONS

- Tours: Appointment Necessary
  Open Houses - Fire Prevention Week in October
- Admission: FREE

Visit one of the many local fire stations. Choose the one servicing your neighborhood and meet a few of the fire fighters or medics who would help you in an emergency. The department is willing to set up an exciting tour to meet your group's interest. Some groups choose to watch a video and ask questions. Most popular is to talk to fire fighters, see where they "hang out", hop aboard a real fire engine truck and pretend they are real fire fighters by putting on hats and other gear. Learn fire safety.

HOSPITALS

DOCTORS HOSPITAL NORTH

C - 1087 Dennison Avenue, **Columbus**. (614) 297-4196.

GRANT RIVERSIDE / METHODIST

C - 3535 Olentangy River Road (Route 315 to North Broadway Exit), **Columbus**. (614) 461-3325. Appointment necessary for tours. Kindergarten and up. FREE admission. (Monday-Friday).

CLEVELAND CLINIC

NE - **Cleveland**. (216) 444-2200.

UNIVERSITY HOSPITALS

NE - **Cleveland**. (216) -844-1000. Your guide will show you around the Emergency Department. This will include the cast room and X-ray. Choose an area of interest for your children or group.

CHILDREN'S HOSPITAL MEDICAL CENTER

SW - 3333 Burnett Avenue, **Cincinnati**. (513) 559-4200.

HUMANE SOCIETY / ANIMAL SHELTERS

- Columbus: (614) 777-7387
- Richland County: (419) 747-4174
- Cincinnati: (513) 541-6100

This is a great tour for a new pet owner or a child who is anxiously waiting for their first pet. Not only will you see many cats and dogs available for adoption, but a knowledgeable guide also shows you the Humane Society clinic and surgery rooms and explains the needs of your pet and how to be a good pet owner. Be prepared to have the children fall in love with one of the animals while they are there!

MILLS

INDIAN MILL

State Route 23 and State Route 67 to Route 47. **Upper Sandusky**

- Area: **C**
- Telephone Number: (419) 294-3349
- Hours: Friday – Saturday, 9:30 a.m. – 5:00 p.m. Sunday, 1:00 – 6:00 p.m., June – October
- Admission: $1.00 Adult, $.50 Youth (6-12)
- Miscellaneous: Original Ohio Historical Society museum of milling housed in a converted gristmill.

BEAR'S MILL

Bear's Mill Road, Greenville (5 miles East on US 36 then South), **Arcanum**

- Area: **CW**
- Telephone Number: (513) 548-5112
- Tours: Friday and Sunday, 11:00 a.m. – 5:00 p.m. Saturday, 9:00 a.m. – 5:00 p.m.; April – November
- Miscellaneous: Store-sells flours ground at the mill, gift baskets, handmade pottery.

Tour the mill built in 1849 by Gabriel Bear where grinding stones (powered by water flowing beneath the building) grind flour and meal. The process is slow and kept cool to retard deteriorating wholesome nutrients.

CLIFTON MILL

75 Water Street (I-70 West to Route 72 South), **Clifton**

- Area: **CW**
- Telephone Number: (513) 767-5501
- Hours: Monday – Friday, 9:00 a.m. – 5:00 p.m.
  Restaurant, 9:00 a.m. – 3:00 p.m.
  Saturday – Sunday, 8:00 a.m. – 5:00 p.m.
  Restaurant, 8:00 a.m. – 4:00 p.m.
- Miscellaneous: Restaurant (see separate chapter) and store

A surprise treat tucked away in a small town where Woody Hayes grew up. Built in 1869 on the Little Miami River, it is the largest operating water powered gristmill in the nation. Before or after a yummy breakfast or lunch overlooking the river, take a self-guided tour for a small fee. There are 5 floors to view. Start in the basement where the turbine takes the flowing water's energy to move a system of belts to the grindstones. As the stones rotate, raw grain is poured into the hopper, through a chute and into a space between the stones which grind it. The most interesting part of the tour is the belt to bucket elevators that are the "life of the mill" transporting grain and floor up and down 5 levels. Be sure to buy some pancake mix to take home!

GARRETTS MILL

8148 Main Street (Route 82 and Route 88) **Garrettsville**

- Area: **NE**
- Telephone Number: (330) 527-2705
- Hours: Monday – Friday, 11:00 a.m. – 9:00 p.m.
  Weekends, 11:00 a.m. – 10:00 p.m.
- Admission: FREE
- Miscellaneous: Food Service Store

Take a self-guided tour of a working gristmill built in 1804 on the banks of the rushing Silver Creek. The first floor grinds grain to flour with milling stones that are 3000 pounds each. The second floor is where they sift, bag and store flour. A system of flights (cup conveyor mechanism) transports the grain and flour to different floors.

ISAAC LUDWIG MILL

Providence Park (State Route 65 and State Route 578) **Grand Rapids**

- Area: **NW**
- Telephone Number: (419) 535-3050
- Hours: Wednesday – Friday, 10:00 a.m. – 4:00 p.m.
  Saturday – Sunday, 11:00 a.m. – 5:00 p.m.
  May – October
- Admission: FREE demonstrations of mill
  45 minute mule drawn canal boat rides leave every hour until 4:00 p.m. Narrated.
  $4.00 Adult, $3.00 Senior (59+)
  $2.00 Children (3-12)

Another one of the few mills left in Ohio. This 19th century mill sits on the Maumee River and demonstrates how a flour mill, sawmill and electric generator can be powered by water from the old canal below.

NEWSPAPERS

THE COLUMBUS DISPATCH

5300 Crosswind Drive (I-270 to Georgesville Road – West), **Columbus**

- Telephone Number: (614) 461-5577
- Tours: Tuesday, 1 hour
  5th grade and above
  35 people maximum

You'll be amazed at all the new technology in newspaper printing. The monster printers and the robots that run beneath will catch your child's attention. Ask lots of questions in the layout department. See samples of different parts that make up just one page. Maybe try to put together your own sample page. After seeing a newspaper made, most companies give you a free copy (dated that day) as your souvenir. National Newspaper Week is in October.

THE CHILLICOTHE GAZETTE

50 West Main Street, **Chillicothe**

- Area: **SC**
- Telephone Number: (740) 773-2111
- Tours: By Appointment (weekdays)
- Miscellaneous: The oldest newspaper (1800) west of the Alleghenies. Tour includes lobby display of printing through the ages.

THE CINCINNATI ENQUIRER

312 Elm Street, **Cincinnati**

- Area: **SW**
- Telephone Number: (513) 721-2700.
- Tours: NOON (Printing Tour), Tuesday and Thursday (1 hour tour)
  6th grade and above
  20 person limit

CINCINNATI POST

125 East Court, **Cincinnati**

- Area: **SW**
- Telephone Number: (513) 352-2788
- Tours: 45 minutes, 15 person maximum

- ❏ Miscellaneous: Editorial tour, newsroom, sports and feature department, and graphics.

PARENT'S PLACE OF WORK

Invite your child or children to spend some time with you at your work place. Some large companies encourage families to attend an organized Open House held annually. Others welcome employees to bring children occasionally for a short visit. You may be surprised at what will delight and amaze your child (drinking fountain, swivel chair!).

POTTERY TOURS

ALPINE POTTERY

C - State Route 93, **Roseville**. (800) 4-ALPINE. Tours: 9:00 a.m. - 3:00 p.m. (Monday - Friday).

THE ROBINSON RANSBOTTOM POTTERY COMPANY

Ransbottom Road, (State Route22 south to State Route 93 south to County Road 102 east - Follow signs) **Roseville**

- ❏ Area: **C**
- ❏ Telephone Number: (740) 697-7355
- ❏ Tours: Weekdays, 9:00 a.m. - 5:00 p.m. (except for 2 week plant shutdown in the summers and holidays).
  Guided - By Reservation
  Weekends watch the video tour
- ❏ Miscellaneous: Pot Shop Gift Shop with below retail prices

Their clay is a special combination of top and bottom clay (what material lies in the middle but isn't used for pottery?).

They use 27 tons of clay daily using the processes of casting, ram and spindle pressing, and jiggering. During the tour, you come very near the process, including hot kilns and large press machines. Stay in groups and hold onto small children. Talking with mold castors and watching clay being molded was most interesting. Also very interesting were the beehive kilns (look like brick igloos). Once the items were loaded, the man sealed the doorway with bricks. The pieces are left to heat dry for three days and then four days cooling. This kiln is used for large outdoor pieces (birdbaths, flower pots) that need slow hardening for durability against elements.

THREE RIVERS POTTERY

CE - 235 Main Street, **Coshocton**. (740) 622-6767. Tours by appointment. Hand thrown pots.

HALL CHINA COMPANY

CE - Anna Street, **East Liverpool**. (330) 385-2900. Tours: 9:00 - 11:00 a.m. and 1 - 1:30 p.m. (Monday - Friday).

PIONEER POTTERY

CE - 761 Dresden Avenue, **East Liverpool**. (330) 385-4293. Tours by appointment.

RESTAURANT TOURS

DOMINO'S PIZZA

Various locations
- Telephone your local shop for tour status
- Tours: Saturday morning
  Age 4 and up
  15-20 minute tour per small group
- Admission: FREE

Your children can be pizza bakers! While the group is instructed on ingredients and pizza secrets, they will get to make their own special pizzas. After the custom made pizza bakes, your tour guide will take it out of the special pizza oven, box it up and you get to take it home!

MCDONALD'S RESTAURANTS

Participating locations

- ❑ Tours: Appointment Necessary
  Large groups are divided into groups of 6 or 7
  Prefer Monday or Tuesday
- ❑ Admission: FREE

What child doesn't love McDonald's food? This is your child's chance to go behind the counter and look at all the machines that make all the fun food. You will be shown the freezer and it's alarm, the fryer, beverage machines and hamburger flipping on the grills. There is a free snack at the end of the tour and the children are allowed to make their own beverage.

PIZZA HUT

Many participating restaurants

- ❑ Telephone Number: Any Store Manager
- ❑ Tours: Monday, Tuesday, Wednesday
  2:30 p.m. to 5:00 p.m.
  Minimum 10 people
- ❑ Admission:$3.50 per person

All children love pizza - especially when they can create their own! As the children tour the kitchen, they learn how to make a pizza, bake it, and then eat it. The admission charge includes lots of pizza "creations", beverage and coloring book with stickers.

SUPERMARKETS
Any local store

- Tours: Appointment Necessary
  Tuesday or Wednesday is usually best
  45 minutes to 1 hour
  Maximum 25 people
  No age restriction
- Admission: Free

Kids are fascinated to go behind the scenes of the same store where Mom or Dad shops. During a tour, you will usually grind meat, walk into large freezer rooms, watch cakes and breads bake and receive free samples along the way. The children on our tour even got to pet a live lobster! The tour ends with a surprise snack for each child.

TV / RADIO STATIONS

WBNS RADIO

62 East Broad Street, **Columbus**

- Area: **C**
- Telephone Number: (614) 460-3850
- Tour: By Appointment, 9:00 a.m. - 5:00 p.m.
  15 minute tour, Max 12 persons
  Suggest 12 years old and up
- Admission: FREE

Visit an AM/FM broadcasting station. During this brief tour, you'll see the station's offices first and then go to the studio which is totally computerized (kids love the wall of lights and buttons). Finally, you will be able to watch a DJ in action.

WOSU RADIO AND TV

2400 Olentangy River Road (near Ohio State University, State Route 315 North to Lane Avenue exit), **Columbus**

- ❏ Area: **C**
- ❏ Telephone Number: (614) 292-9678, Ask for Tour Coordinator
- ❏ Tours: Ages 10 and up
  1-25 people
  Day and Evening tours
- ❏ Admission: FREE

Start your tour with a look at the radio station and newsroom. Then venture into the world of TV and see the rooms where local public television is broadcast.

WTTE – CHANNEL 28

6130 Sunbury Road (I-270 north to State Route 161 / New Albany exit), **Columbus**

- ❏ Area: **C**
- ❏ Telephone Number: (614) 895-2800
- ❏ Tours: Groups up to 20 persons
  30 minutes, Monday afternoons, 4:00 and 4:30 p.m.
  Ages: Newborn to age 16
- ❏ Miscellaneous: The highlight of this tour is to see the set for the Kids Club. Kids get prizes. Kids Club room.

WCVO RADIO

4400 Reynoldsburg-New Albany Road (State Route 161 East to Reynoldsburg-New Albany Road exit – South), **New Albany**

- ❏ Area: **C**
- ❏ Telephone Number: (614) 855-9171 (ask for Tour Coordinator)
- ❏ Tours: Appointment Necessary

No minimum number of persons
Day or evening

Visit the control room, watch the interviews while on the air, visit their Prayer Room outlined in stained glass windows depicting the Lord's Supper. And be sure to see the 50 pictures by a well know artist of scenes from the Bible, both old and new testaments.

WCPO – TV (ABC Channel 9)

SW - 500 Central Avenue, **Cincinnati.** (513) 721-9900. Tours: Ages 5 and up, 45 minutes, Maximum 10 persons. (Wednesday)

WKRC – TV (CBS Channel 12)

SW - 1906 Highland Avenue, **Cincinnati.** (513) 763-5500. Tours: Ages 5-12, 1 hour. Weekdays by appointment.

WLW-AM 700 (Radio)

SW - 1111 St. Gregory, **Cincinnati.** (513) 241-9597. Tours: Call for details. Listen and watch "Sports or Consequences" aired. 30 minutes.

WSTR – TV 64

SW - 5177 Fishwick Drive, **Cincinnati.** (513) 641-4400. Tours: Ages 5-18, 15 person maximum, 1 hour. Make your own commercial!

If you have a favorite TV or Radio Station in your area, call them and ask for details on tours they may offer.

WATER TREATMENT PLANTS

COLUMBUS

910 Dublin Road (State Route 315 to Dublin Road exit – West)
- ❏ Area: **C**

- ❏ Telephone Number: (614) 645-6186
- ❏ Tours: Tuesday and Wednesday mornings
    2nd grade and up
    30 person maximum

A giant science experiment! You will watch the seven stages of water treatment from settling, flocculation, softening, filtration, chlorine, fluoride and finally corrosion inhibitor. The favorite is usually the huge wall of bright buttons flashing that monitor the different processes.

CLEVELAND

- Call for location offering tours
- ❏ Area: NE
- ❏ Telephone Number: (216) 664-2444 ext. 5663
- ❏ Tours: Year round
    Open House during National Drinking Water Week (early May) or by appointment
    1 hour, ages 6 and up
    Video and tour
- ❏ Admission: FREE

CINCINNATI WATER WORKS

5651 Kellogg Avenue, Cincinnati

- ❏ Area: SW
- ❏ Telephone Number: (513) 591-7700
- ❏ Tours: Monday – Friday, 1 ½ hours
    3rd grade and up (5-30 persons)
- ❏ Miscellaneous: Slide show and museum. Settling ponds and filter galleries.

U.S. MAIN POST OFFICES TOURS

COLUMBUS MAIN POST OFFICE
850 Twin Rivers Drive (State Route 315 and Dublin Road)
- Area: C
- Telephone Number: (614) 469-4521
- Tours: Weekday mornings
  Group size 10-50
  Ages 6 and up
  By appointment only

Did you know you can ship live baby chicks through the mail? Did you know Ben Franklin was the first Postmaster General (over 200 years ago)? Most interesting is the high-speed automated mail processing equipment. Learn how to address envelopes so they will be sent quicker (there are secrets). Be sure you look for the mail receiving area where bundles come in and slide down giant mail slides. To make your tour more interesting, have your children write a letter to themselves and address it with special colorful markers. Mail it early that day before the tour starts. They will stay interested trying to locate their letter in all the high-speed machinery. Comfortable shoes are a must.

CLEVELAND MAIN POST OFFICE

NE – Downtown, 2400 Orange Avenue. (216) 443-4241. Tours: Year round, Monday – Thursday preferred. Ages 12 and up. Reservations required.

CINCINNATI MAIN POST OFFICE

SW – 900 Dalton Avenue. (513) 723-9900. Tours: Call for details, after 3:00 p.m.

Chapter 12

TRANSPORTATION ADVENTURES

CANAL BOAT CRUISES

ST HELENA III

103 Tuscarawas Village Park, (I-77 to Exit 111 Portage Street West, follow signs), **Canal Fulton**

- Area: **NE**
- Telephone Number: (800) HELENA-3
- Hours: Daily, 1:00 – 3:00 p.m. (Summer)
  Weekends, 1:00 – 3:00 p.m. (May, September, October)
- Admission: $5.00 Adult, $4.00 Senior
  $3.00 Children (3-11)

A one-hour horse drawn canal boat freighter ride with a narrative history of the canal system and the local area. Appearing as it did in the 1800's, the view also includes Lock IV, one of the few remaining working locks on old canal routes. Included in the tour is a Canal Museum with pictorial stories of colorful local history and canal memorabilia including tools used to build and repair canal boats.

SANDPIPER CANAL BOAT

Toledo Riverfront

- Area: **NW**
- Telephone Number: (419) 537-1212
- Hours: Hourly, Wednesday – Sunday, 10:00 a.m. – 4:00 p.m. (May – October)
- Admission: $4.00 Adult, $3.00 Senior
  $2.00 Children (12 and under)

Replica of a Miami and Erie Canal boat. Cruise up river past riverside estates or down river to Lake Erie.

LAKE ERIE ISLAND BOAT TOURS

EMERALD EXPRESS
Sandusky

- Area: **NC**
- Telephone Number: (800) 876-1907 or (419) 626-5557
- Admission: $5.25 - $29.95

Lazy Day Cruise – Put-In-Bay and Kelley's Island with breakfast and lunch en route.

Lunch Break Cruise and Dinner Cruise – 1 ½ hour sightseeing cruise around islands with buffet.

Lake Break Cruise – sightseeing

GOODTIME I
Sandusky (docked at Jackson Street Pier)

- Area: **NC**
- Telephone Number: (800) 446-3140
- Hours: Daily, 9:30 a.m. – 6:30 p.m. (Memorial Day – Labor Day)
- Admission: $10.00 - $20.00 (ages 4 and up)

Island hopping 40-meter sight seeing cruise to Kelley's Island and Put-In-Bay.

M/V "CITY OF SANDUSKY"
Columbus Avenue (downtown **Sandusky**)

- Area: **NC**
- Telephone Number: (800) 426-6286
- Hours: Departs at 9:30 a.m.

Full day sightseeing "Island Hopping Cruise" to Islands.

RIVERBOAT CRUISES

LORENA STERNWHEELER

Moored at Zanis Landing. (West End of Market Street – I-70 to Downtown Zanesville Exit – Follow signs), **Zanesville**

- Area: **C**
- Telephone Number: (800) 246-6303 or (740) 455-8883
- Hours: Wednesday – Sunday at 1:00, 2:30, and 4:00 p.m. (Noon on Wednesday) – (June – August) Weekends Only (September)
- Admission: $3.50 Adult, $1.50 Children (2-12) $6.50 Carnival Cruise (one Saturday each month, includes entertainment, pizza and pop)

There was a mythical sweetheart of the Civil War named Lorena who inspired a song written by the famous Zanesvillian, Rev. Henry Webster. The 104' long, 59-ton boat was christened "Lorena" after that popular song. A one-hour cruise on the Muskingum River at a very reasonable rate.

GOOD TIME III

825 East 9th Street Pier (Behind Rock & Roll Hall of Fame), **Cleveland**

- Area: **NE**
- Telephone Number: (216) 861-5110
- Hours: Daily, Noon, 3:00 p.m., Sundays at 6:00 p.m.
- Admission: $10.00 Adult, $9.50 Senior $6.00 Children (2+)
- Miscellaneous: Food Service Available. Lower deck is air-conditioned and heated.

The triple deck, 1000 passenger boat takes a two hour excursion of city sights along the Cuyahoga River and Lake Erie. The word *Cuyahoga* is Indian for "crooked". You'll see tugboats and the largest yellow crane boats in the country. See all the industry in the Flats including concrete, pipe, transportation, limestone, and coke businesses. Collision Bend used to be so narrow that many boats got tangled up. Since then, they have dredged the curve and it's now very wide.

NAUTICA QUEEN

1153 Main Avenue (West Bank Flats), **Cleveland**

- Area: **NE**
- Telephone Number: (800) 837-0604 or (216) 696-8888
- Hours: Monday – Thursday, Noon, 7:00 p.m.
  Friday and Saturday, 11:00 a.m., 7:30 p.m.
  Sunday, 11:00 a.m., 4:00 p.m.
  Reservation Required
  (April – New Years Eve)
- Admission: Starts at $21.00

3 Hour Dinner Cruise or 2 hour Lunch/Brunch Cruise. Many cruises include entertainment.

ARAWANNA II

Rossford City Marina, **Toledo**

- Area: **NW**
- Telephone Number: (419) 255-6200
- Hours: Weekends, Departs at 1:00 p.m. (April – November)
- Admission: $4.50 Adult, $4.00 Senior
  $2.50 Children (12 and under)

Narrated tour of Maumee Valley river estates or skyline of downtown Toledo. 2 deck boat (lower deck is sheltered)

NORTHERN STAR CRUISE LINES
Toledo

- Area: **NW**
- Telephone Number: (419) 666-4000

Paddlewheel boat rides on the Maumee River.

VALLEY GEM STERNWHEELER
601 Front Street, (State Route 60 and State Route 7) (Docks next to the Ohio River Museum under the Washington Street Bridge), **Marietta**

- Area: **SE**
- Telephone Number: (740) 373-7862
- Hours: Tuesday – Sunday. Departs every hour from 1:00 – 5:00 p.m. No 5:00 p.m. departure on Saturday. (Summer) Rest of Year and Holidays, call for schedule.
- Admission: $5.00 Adult, $3.00 Children (2-12)
- Miscellaneous: Gift and snack area on board. Fall foliage cruises very popular in October. Heated main cabin.

Take the 300 passenger, 50 minute cruise on the Valley Gem where the captain points out historic interests. See who can find the large stone blocks spelling "Marietta" on the landing welcoming steamboats. Why was the boat named after a piano company?

BB RIVERBOATS
Covington, KY (Cincinnati area)

- Area: **SW**
- Telephone Number: (606) 261-8500
- Admission: $7.00 Adult
  $6.00 Senior (60+) and Children (4-12)

TRANSPORTATION ADVENTURES   273

- Tours: 1 hours sightseeing cruises on the Ohio River. Several times daily. Reservations Required – (May – October).

Docked at the foot of Madison Street see the Modern "Funliner", "Mark Twain" sternwheeler or steamboat "Becky Thatcher". Also theme cruises like mini-vacation, holiday or "Skyline Chili".

DELTA QUEEN STEAMSHIP COMPANY

- Area: **SW**
- Telephone Number: (800) 543-1949

"Mississippi Queen", "Delta Queen", or "American Queen". Overnight paddlewheel steamboat trips with regional food service and old time river music played on the calliope and banjo. Also can explore tour of the engine room and pilothouse. Many theme cruises. Usually 3-7 night cruises start at $500.00/person.

OHIO RIVER CRUISES

303 O'Fallon Drive, Dayton, KY (Cincinnati area)

- Area: **SW**
- Telephone Number: (606) 292-8687

"Spirit of Cincinnati" and "Queen City Clipper"

RAILROAD TRANSPORTATION

BUCKEYE CENTRAL SCENIC RAILROAD

US 40 (3 miles East of **Hebron** – I-70 to Route 79 North Exit to US 40)

- Area: **C**

- Telephone Number: (740) 366-2029
- Hours: Weekends and Holidays, 1:00 and 3:00 p.m. Departures (Memorial Day – October)
- Admission: $6.00 Adult, $5.00 Children (2-11)

Take a trip through Ohio farmland for a one hour, 10 mile ride on the same route the train traveled in the mid-1800's on the Shawnee line (important line for pioneers heading west). School-aged kids will want to check out the Wild West/Great Train Robbery. Be part of the action as the train is boarded and held up by outlaws. Will the sheriff save the day?

THE ELDERBERRY LINE

Carrollton – Oneida – Minerva Railroad, **Carrollton**

- Area: **CE**
- Telephone Number: (800) 956-4684
- Hours: Friday, 5:30 p.m., Saturday, 10:00 a.m. and 2:00 p.m. Sunday, 10:00 a.m. and 2:00 p.m. (Memorial Weekend – October)
- Admission: $10.00 Adult, $7.00 Children (2-12)
- Miscellaneous: No restroom on train. No cooling or heat. Elderberry Patch Gift Shop

A scenic round trip of 22 miles lasting 3 hours including the 1 hour layover in Minerva (half-way). The train crosses the historic "Great Trail" of the late 1700's and passengers will pass villages, historic areas, farmland and spacious forests.

OHIO CENTRAL RAILROAD

111 Factory Street (I-77 to Dover Exit, West on State Route 39), **Sugarcreek**

- Area: **CE**
- Telephone Number: (330) 852-4676

- Hours: Departures, 11:00 a.m., 12:30, 2:00, 3:30, and 5:00 p.m. (May – October)
- Admission: $7.00 Adult, $4.00 Children (4-12)
- Miscellaneous: Gift Shop with train memorabilia and Ohio Central souvenirs.

A steam locomotive built in 1912 takes you on a one-hour excursion through Amish Country. Get a real feeling of an old time passenger when the uniformed conductor comes through each car to punch your ticket. Along the way, the trainman points out sites such as many Amish farms with men working in the fields and women hanging laundry. The railroad brought and sent business to the area and many types of manufacturer's factories and warehouses can be seen along the tracks.

PUT-IN-BAY TOUR TRAIN
Put-In-Bay, South Bass Island
- Area: **NC**
- Telephone Number: (419) 285-4855
- Hours: Daily, 10:00 a.m. – 5:00 p.m. (Memorial Day – Labor Day)
  Weekends Only (May and September)
- Admission: $8.00 Adult, $1.50 Youth (6-11)

A one-hour narrated tour of the island. Departing every 30 minutes, the train trolley allows passengers to depart and re-board (without additional cost) at any time.

AC & J SCENIC RAILROAD
State Route 46 to East Jefferson Street, **Jefferson**
- Area: **NE**
- Telephone Number: (440) 576-6346
- Hours: Weekends, 12:30, 2:00, and 3:30 p.m. (Mid June – October)

- ❏ Admission: $7.00 Adult, $6.00 Senior (60+)
  $5.00 Children (3-12)
- ❏ Miscellaneous: Gift Shop/ Concessions

Ride on a 1951 Nickel Plate train with a bright red caboose on a one hour ride through woodlands and farmland. Stop halfway at a staging yard for coal and iron ore in Ashtabula Harbor.

CLEVELAND TROLLEY TOURS

North Marginal Road (Burke Lakefront Airport) Downtown, **Cleveland**

- ❏ Area: **NE**
- ❏ Telephone Number: (216) 771-4484
- ❏ Hours: Late morning or Early afternoon departures
- ❏ Tours: 1 or 2 hours, Reservations Required. 1 hour tour is suggested for preschoolers.
- ❏ Admission: $5.00 and up

"Lolly the Trolley", an old fashioned bright red trolley, clangs its bell as you take in over 100 sights around the downtown area. A great way to show off the city to visitors!

CUYAHOGA VALLEY SCENIC RAILROAD

Cuyahoga Valley National Recreation Area, (**Peninsula** and **Independence** – off I-77 or I-271, follow signs)

- ❏ Area: **NE**
- ❏ Telephone Number: (800) 468-4070
- ❏ Hours: Departs Wednesday – Sunday, Morning and early Afternoon (Summer – October)
  Weekends, Morning and early Afternoon (Rest of the Year)
- ❏ Admission: $11.00 - $20.00 Adult

TRANSPORTATION ADVENTURES 277

$10.00 - $18.00 Senior
$7.00 - $12.00 Children (3+)
- Miscellaneous: Gift Shop at Depot, Gift Shop Car, Concession Car, Park Ranger/Volunteer available for transportation or nature information.

Ride in climate controlled coaches built between 1939 and 1940 on the very scenic 2 - 6 ½ hour ride to many exciting round trip destinations. Meadowlands, pinery, marsh, rivers, ravines, and woods pass by as you travel to Hale Farm and Village, Quaker Square, Inventure Place, Canal Visitor Center, Stan Hywet Hall or just a basic scenic tour (best if small kids take shorter trips or one's with layovers). This is a fun way to spend the day family style (grandparents too!) and see one other attraction along the way. Be sure your little engineers get a blue or pink cap to wear along the trip as a memory of their first train ride!

TROLLEYVILLE, USA

7100 Columbia Road. (State Route 252 off I-480 West) **Olmstead Township**

- Area: **NE**
- Telephone Number: (440) 235-4725
- Hours: Wednesday, Friday, 10:00 a.m. – 3:00 p.m. (Late May – September)
  Saturday, Sunday, and Holidays, Noon – 5:00 p.m. (May – November)
- Admission: $5.00 Adult, $4.00 Senior, $3.00 Children Includes unlimited rides in all cars.

The 1914 Cleveland Station Railway Depot is home to more than 34 pieces of electric railway equipment. Note the switchboard from the Penn Railroad Station downtown. Take rides on the 2 ½ mile train ride on a #304, #409 or #460 Interurban (electric rail car) at 72 M.P.H. speeds. You'll have a chance to stop at a depot built in 1896 with a replica of a Pittsburgh streetcar.

BLUEBIRD PASSENGER TRAIN

49 North 6th Street, Waterville (3rd and Mill Street), **Grand Rapids**

- Area: **NW**
- Telephone Number: (419) 878-2177
- Hours: Tuesday, Thursday, Saturday, Sunday and Holidays Afternoon Departures (Summer). Weekends and Holidays Only – (May, September, October)
- Admission: $8.00 Adult, $7.00 Senior (65+) $4.50 Children (3-12)

Can you guess why they call it "Bluebird"? Answer: The bluebirds come back to Ohio in the spring and leave in the early fall. That's when the train runs. The 45-minute trip (each way) on a 1930's era passenger train includes a spectacular view from a 900-foot long bridge over the Maumee River.

MAUMEE/TOLEDO TROLLEY TOUR

Downtown, **Toledo**

- Area: **NW**
- Telephone Number: (419) 245-5218
- Tours: Wednesday and Sunday (Weekly, June – September). 2 ½ hours long

Tour downtown Toledo and Maumee on an 1880 streetcar replica.

HOCKING VALLEY SCENIC RAILWAY

(Off Route 33), **Nelsonville**

- Area: **SC**
- Telephone Number: (513) 335-0382 (Monday – Friday) (513) 753-9531 (Saturday and Sunday) Weekends, Noon and 2:30 p.m., (June – October) Special Holiday Schedule
- Admission: $6.50 - $9.50, Adult

TRANSPORTATION ADVENTURES

$4.00 - $6.50 Children (2-11)

Ride through the hills of scenic Hocking Valley on an authentic 1916 steam locomotive or a 1950 diesel locomotive (both trips are 25 miles roundtrip). Both rides include a 30-minute stop over at Robbins Crossing Visitor's Center (small settler village).

MARIETTA TROLLEY TOURS

Ohio and 2nd Streets, Levee House Café, Marietta

- Area: **SE**
- Telephone Number: (740) 374-2233
- Hours: Afternoon, 12:30 and 2:30 p.m. (April – October)
- Admission: $7.50 Adult, $7.00 Senior (55+)
  $5.00 Youth (5-12)

Narrated one-hour tours describing and viewing historic architecture, shops along Front Street, Marietta College and more.

TURTLE CREEK VALLEY RAILWAY

198 South Broadway (US 42), **Lebanon**

- Area: **SW**
- Telephone Number: (513) 398-8584
- Departures: Late Morning, Noon, Early Afternoon
  Wednesday, Friday, Saturday, Sunday (May – October)
  Saturday, Sunday (April, November, December)
- Admission: $9.00 Adult , $8.00 Senior (60+)
  $5.00 Children (3-12)
- Miscellaneous: Station Depot with Gift Shop. Discount Days – Holidays (Summer)

A one-hour ride in a refurbished train car reminiscent of yesteryear in the old Indiana and Ohio Railroad through rural countryside (fields and farmlands). Turtle Creek was named for the famous Indian Chief "Little Turtle".

PUBLIC SERVICE TELEPHONE NUMBERS

Call the services of interest and request to be added to their mailing lists.

- ❏ Ashtabula County Metroparks (800) 3-Drop-In
- ❏ Butler County Metroparks (513) 867-5835
- ❏ Canton Park District (330) 489-3015
- ❏ Cincinnati Recreation Department (513) 352-4001
- ❏ Cincinnati Parks Department (513) 352-4080
- ❏ Cleveland Discount Card (800) 321-1004
- ❏ Cleveland Metroparks (216) 351-6300
- ❏ Columbus Metro Parks (614) 891-0700
- ❏ Columbus Recreation & Parks (614) 645-3300
- ❏ Dayton/Five Rivers Metroparks (937) 275-Park
- ❏ Great Cincinnati Getaways/Discounts (800) Cincy-USA
- ❏ Greene County Parks (937) 376-7440
- ❏ Hamilton County Park District (513) 521-Park
- ❏ Lake Metroparks (800) 669-9226
- ❏ Lima/Johnny Appleseed Metroparks (419) 221-1232
- ❏ Lima City Parks & Rec (419) 221-5195
- ❏ Medina County Parks (330) 722-9364
- ❏ Ohio Boating (800) 446-3140
- ❏ Ohio Division Of Travel & Tourism (800) Buckeye
- ❏ Ohio State Parks (614) 466-0652
- ❏ Port Clinton Parks & Rec (419) 732-2206
- ❏ State Park Lodges & Resorts (800) 282-7275
- ❏ Toledo Area Metroparks (419) 535-3050

INDEX

100th Bomb Group 217
356th Fighter Group Restaurant 215
94th Aero Squadron 214
A Quick Look/Special Events/Season 177
A World A'fair 148
A.W. Marion 132
Ac & J Scenic Railroad 275
Adams County Heritage Center 113
Adena State Memorial 97
African-American Homecoming Fest 152
African American Museum 200
African Wildlife Safari Park 21
Airports 244
Akron Art Museum 199
Akron Recreation Bureau 199
Akron Symphony Orchestra 199
Akron Zoological Park 22
All About Kids Show 162
All American Qtr Horse Congress 169
All American Soap Box Derby 160
All Ohio Balloon Festival 158
Allen County Museum 109
Allen Memorial Art Museum 199
Alpaca Farms 28
Alpine - Alpa 119
Alpine Hills Museum 107
Alpine Pottery 258
Alum Creek 132
Alverta Green Museum 114
American Soya Festival 163
American Whistle Corporation 222
Americana Amusement Park 11
Annie Oakley Days 156
Anthony Thomas Candy Company 246
Appalachian Down Home Days 153
Apple Festivals 167
Apple Hill Orchards 29
Arawanna Ii 271
Arboretums & Gardens 125
Ariel Theatre 208
Art For Community Expressions 188
Artspace/Lima 197
Ashland Balloonfest 156
Ashland County Historical Museum 110
Ashland Symphony Orchestra 198
Ashland Wooster Drive-In 214
Ashtabula Arts Center 200
Ashtabula County Covered Bridge
  Festival 170
Asian Festival 147
Atwood Lake 135
Auglaise Village Farm Museum 95
Auto Sports 183

Baldwin-Wallace College Aces 200
Ballet Theatre Ohio 204
Balletmet 188
Balloon A-Fair 166
Ballreich's Potato Chips 236
Baltimore Community Museum 103
Banks 245
Barbara Barbe Doll Museum 53
Barber's Museum/Hall Of Fame 48
Barkcamp 134
Bb Riverboats 272
Bear's Mill 254
Beaver Creek 134
Beck Center For Cultural Arts 203
Behalt 192
Belmont County Vict'n Mansion 105
Berea Summer Theatre 200
Bethlehem Experience 172
Big Bear Warehouse 223
Birdwatching 131
Black Cultural Festival 155
Black Nativity 175
Blue Ash Airport 245
Blue Jacket 198
Blue Rock 135
Bluebird Passenger Train 278
Bob Evan's Farm 27
Boulevard Of Flags 93
Bowling Green State University
  Fine Arts Center Galleries 205
Boyd's Crystal Art Glass Co. 228
Broad Run Cheesehouse 250
Buck Creek 136
Buckeye Central Scenic RR 273
Buckeye Flint Festival 164
Buckeye Furnace Museum 60
Buckeye Hall Of Fame Café 214
Buckeye Lake 133
Burke Lakefront Airport 245
Burr Oak 132
Butch's Coca-Cola Museum 60
Butler County H.S. Museum 114
Butler Institute/American Art 204
Buzzard Day 145
Byesville Museum 105
Caesar Creek 142
Cambridge Glass Museum 105
Camping 127
Campus Martius: Museum NW 97
Canal Boat Cruises 268
Canal Festival 158
Candy Factories 246
Canton Ballet 193

Canton Classic Car Museum 61
Canton Museum Of Art 193
Canton Symphony Orchestra 193
Capital Holiday Lights 175
Captain Hook's Tomb 123
Caramel Festival 163
Carew Tower 124
Carillion Historical Park 84
Carnation Basket Company 237
Carolfest 176
Carriage Hill Farm And Museum 17
Carriage Hill Reserve 135
Carriage House Museum 106
Castle Feast 216
Catawba Island 136
Caverns 128
Cedar Bog And Nature Preserve 120
Cedar Point 4
Celeryville Vegetable Farms 22
Celtic Heritage Fair 157
Celtic Music & Cultural Festival 167
Central Ohio Symphony Orchestra 190
Central Ohio Kite Flyers Assoc. 180
Cent.Cultural Hispano De Cleveland 201
Century Village Museum 92
Charles Mill Lake 133
Chateau LaRoche "Loveland Castle" 243
Cheesehouses 250
Chickenfest! 166
Children's Hospital Medical Center 253
Chocolate Fantasy Fair 144
Christmas Candlelightings 175
Christmas Decorations/Open Houses 172
Christmas Festival 176
Christmas In The Village 176
Christmas Music Spectacular 175
Christmas Tree Farms 173
Cincinnati/N.Kentucky Int'l Airport 245
Cincinnati Art Museum 209
Cincinnati Ballet 210
Cincinnati Bengals 182
Cincinnati City Hall 102
Cincinnati Cyclones & Silverbacks 182
Cincinnati Fire Museum 44
Cincinnati History Museum 45
Cincinnati Main Post Office 265
Cincinnati Museum Of Natural History
    And Science 46
Cincinnati Opera 210
Cincinnati Playhouse In The Park 210
Cincinnati Polo Club 182
Cincinnati Post 257
Cincinnati Reds 182

Cincinnati Symphony Orchestra 210
Cincinnati Water Works 264
Cincinnati Zoo And Botanical Gardens 27
Circle "S" Farms 29
Citizen's Motorcar Packard Museum 62
City Halls 102
Clark State Performing Arts Center 197
Classic Car Museums 61
Clendening Lake 134
Cleveland 264
Cleveland Ballet 201
Cleveland Botanical Garden 126
Cleveland Cavaliers 181
Cleveland Center/Contemporary Art 201
Cleveland Chamber Orchestra 201
Cleveland Children's Museum 41
Cleveland Clinic 253
Cleveland Indians 181
Cleveland Institute Of Music 201
Cleveland Lakefront 138
Cleveland Lumberjacks 181
Cleveland Main Post Office 265
Cleveland Metroparks Zoo 24
Cleveland Museum Of Art 201
Cleveland National Air Show 161
Cleveland Opera 201
Cleveland Orchestra 202
Cleveland Playhouse 202
Cleveland Polo Club 181
Cleveland Signstage Theatre 202
Cleveland State Univ.Dance 202
Cleveland Trolley Tours 276
Cleveland's Irish Cultural Festival 156
Cleveland-Hopkins Int'l Airport 245
Clifton Mill 255
Clifton Mill Restaurant 216
Coblentz Chocolate Company 247
College Tours 252
Columbus 263
Columbus Assoc./Performing Arts 188
Columbus Chill 180
Columbus City Hall 102
Columbus Clippers 180
Columbus Crew 180
Columbus Cultural Arts Center 188
Columbus International Festival 171
Columbus Invaders 180
Columbus Junior Theatre 188
Columbus Main Post Office 265
Columbus Motor Speedway 183
Columbus Museum Of Art 188
Columbus Polo Club 180
Columbus Quest 180

INDEX

Columbus Southern Power Plant 223
Columbus Symphony Orchestra 189
Columbus Zoo 14
Community Museums 103
Coney Island 8
Conneaut Histor'l Railroad Museum 72
Conneaut Lake Park 6
Contemporary Arts Center 210
Cooper's Mill And Jelly Factory 222
Corn Festival 155, 160, 165
COSI Toledo 44
Court Watching 114
Covered Bridge Pizza 217
Cowan Lake 142
Cox Arboretum 126
Cranberry Bog Annual Open House 149
Crane Creek 137
Creegan Co. Animation Factory 231
Croatian Heritage Museum &Library 203
Culbertson's Mini Zoo 25
Cultural Center For The Arts 193
Cuyahoga Valley Scenic Railroad 276
Cuyahoga Valley Youth Ballet 203
Dairy Barn Cultural Arts Center 207
Dance Cleveland 202
David Warther Museum 55
Dawes Arboretum 126
Dayton Art Institute 195
Dayton Ballet 196
Dayton Holiday Festival 172
Dayton International Airport 244
Dayton Museum Of Discovery 38
Dayton Opera 196
Dayton Philharmonic Orchestra 196
Dayton Visual Arts Center 196
Decker Arboretum 125
Deer Creek 133
Defiance College 205
Delaware 132
Delaware County Histor'l Museum 103
Delphos Canal Museum Center 106
Delta Queen Steamship Company 273
Der Dutchman/Dutch Valley Rest. 216
Dietsch Brothers 250
Dillon 133
Dixon Ticonderoga Crayon Factory 235
Doctors Hospital North 253
Dodge Skate Park 184
Domino's Pizza 259
Duffy Liturgical Dance Ensemble 204
East Cleveland Theater 202
East Fork 141
East Harbor 137

Easter Egg Hunts 146
Ebbert's Farm Market 30
Ehrhart Museum 112
Eldora Speedway 184
Electric Company 244
Emancipation Day 166
Emerald Express 269
Enchanted Forest 169
Engine House No. 5 214
Ensemble Theatre/Cincinnati 210
Erieview Park 8
Ethnic Festival 165
Fairborn Summer Park Series 196
Fairport Harbor 138
Fairport Marine Museum 68
Farm Festival 170
Festival Latino 149, 153
Festival Of Fish 152
Festival Of Trees 171
Festivals Of Lights 173
Fiesta Latino-Americana 153
Fiesta Mexicana 162
Findlay Area Arts Council 206
Findley 137
Fire Stations 252
Firelands Assoc. / Visual Arts 199
Firelands Museum 110
Firelands Symphony Orchestra 199
Flight Museums 63
Flint Ridge State Mem. Museum 74
Folklife Celebration 159
Follett House Museum 111
Forest View Gardens 218
Forked Run 141
Fort Ancient State Memorial 100
Fort Laurens State Mem. Museum 81
Fort Meigs 96
Fort Recovery State Memorial 85
Fort Steuben Festival 150
Franciscan Center 206
Franklin Park Conservatory &
    Botanical Gardens 125
Freed Center/Performing Arts 205
Freshwater Farms Of Ohio 18
Frisch's Commissary 242
Fulton Farms 30
Gallery Players 189
Garlic Festival 151, 152, 166
Garlic Lovers Festival 152
Garretts Mill 255
Garst Museum, Darke Cty H.S. 109
Geauga County Maple Festival 146
Geauga Lake 5

General Motors Assembly Plant 234
German Village Oktoberfest 163
German-American Festival 156, 162
Geveva 138
Ghost Town Museum Park 96
Glamorgan Castle 238
Glass Axis 189
Good Time Iii 270
Goodtime I 269
Goodyear World Of Rubber 237
Gorant Candies 249
Governor Bebb Preserve 99
Grand Lake St. Mary's 136
Grand Prix Of Cleveland 156
Grandparents Living Theatre 189
Grant Riverside / Methodist 253
Granville Historical Museum 103
Granville Life Style Museum 103
Grape Jamboree 166
Great Balloon Chase 148
Great Lakes Marine & Coast Guard Memorial Museum 67
Great Lakes Medieval Faire 152
Great Lakes Science Center 42
Great Lakes Theater Festival 202
Great Lakes Wood Sailboat Regatta 160
Great Mohican Indian Pow-Wow 155
Great Outdoor Underwear Festival 170
Great Seal 139
Greater Canton Amateur Sports HOF 106
Greater Youngstown Italian Fest 156
Grecian Festival 159
Greek Festival 157
Green County H.S.Museum 110
Green's Heritage Museum 104
Greenbrier Theatre 204
Guernsey County Histor'l Museum 106
Guggisberg Cheese Factory 251
Guilford Lake 134
Hale Farm And Village 91
Hall China Company 259
Hamburger Inn 214
Hanby House 80
Harding Memorial And Home 78
Harriet Beecher Stowe House 98
Harrison Lake 139
Harry London Chocolate Factory 247
Harvest Festivals 168
Hayes Presidential Center 88
Headlands Beach 138
Hickories Museum 110
Hidden Valley Fruit Farm 31
Hillside Orchard 30

Historic Putnam Tour 105
Historical Harmar Model RR Museum 72
Hobart Welded Sculpture Park 120
Hobbies 131
Hocking Fall Color Tour 171
Hocking Hills 130, 140
Hocking Valley Scenic Railway 278
Holden Arboretum 126
Holidays At Ohio Village 175
Homestead Park 2
Hoover Historical Center 229
Hopalong Cassidy Festival 147
Hopewell Culture Nat'l Historical Park 122
Hopkins Hall Gallery 189
Hornblower's 217
Hospitals 253
Hot Air Balloon Festival 150,156,166,158,148
Hot Rod Super Nationals 184
Hower House 111
Hubbard House/Underground RR Museum 91
Hudson Bandstand Concert Society 204
Hueston Woods 136
Human Race 196
Humane Society / Animal Shelters 28, 253
Huntington Beach 136
Ice Festival 145
Images Images Images 210
Independence Dam 139
Indian Festival 165
Indian Lake 135
Indian Mill 254
Indian Museum Of Lake County 112
Indian Summer Campout 171
Inland Seas Maritime Museum & Lighthouse 66
Institute Of Industrial Technology 35
International Festival 151, 171, 149
Int'l Mining & Manuf.Festival 164
International Street Fair 149
Int'l Women's Air/Space Museum 64
Inventure Place 40
Irish Fest 161
Irish Festival 158, 152, 156
Irons Fruit Farm 31
Isaac Ludwig Mill 256
Italian American Festival 150, 157
Italian American Heritage Festival 161
Italian-American Festival of Summit 157
I-X Center Indoor Amusement Park 7
Jackson Lake 140
Jaggin' Around 215
James M. Thomas Telephone Museum 59
Japan Mini-Tour/Educational Center 226

INDEX

Jefferson County Historical Museum 107
Jefferson Lake 135
Jewish Comm. Center Jr. Theatre 206
Jiggs Drive In 218
Jim's Drive In Restaurant 216
John Bryan 136
Johnny Appleseed Festival 170
July 4th Celebrations 154
Kahiki Restaurant 214
Karamu House 203
Kelley's Island 137
Kelton House Museum And Gardens 49
Kent State University Museum 203
Kettering-Moraine Museum 109
Kewpee 216
Kids Day 149, 151
Kids Fest 149, 153, 161
Kidspeak Kidsfest 163
Killbuck Valley Museum 104
King Arts Complex 189
Kingwood Center 125
Kiser Lake 136
Kite Festival 160
Kite Flying 131
Krohn Conservatory 127, 176
Kwanzaa Festivals 174
Lagoon Deer Park 22
Lagrange Street Polish Festival 157
Lake Alma 141
Lake Erie College Fine & Performing Arts Department 204
Lake Erie Island Boat Tours 269
Lake Erie Islands Museum 111
Lake Farm Park 24
Lake Hope 140
Lake Logan 140
Lake Loramie 136
Lake Milton 138
Lake Vesuvius 140
Lake White 141
Lakeside Association 198
Lakeview Park 137
Lancaster Chorale 190
Lane-Hooven House 114
Lawnfield Museum 93
Lawrence County Museum 113
Lawrence Orchards 29
Lee Middleton Original Doll Factory 240
Leesville Lake 134
Licking County Art Association 191
Licking County H.S. 104
Lima Symphony Orchestra 197
Limaland Motor Speedway 184

Linder Family Omnimax Theater 9
Lithopolis Fine Arts Association 190
Little Brown Jug 164
Little Miami 141
Living Christmas Tree Concerts 175
Lockington Locks State Memorial 86
Logan County Hist'l Museum 108
Longaberger Museum & Factory Tour 225
Lorain Palace Civic Center 198
Lorena Sternwheeler 270
Loveland Museum 114
Lyme Village 87
Lynd Fruit Farm 29
Lyric Opera Cleveland 203
M/V "City Of Sandusky" 269
Mac-O-Chee And Mac-O-Cheek Castles (Piatt Castles) 235
Mad River/NKP RR Museum 71
Mad River Theater Works 197
Madison Lake 132
Magical Farms 28
Mahoning Valley H.S. Museum 112
Malabar Farm State Park 16, 133
Malley's Chocolates 248
Mansfield Art Center 191
Mansfield Playhouse 191
Mansfield Symphony Society 191
Maple Syrup Festivals 145
Mapleside Farms 216
Maps Air Museum 64
Marietta Trolley Tours 279
Marigold Festival 158
Marine Museums 66
Marion County Int'l Raceway 183
Marmon Valley Farm 20
Martin Luther King Festival 144
M. Luther King March/Program 144
Mary Jane Thurston 139
Massillon Museum 107
Massillon Museum 194
Maumee Bay 137
Maumee/Toledo Trolley Tour 278
McCook House 106
McDonald's Restaurants 217, 260
McDonough Museum Of Art 205
McGuffey Museum 70
McKinley Museum/Discvr World 36
Medieval & Renaissance Festival 147
Medina County H.S.Museum 104
Melon Festival 160
Memorial Golf Tournament 181
Memphis Kiddie Park 7

Mercer County H.S. Museum 108
Merry-Go-Round Museum 56
Miami University 252
Miami University Art Museum 211
Miami Whitewater Forest 141
Miami-Erie Canal Museum 114
Miamisburg Mound 119
Mid Ohio Sports Car Course 183
Middfest International Celebration 171
Middlefield Cheese House 251
Mid-Ohio Historical Museum 48
Milan Historical Museum 89
Mill Creek Park 122
Miller's Country Garden 29
Mills 254
Minges Farm 30
Mitchellace Shoestring Factory 239
Moch Series Hydroplane Racing 181
Mohican 133
Mom's Diner 218
Mosquito Lake 139
Motorcycle Heritage Museum 52
Mount Gilead 133
Murphy Theatre For The Arts 211
Murphy's Lighthouses, Inc. 238
Museum Of Cambridge Glass 106
Museum Of Ceramics 106
Museum Of Postal History 56
Museum Of Troy History 110
Music In The Air 189
Musique Mechanique 50
Muskingum College Cultural Series 194
Muskingum River 133
Mysterious Revolving Ball 118
NASA Lewis Research Visitor Center 66
National Afro-American Museum 87
National Folk Festival 151
National McKinley Birthplace/Mus. 94
National Road Zane Grey Museum 54
National Threshers Annual Reunion 153
National Tractor Pull Championships 182
National Trail Raceway 183
Native American Powwow 145,155,158, 160,162
Nautica Queen 271
Neil Armstrong Air/Space Museum 39
New Bremen Historic Museum 109
New Years Eve Celebrations 176
Newark Earthworks 79
Newspapers 256
Noah's Ark Animal Farm 26
Northeast Ohio Polka Fest 152
Northern Ohio Garlic Festival 166

Northern Star Cruise Lines 272
Oakland Center/Arts 205
Oberhaus Enterprises 63
Oberlin Historic Sites Tour 110
Ohio Agricultural Research & Development Center 232
Ohio Ballet 200
Ohio Central Railroad 274
Ohio Department Natural Res. 127
Ohio Gourd Show 169
Ohio Historical Center 75
Ohio History Of Flight Museum 63
Ohio Honey Festival 162
Ohio Irish Festival 152
Ohio Light Opera 195
Ohio National Championship AMA Motorcycle Races 182
Ohio Pumpkin Festival 164
Ohio Railway Museum 70
Ohio Renaissance Festival 163
Ohio River Cruises 273
Ohio River Museum 69
Ohio River Sternwheel Festival 167
Ohio Sauerkraut Festival 171
Ohio Scottish Games 151
Ohio Society Of Military History 82
Ohio State Fair 158
OS Hwy Patrol Training Facility 224
Ohio State Univ. Entomology Dept 14
Ohio State Univ. Veterinary Hosp. 15
Ohio Statehouse 76
Ohio Swiss Festival 165
Ohio Theatre 206
Ohio University 252
Ohio University Art Gallery 207
Ohio University Office Public 207
Ohio Village 76
Ohio Village Muffins 181
Ohio Waterfowlers Festival 165
Ohio's Agricultural Fairs 157
Ohio's Center Of Science And Industry (COSI) 34
Oktoberfest 163,167,168
Oktoberfest-Zinzinnati 167
Old Courthouse/Montgomery County Historical Museum 108
Old-Fashioned Ice Cream Festival 147
Olentangy Indian Caverns 128
Olympia Gourmet Chocolates & Caramel Corn 248
Opera/Columbus 190
Orange Johnson House 80
Orchard / Crop Farms 29

INDEX

OSU Dance 190
OSU Music 190
OSU Theatre 190
Ottawa County Historical Museum 111
Our House Museum 113
Painesville Speedway 184
Paint Creek 140
Palace Cultural Arts Association 191
Paper Festival 153
Paramount's Kings Island 10
Parent's Place Of Work 258
Parky's Farm 30
Patterson Homestead And Gardens 108
Paul Bunyan Show 170
Paul Lawrence Dunbar State Mem. 55
Pepsi Country Music Festival 156
Perkins Mansion 111
Perkins Observatory 34
Perry's Cave 129
Perry's Victory & Int'l Peace 90
Piatt 135
Pickaway County H.S.Museum 103
Pickerington-Violet Twp. Museum 105
Piedmont Lake 135
Pike Lake 139
Pine Crest Farms 29
Pioneer Days 159
Pioneer Pottery 259
Pioneer Waterland 6
Piqua Historical Area Tour 86
Piqua Historical Museum 109
Pizza Hut 260
Players Guild Ctr. For Public Theatre 193
Pleasant Hill Lake 133
Pomerene Center For The Arts 194
Popcorn Festival 164, 165
Popeye's Restaurant 215
Pork Rind Heritage Festival 153
Port Columbus International Airport 244
Port Washington Union Hall 107
Portage Lakes 137
Portsmouth Murals 208
Possum Creek Reserve 135
Potato Festival 166
Potter Players Theatre 194
Pottery Tours 258
Poultry Days 151
Prairie Peddler 149
Preble County Historical Farm 108
Preble County Pork Festival 165
Prehistoric Forest 4
Pretzel Festival 165
Pro Football Hall Of Fame 37

Professional Football HOF Fest. 155
Pufferbelly Restaurant 217
Pump House Art Gallery 208
Pumpkin Festivals 164, 169
Pumpkin Patches/ Hayrides/
    Corn Mazes/ Fall Playlands 168
Punderson 138
Put-In-Bay Tour Train 275
Pymatuning 137
Pyramid Hill Sculpture Park 124
Quail Hollow 138
Railroad Festival 148
Railroad Museums 70
Railroad Transportation 273
Rankin House State Memorial 101
Recreation Areas 132
Red Hawk American Indian
    Powwow 162
Restaurant Tours 259
Rhodes State Office Tower 77
Rhythm & Food Festival : A Taste
    Of Columbus 147
Richland Academy Of The Arts 191
Richland Carousel Park & Carousel
    Magic Factory 3
Richland County Museum 104
Ritz Theatre 206
River Days 162
Riverboat Cruises 270
Riverfest 162
Rockwell Orchards 30
Rocky Fork 140
Rodeos 183
Rolling Ridge Ranch 17
Rookwood Pottery 218
Roscoe Village 81
Rose Festival 150
Ross County Hist'l Museum 113
Rossi Pasta 241
Rothschild Berry Farm 30
Rousters Apple House 31
Salt Fork 134
Sandpiper Canal Boat 268
Santa Maria 78
Sauder Farm & Craft Village 94
Savannah Sweets Chocolate 246
Scarecrow Festival 166
Schoepfle Arboretum 126
Schrock's Amish Farm/Home 226
Scioto Trail 140
Sea World 23
Secrest Arboretum 126
Sedgwick House Museum 107

Seneca Caverns 129
Seneca County Museum 111
Senecaville Lake 134
Serpent Mound State Memorial 123
Seven Caves 130
Shady – Nook 218
Shaker Historical Museum 112
Shandy Hall 112
Sharon Woods 141
Sharon Woods Village 101
Shawnee 140
Shawnee Lookout 141
Shoenbrunn Village State Memorial 82
Showboat Becky Thatcher 209
Showboat Majestic 210
Skiing 185
Sky Cream & Deli 219
Slate Run Historical Farm 74
Slavic Village Harvest Festival 161
Sorg Opera House 211
South Bass Island 137
S. Ohio Museum & Cultural Center 209
Spectator Sports 180
Spring Four-Wheel Jamboree Nat'ls 148
Spring Plowing Days 147
Springfield Museum Of Art 197
Springfield Summer Arts Festival 197
Springfield Symphony Orchestra 197
Ss Willis B Boyer Maritime Museum 68
St Helena Iii 268
St. Mary's Fish Farm 18
St. Patrick's Parades/Celebrations 145
Stamp Collecting 131
Stan Hywet Hall 57
Steubenville City Of Murals 195
Stonelick 142
Strawberry Festival 148,150,151,152
Stroud's Run 139
Sugarcreek Reserve 135
Sugarplum Festival Of Trees 172
Sumburger Restaurant 218
Summit Choral Society 200
Sunwatch 84
Supermarkets 260
Surf Cincinnati 9
Sweet Corn Festival 159, 160
Sycamore 136
Taft Museum 211
Tappan Lake 134
Tar Hollow 139
Tecumseh 207
Ted Lewis Museum 49
Tender Shepherd Farms 28

Thanksgiving Day Parades 172
The Alaskan Birdhouse Wildlife 21
The Apple Barn 30
The Apple Cabin 29
The Barn 209
The Beach 10
The Buggy Haus 231
The Butterfly Box 20
The Castle 113
The Chillicothe Gazette 257
The Cincinnati Enquirer 257
The Cleveland Museum of Natural
   History 41
The Columbus Dispatch 256
The Depot Canteen Restaurant 215
The Depot Restaurant 216
The Elderberry Line 274
The Georgian /The Sherman House
   Museum 104
The Heath Museum 42
The Living Bible Museum 51
The Living Word Passion Play 192
The Mailbox Factory 121
The Most Magnificent McDonald's In
   America 217
The Ohio State University Buckeyes 180
The Ohio State Univ.Main Campus 252
The Packard Museum 62
The Popcorn Gallery 233
The Popcorn Outlet 224
The Robinson Ransbottom Pottery Co.258
The Spirit Of '76 Museum 199
The Stables 215
The Sullivan-Johnson Museum
   Of Hardin County 109
The Tin Man 234
The Western Reserve H.S. 92
The Wilds 16
The W.H. Taft National Historic Site 99
Thomas Edison's Birthplace Museum 89
Three Rivers Pottery 259
Thunder-In-The-Hills Hydro Race 167
Thurber House 50
Tinker's Creek 138
Toboggan Run 176
Toledo Botanical Gardens 127
Toledo Firefighters Museum 59
Toledo Mud Hens Baseball 182
Toledo Museum Of Art 206
Toledo Opera 206
Toledo Speedway 184
Toledo Storm 182
Toledo Symphony Orchestra 207

INDEX

Toledo Zoo 26
Tomato Festival 164
Tony Packos Café 218
Topiary Garden 125
Tower City Center Observation 121
Toy & Hobby Museum 54
Train – O – Rama 71
Train Rides With Santa 174
Trains, Planes & Automobiles Fest 152
Trolleyville, USA 277
Trout Derby 146
Trout Derby 148
Trumbull County H.S. Museum 112
Trumpet In The Land 194
Turtle Creek Valley Railway 279
Tuscarawas County Italian-American Festival 159
Tuscarawas Philharmonic 195
TV / Radio Stations 261
Twins Days Festival 161
U. S. Air & Trade Show 155
U.S. Glass Specialty Outlet 239
U.S. Main Post Offices Tours 265
U.S. Playing Card Museum 61
U.S.S. Cod 67
Ulysses S. Grant Homestead Museum 100
Union Depot Railroad Museum 70
United Dairy Farmers 242
United States Air Force Museum 38
United States Plastic Corporation 233
University Hospitals 253
University Of Akron Theatre 200
University Of Cinti – Athletics 183
University Of Rio Grande Valley Artists Series 209
University Of Toledo 252
Valley Gem Sternwheeler 272
Van Buren Lake 139
Victorian House 107
Victorian Perambulator Museum 58
Village Of Mt. Pleasant 107
Vinton County Wild Turkey Festival 149
Violet Festival 159
Wahkeena Nature Reserve 118
Walleye Derby 146
Walleye Festival 148
Warren Civic Music Association 204
Warren County H.S. Museum 114
Warther Carvings Tour 229
Wassenberg Art Center 207
Water Treatment Plants 263
Wayne Center For The Arts 195
Wayne County H.S. Museum 108

WBNS Radio 261
WCPO – TV (ABC Channel 9) 263
WCVO Radio 262
Weathervane Playhouse 200
Wendall August Forged Tour 227
West Branch 138
Western Reserve Fine Arts 203
Westerville Civic Symphony 191
Wexner Center For The Arts 190
Wildlife Festival 148
Wildwood Waterpark 7
William G. Mather Museum 43
Willoughby Fine Arts Assoc. 204
Windmill Farm Market 31
Winterfest / Martin Luther King Jr. Celebration 144
Winterfest 144, 175
Winton Woods 141
WKRC – TV (CBS Channel 12) 263
WLW-AM 700 (Radio) 263
Wolcott House Museum 113
Wolf Run 134
Woollybear Festival 170
Worden Heritage Homestead 112
WOSU Radio And TV 262
Wright B. Flyer 65
Wright Cycle Company 65
Wright State University Artist 196
WSTR – TV 64 263
WTTE – Channel 28 262
Wyandot County H.S. 105
Wyandot Lake Amusement & Waterpark 2
Wyandot Popcorn Museum 51
Ye Olde Mill Ice Cream Museum 52
Yoder's Amish Home 230
Young's Jersey Dairy Farm 19
Youngstown Historical Center Of Industry & Labor 58
Youngstown Playhouse 205
Youngstown Symphony 205
Zane Caverns 128
Zanesville Art Center 191
Zanesville Greys 181
Zivili 190
Zoar Village 83
Zoo Blooms 157
Zucchini Festival 156, 159

THE OHIO STATE REFORMATORY
100 Reformatory Road, (US 30 & SR 545 North), **Mansfield**
- Area: **C**
- Telephone Number: (419) 522-2644
- Hours: Sunday, 1-4 p.m. (May – October)
- Tours: Phone Reservations Preferred
  Children under 9 not admitted
  Groups by reservation only
- Admission

A castle prison? Well, maybe from the outside only. This 1886 structure was built as a boy's reformatory. The original cellblocks and offices remain intact and were used to film 3 major motion pictures including "The Shawshank Redemption".

MOSSER GLASS
(I-77 exit 47. US 22 West) **Cambridge**
- Area: **CE**
- Telephone Number: (740) 439-1827
- Tours: Monday – Friday, 8:15, 9:15, 10:15 a.m., Noon, 1,2,3:00 p.m. Except plant shutdown in July and Christmas Week. Best not to tour if it's extremely hot outside since the plant is not air conditioned.

Mosser makes glass pitchers, goblets, lamps, figurines, auto parts (headlights), and paper weights. Your guide starts the tour explaining the glassmaking process from the beginning when glass powder (sand and cullet-broken glass) are heated to 2000 degrees F. in a furnace. Once melted, the molten glass is pulled on a stick and then iron molded or pressed, fire glazed and finally cooled in a Lehr which uniformly reduces the temperature of the object to prevent shattering. We saw them make old Ford car headlight covers and red heart shaped paperweights. They add selenium to make red glass. A little toothpick holder or doll's glass was our free souvenir of this great tour.

OLD BARN OUT BACK

3175 West Elm Street, **Lima**

- Area: **CW**
- Telephone Number: (419) 991-3075.

A local favorite with large timbers, cedar aged barn siding, and lanterns hanging from wagon wheels create a true feeling of being "down on the farm". Groups can eat together in the "Chicken Coop", "Milking Parlor", or "Pig Pen". Grandma's famous recipe fried chicken or cinnamon rolls along with great homemade favorites and a large variety of fresh food served on their salad bar. Local area family owned. Come with ready appetites, as the portions are farm style generous. Don't miss this family friendly Lima tradition!

BICYCLE MUSEUM OF AMERICA

7 West Monroe Street, **New Bremen**

- Area: **CW**
- Telephone Number: (419) 629-9249
- Hours: Monday – Thursday, 11:00 a.m. – 5:00 p.m.
  Friday, 11:00 a.m. – 8:00 p.m.
  Saturday, 12:00 – 3:00 p.m.
- Admission: $3.00 Adult, $2.00 Senior, $1.00 Student

A department store has been converted into a showcase of the world's oldest bike (w/out pedals) to the Schwinn family collection (including the 1,000,000 th bicycle made). Dayton based Huffy Company also donated many pieces and the owners continue to acquire celebrity bikes.

GROUP DISCOUNTS AND FUNDRAISER OPPORTUNITIES!

Dear Coordinator:

We're excited to introduce our new book to your group! This new guide for parents, grandparents, teachers and visitors is a great tool to discover hundreds of fun places to visit around Ohio. **KIDS ♥ OHIO** is one resource for all the wonderful places to travel either locally or across the state.

We are two parents who have researched, written and published this book. We have spent over 1000 hours collecting information and, very often, visiting every site listed in this guide. This book is kid-tested and the descriptions include great hints on what kids like best!

After you have reviewed your copy of **KIDS ♥ OHIO**, please consider the following options:

- ❑ **Fundraiser and/or Group Discount** – You may sell **KIDS ♥ OHIO** to your members and friends at the price of $12.95 and keep the 23% per book discount as an organizational fundraiser OR sell the book at the price of $10.00 and offer the 23% savings off the suggested retail price to members/ friends. Minimum order is ten books.
- ❑ **Available for Interview/Speaking** – The authors have a treasure bag full of souvenirs from favorite places in Ohio. We'd love to share ideas on planning fun trips to take children while exploring Ohio. The authors are available, by appointment, at (614) 898-2697. The minimum guaranteed order is twenty-five books. There is no additional fee involved.

Call us soon at (614) 898-2697 to make arrangements!
Happy Exploring!

Attention Parents:
(Please pass this page on to a friend)

KIDS ♥ OHIO

- **Discover places like hidden castles & whistle factories.** Well-known attractions + tours & special events you probably never knew
- **Wonderful resource to make short vacation plans or get to know your hometown area better.** You will probably find there are at least 100 things to do within an hour of your home! Nearly 1000 listings in one book about Ohio travel for kids ages 2 – 15!
- **Formatted in 9 geographical zones** providing addresses, telephone numbers, directions, and descriptions to save you lots of time!
- **Great tool for moms, dads, grandparents, teachers, babysitters and visitors** to plan exciting days all around Ohio. Kid-tested!
- **Economy.** We have found lots of places to visit for little or no charge!

Name_____

Address_____

City_____

State_____ Zip_____

Enclose check or money order payable to <u>U.S. Voice Communication</u> and send to:

U.S. Voice Communication
7438 Sawmill Road, Suite 500
Columbus, Ohio 43235

Quantity	Price (ea)	TOTALS
	$12.95	$
	Ohio Sales Tax $0.75/bk	$
	S/H	FREE
	TOTAL	$